A GUID
NATURAL

*Dedicated to the people of Cumbria and
Carlisle City Council without whom
A Guide to Natural Burial would not have emerged*

A GUIDE TO
NATURAL BURIAL

Ken West MBE,
DMS, Life Member ICCM (Dip.), ILAM (Dip.)

Shaw & Sons

Published in 2010 by
Thomson Reuters (Legal) Limited (Registered in England and Wales,
Company No 1679046. Registered office and address for service:
100 Avenue Road, Swiss Cottage,
London NW3 3PF), under the Shaw & Sons imprint

For further information on our products and services, visit
http://www.sweetandmaxwell.co.uk

Printed and bound in Great Britain
by CPI Antony Rowe, Chippenham, Wiltshire

ISBN 978 0 4140 4490 6

No natural forests were destroyed to make this product;
only farmed timber was used and replanted.

A CIP catalogue record for this book is available
from the British Library

SUMMARY OF CONTENTS

ACKNOWLEDGEMENTS

I would like to thank all who helped in the preparation of this book, in particular, Cynthia Beale, Rupert Callender, Charles Cowling, Dr. Boyd Dent, James Leedham, Tim Morris, Kevin Pilkington, Ed Ranger, Dr. Julie Rugg, Justine Smith, Dr. Kate Woodthorpe and, especially, my wife Ann.

TABLE OF CONTENTS

THE AUTHOR

The author has worked in the death industry for 45 years and has been involved in over 100,000 funerals. He began full-time work on his 15th birthday at Shrewsbury Cemetery in 1961, where he trained in horticulture. He later worked as the sexton, cremator technician and deputy manager of the cemetery and crematorium. He worked for Sheffield Council from 1972 to 1974, as deputy manager, and from 1974 to 1983 as manager for Wolverhampton Council.

In 1983 he obtained the post of Bereavement Services Manager for Carlisle City Council and managed a crematorium, three cemeteries and seven closed churchyards. While in this post he devised and opened the first woodland burial site (now called natural burial) in the UK in 1993, and gradually developed what are now called green funerals. Much controversy arose at this time especially with funeral directors, who remained opposed to all these initiatives.

While managing at Carlisle, the cemetery won the first "Cemetery of the Year" award from the Memorial Advisory Board in 1998, and several awards from the Natural Death Centre for service innovation. During this period the author wrote the Charter for the Bereaved, and the Assessment Process, which enables cemeteries and crematoria to adopt defined standards against which they could be measured. He gave evidence to the Parliamentary Select Committee during an investigation into cemetery provision in 2000. In 2001 he obtained the post of Bereavement Operational Manager at Cardiff and then moved to the London Borough of Croydon as Bereavement Services Manager in 2003, where he retired in 2006.

The author has obtained the following qualifications:

- Institute of Cemetery & Crematorium Management Diploma (ICCM) (1974);

- Royal Horticultural Society Certificate General Examination in Horticulture (1977);

- Diploma in Management Studies with Credit (DMS) (1991);

- Institute of Leisure & Amenity Management Diploma with Distinctions (1991).

During this period he was awarded:

- ICCM Fellowship – 1989, President – 1993, Life Membership (1996);
- MBE for Services to Burial and Cremation (2002).

The author has also written and presented many papers. Since retirement he has acted as judge for the Cemetery of the Year award and is currently a Crematorium Technicians Training Scheme Assessor for the ICCM. He acted as an honorary advisor to the Natural Death Centre until 2008. He was awarded the 2007 Best Article in ICCM *The Journal* for 'How Green is Your Funeral', and in 2008 was commissioned to complete the Carbon Footprint questionnaire for cemeteries and crematoria by the Burial and Cremation Education Trust (BCET).

FOREWORD

Since 2000, natural burial has been called 'the single greatest environmental initiative in the UK'. Whether an exaggeration or not, the concept has advanced and daily becomes a realistic funeral option for people in many parts of the UK. This book is the first to offer a perspective on natural burial and its effect on the whole death industry. It is a book for those who are unsure whether natural burial is their personal funeral choice. It is also the principal source of advice for present and future site owners to enable them to understand their obligations and to avoid the problems that crippled traditional cemeteries.

This book is invaluable to anyone who wants to have a greater understanding of the funeral market. This might be to appreciate the historical perspective of funerals and their current commercial, environmental and social impact; or it might just be a desire for the empowerment to control personal funeral arrangements.

There are detractors of natural burial; others who find it a step too far, and those who are unable to access a site because they reside in an urban area. For them, this book will give an awareness of natural burial, and how its principles can also help to create a conventional burial or cremation that is less damaging to the world and more financially and environmentally sustainable. For the eco-warriors out there and those concerned about ever-rising funeral costs, it will give the information to lobby councillors and politicians for change.

The seed of natural burial was set in a different period. It was when we all shopped at Liptons and Home & Colonial and, if poor, bought broken biscuits at Woolworths. It was a period when farm workers were forced off the land to become the mainstay of the cemetery workforce, when 80-year-old men still went to work on 'sit up and beg bicycles', the last of those who could use a scythe. They lived in towns where a barn owl screeched at night; where children in new socialist council houses played in long grass full of butterflies and blood suckers, those harmless soldier beetles; where bats clustered around street lamps clouded with moths. This arcadia was not hundreds of years ago, but the 1960s, the era of the Beatles and Twiggy. The 1960s is not so far away that the good from that period cannot be recreated! Natural burial is not about harking back to some dreamy arcadia but about taking the best from the past, adding present day knowledge, and creating a new sustainable way forward.

This is the history of the death industry based on the experiences of one man's working life. It reflects a society in transition, from a simple way of life to one dominated by commercialism and marketing. It is a story in which even a bunch of flowers and a wreath can no longer be bought in innocence; of how a relatively clean industry becomes part of the problem of pollution and global warming.

Our society is based on constant annual growth, on increasing population and increasing demand, regardless of sustainability. The death industry with all its inherited problems is now poised for expansion due to the baby boomers and the burger boomers. These two cohorts of current society, each reflective of great changes, the former of optimism for the future, the latter of a fat-eating consumer society living on a struggling planet!

This book is also a tribute to Carlisle City Council and its staff, and to the residents and media of Cumbria in the early 1990s, without whom I could never have started natural burial. My experience of other local authorities since that period assures me that it could not have been developed anywhere else. Carlisle City Council was innovative, brave and supportive, all essential ingredients when opposition was aggressive and at times vindictive.

The natural burial site in Carlisle cemetery was opened in 1993 and is now flourishing, with oak trees, and bluebells appearing each spring, an entirely new habitat precisely one mile from the centre of the city. The Council wanted to widen burial choice for the community, with easy access for the bereaved. It will be a future green lung and an educational resource.

The natural burial site in Carlisle was a response to an environmental challenge that did not lose sight of human needs. Excessive eco actions that demand responses that actually make day-to-day life difficult or impossible are no real solution. However, people now realise that we must treat the earth more lightly in the future, and natural burial can fit this perspective. The fact that over 220 natural burial sites now operate in the UK is evidence that people believe that this is a way forward. In the UK there are a variety of natural burial choices. They include burial within established woodland, in fields to create nature reserves, forests and orchards, and in farmland to be grazed by stock. New and innovative ideas arise and each burial, by replacing conventional burial or cremation, reduces harmful emissions, the use of finite fuels and unsustainable practices. It can also give deep psychological satisfaction to people who feel that through their death they are supporting the collective good of humanity and often expressing their philosophy in life.

Finally, I want to apologise for at times using the all-embracing word green when I refer to something which has environmental, sustainable, or iconic value. Most readers will accept the word, even if it is seen by some as superficial and literally careless. I also have to remind the reader that in the absence of relevant research, many of my assertions are based on anecdotal evidence arising through my experience.

Chapter 1

UNDERSTANDING THE MARKET

1.1 HOW HAVE WE ARRIVED WHERE WE ARE TODAY?

1.1.1 Cremation and conventional burial

Cremation

Natural burial is the right way forward, and by implication it suggests that the 73% who choose cremation are wrong. In truth, cremation is wrong in many ways, not least because it reinforces our reliance on fossil fuels to the very end; it wastes the benign, biodegradable components of our body and the coffin and turns them into harmful emissions; it wastes technology to manufacture the cremators and abatement equipment. It also removes us from that important state, that of being natural.

When the first crematorium in the UK opened in 1885 in Woking, the majority of people objected to it, taking the view that the process is unchristian and unnatural. In contrast to the dramatic increase in natural burial, it took until the 1960s, over 75 years, before cremation numbers exceeded conventional burial numbers. The reasons for the success of cremation are not clear and it could be considered the ultimate denial of death, a clinical process completed by increasingly automated machines. Routinely, the bereaved partner or family neither see, nor touch, nor have any other involvement in the process. Sitting in a comfortable chapel, the coffin is screened by curtains and they are spared the open grave, the cloying soil and the elements. Perhaps the bereaved feel sheltered from the world and mortality and they can walk back out into life as if nothing had happened. Constant criticism arises from the bereaved about this conveyor belt system that is perceived as slick and uninspiring.

Much as I oppose the process of cremation, I recognise that it cannot be discontinued in the short term. It is a requirement for some religions such as Hindus, Sikhs and Buddhists. Also, following a Papal declaration in 1963, it is now acceptable to Roman Catholics and because of its science base, has been favoured by atheists and humanists. Cremation must also continue in large urban areas where land does not exist to create natural burial sites. It ought, though, be

1

subject to Government targets to reduce carbon emissions. As scientific as it may appear, cremation is just a crude means of incinerating bodies with little understanding of the environmental impact.

The slogan 'Save the Land for the living' produced by the Cremation Society may have promoted cremation but it is a false premise. The land used in conventional cemeteries is too insignificant for this to be truly meaningful.

Conventional burial

Burial was the traditional method of disposing of bodies in the UK for the past 5,000 years, until cremations exceeded burials in the 1960s. The earliest known burial cairns and chambered tombs denoted ownership of tribal lands. These chambers appear to have been re-used, perhaps the bodies being left until the soft tissue had decomposed, and then the bones moved elsewhere. This was a sustainable practice that avoided digging graves using antler horn, but whether people utilised the process as a means of saving labour is impossible to know. The Beaker people and the Romans carried out a limited number of cremations.

Cemeteries were used in the dark ages but it was Christianity and its focus on the resurrection of the body that reinforced earth burial. These were concentrated in small areas around churches, what we now call God's Acre. Graves were not memorialised and burials can be anticipated to have been shallow, so decomposition was rapid and graves could be re-used, in a rotation of perhaps 30 to 50 years. The spare soil from each burial was tipped over older graves, so increased burial depth was gained by this practice.

A right of burial in the parish churchyard for any parishioner became enshrined in common law. Where a churchyard retains new grave space, this right still exists for every resident of an English parish, whatever their religion. The Catholic and Free Churches did not have their own churchyards and their poor burial experience, similarly experienced by atheists, caused much social disquiet at times.

Parishioners appear to have accepted this unmemorialised burial process until the 1700s, as the body was considered insignificant when the spirit proceeded to paradise. Memorials then began to appear, often very crudely carved and suggesting a shift in people's attitude to death and burial. Memorials imply ownership, and in confirming a location, generate visits by survivors, so the sexton would avoid reusing graves with a memorial. As these increased, so the churchyard filled and where possible, was extended.

With the migration of rural people to towns and cities, and the cholera and other diseases in the 1800s the urban churchyards were overwhelmed. Graves were re-used containing partly decomposed bodies, limbs often protruded out of the ground, the churchyard often stank, and water drawn from nearby wells became polluted with body fluids. In response, the government created new laws to permit private companies and public authorities to create and open what we now recognise as cemeteries. Many were opened and filled to capacity within as little as 20 to 40 years, due to the vast numbers of poor being interred in the dreaded pauper grave, often with multiple burials with no memorials or rights. The rich were placed in their oak, often lead-lined coffins, in ornate stone tombs alongside the principal drives, usually the gated entrance drive leading to the chapels. The poor were placed in thin wood coffins and interred at the back of the cemetery, often in wet, infrequently mown sections. Various schemes to enable the poor to buy a grave in instalments were introduced. With these the cemetery authority gave an assurance that no further burial of a body of an unrelated person would take place, say for 14 years, during which time the ownership of the grave right could be secured.

These cemeteries overturned the age old routines. The parish minister could no longer decide where you were to be buried and the right to a grave could be purchased where a person wished, and money was king. Memorials became larger and more ornate, especially in the private cemeteries. At this time the undertaker was created to unify what were previously individual actions, such as the carpenter building the coffin, and the carriage master providing the transport. Over time, marketing created the feeling that 'a good send-off' was essential, and that the standard of the funeral ought to reflect the deceased's status during life.

We now consider this conventional burial, and although less routine than cremation due to there being more burial locations, it is nonetheless, outdated and little better than cremation regarding the environment. The need for constant mowing to maintain neat lawns expends considerable fossil fuel and memorial stone is imported from across the world. Conventional burial has declined for decades, partly due to cemeteries filling up, partly due to the cost of mowing, but primarily due to the fact that no sinking funds were reserved for maintenance, unlike in the US, where it is legally required. In view of this the grounds and memorials have gradually deteriorated. A considerable percentage of all Victorian and Edwardian memorials are unsafe in the UK at the current time, and many pose a significant safety hazard as well as making the cemetery look neglected. Local councillors, ever eager to remain electable often promise to maintain the cemeteries, yet, at the crunch, cede the resources instead to where the votes abide, such as in education. This is an example of modern government, the pretence that everything can be resourced. Consequently, many local authorities fear the sensitive issue of removing the unsafe memorials and refuse to give permission but withhold the resources needed for renovation. Consequently, the memorials remain unvisited, unloved and often very unsafe.

Too often park or leisure departments are given control of cemeteries simply because they know how to cut grass, apply herbicides and reduce the need for resources. This horticultural skill becomes the main interest in the cemetery and takes priority over the needs of the bereaved such that bereavement skills are often discounted. The parks manager is no less fearful than the cemetery manager in promoting a new and modern strategy. Global warming and carbon reduction ought to be national, horticultural topics no less important than understanding soil structure or composting. Every manager should be trained to reduce mowing, and in the case of cemeteries, how to integrate that with the need to provide sensitive services to the bereaved.

The Europeans have operated their cemeteries differently and accepted that resources are limited. Unlike the British, who demanded graves in perpetuity, they restricted grave rights to as low as 20 years. Consequently, a grave could be maintained to a high level for the period and then re-used. Not only did the British demand perpetuity, but they also demanded low cost. Even today, many parish cemeteries and all churchyards charge sums that hardly cover maintenance for a decade, let alone the 100 years or more that we can expect to maintain a grave in the UK. This complete absence of financial logic and acumen means that taxpayers, one way or another, fund the deficit.

Over many decades, with frequent local government reorganisation and empire building, conventional burial and cremation has been put under various departments in the local authority structure. As already mentioned it could be put under the 'parks' umbrella; however, as it involved handling the dead some authorities put it under Environmental Services; as it involved law it was occasionally put under Legal Services (perhaps with Births, Deaths and Marriages Registration). In at least one authority it was allied to dog fouling and markets. Wherever it was put, it was too often the butt of jokes as the 'dead centre of town' or the section 'that never got complaints from its customers'. Management that was truly sympathetic with the actual topic of bereavement was rare.

Cemetery management moved into the twentieth century when some UK authorities adopted the name of Bereavement Services. This enabled a new ethos to develop which ensured that no one disposal method took priority over another, and rebalanced the excessive focus on cremation with a more optimistic approach to burial. In part this reflected the environmental ethos of natural burial and the social benefits inherent in the reuse of conventional graves.

1.1.2   Management style

I am aware of some exceptional local authority Bereavement Services managers in the UK, but few of them could be identified as environmentalists. They have a difficult management stance in that most manage and deliver three disparate services, those of cremation, conventional burial and, for increasing numbers, natural burial. Most managers rise through the ranks and no external training course prepares them through university or college. They have all trained in a crematorium or conventional cemetery section, and as far as I am aware, not a single manager has trained uniquely in a natural burial setting. It is then no surprise that they possess a certain conviction that the cremation or burial that they know is the right and best way forward.

Some decades ago there was a view that younger members joining the profession would take more interest in the environment, but that is not apparent at the current time. Few young people now aspire to a profession that deals primarily with old people and outwardly possesses little excitement or relevance to modern life. In the past the profession also saw itself as a calling, one that benefited from a religious, preferably Christian, personal belief. This religious base is now less obvious, but probably exists to a small degree. Suffice to say that people with external qualifications that might benefit the profession, such as on the environment, social services and generic management, are not attracted to it.

I was a product of this old style in-house training and I used the many competent people I worked with as peer figures. Perhaps my strength was in having practicable experience and then integrating this with more academic skills acquired later in life. This has enabled me to analyse my past experience and devise some solutions to the evident problems. An essential skill for managers is listening, and this is how the idea of natural burial arose.

Two women, who opposed cremation and 'boring lines of conventional memorials', sought my advice on burial under a tree in their back garden. I advised them that with a burial in the garden, the house was hardly likely to appeal to a new buyer, and would lose some value. I also explained that were a new owner to secure the house at a reduced price, they might then succeed in having their body exhumed and sent to a conventional cemetery. But I did ask: "If I could offer you a form of tree burial, would it solve your concerns?" Both of them said yes and the seed for natural burial was sewn.

I detail this to show that the impetus came from other people, although I distilled the idea into being. It did, though, upon reflection, strongly influence my own management style at Carlisle. That period was also one in which new cremators were introduced which greatly increased gas consumption to meet the Environmental Protection Act 1990. I realised that cremation was no longer sustainable!

I had also developed wildflower conservation areas at Carlisle, which was partly due to being the ICCM representative on the Living Churchyard initiative, organised by the Church of England. This scheme, run by the truly inspiring Eve Dennis, aimed to get an owl back into every churchyard in the UK. Unlike most managers selling cremation and conventional burial, I turned green. I would love to say I remained ambivalent but I suspect my passion for owls came across. Even though I was selling cremation to 75% of the 2000 people using the service each year, I made it clear that cremation was unsustainable. For those, including many bereaved people, committed to cremation, my approach must have been challenging.

Natural burial is often more than just a concept to many site owners and managers. It becomes a passion, and often relates to their lifestyle, in which they would typically present as green consumers themselves. This deeper understanding of the environment and how all things relate does expand the vocabulary such that responses to questions on the broader environment can be answered with a degree of knowledge.

This undoubtedly gives enquirers and bereaved families much more confidence themselves, and is an important marketing issue.

If passion is evident at private sites, sadly, at some local authority sites the concept is often ill thought-out, and staff interest and awareness rather weak. Too often, natural burial is seen as a token product to meet some higher demand in the authority for a more potent environmental image. Even without natural burial, few local authorities describe with clarity the environmental and sustainability problems related to bereavement issues.

It is evident that where a Bereavement Services Manager is managing three disparate services, passion for any one option might be inappropriate. This makes me recall the word 'disinterested' which is carved on a Victorian memorial at Carlisle. It means freedom from bias or involvement. Perhaps the modern manager needs to disinterestedly manage all cremation and burial services. To be disinterested the least I would expect is that the pros and cons of each of the services is fully described, but that is extremely rare. If the manager is not environmentally aware, then specialised staff, perhaps with a passion, can be appointed to manage that specific part of the service. Even given these approaches, I really wonder whether natural burial can move forward in local authorities when conflicting services have to be packaged together!

I consider that in the new and growing natural burial market, one of the keys to success lies with the passionate owners of small, private sites. They have the freedom to adversely criticise cremation and conventional burial because they do not manage disparate services. The passion, though, must be associated with other skills that are often the strengths within the local government in-house environment. These include horticulture, transparency and understanding bereavement. Providing this knowledge is one of the principal objectives of this book.

1.1.3 Contracted services

One of Margaret Thatcher's most odious and anti-community ideas was the Compulsory Competitive Tendering of all grounds maintenance for local authority services, the memorable CCT. Local authority managers, myself included, suffered much stress when the in-house workforce of skilled, reliable, hard working people, were transferred to a municipal direct works department or private company in order to contract out cemetery grounds maintenance. The long-term effect throughout the country was reflected in the situation at Croydon, where by 2003 they had experienced ten years of grounds contracting to a private company. These companies paid the minimum wage and never provided a single day's training. Consequently, staff turnover was high, the level of skills inadequate and the horticultural standards abysmal. The cemetery memorials became merely obstacles to mowing. Within this changed environment the contract with the grave owner and grave visitor subtly changed and their rights became no more recognised than those of the user of a local park.

When judging cemeteries for the Cemetery of the Year award I immediately note bare soil due to the use of pre-emergence weedkiller or herbicides, and any evidence of perfunctory work. If it is not obvious I ask whether contractors are employed as mobile units, visiting sites periodically. Such arrangements have to be contrasted with permanent, familiar, on-site trained staff and the impact of this to the bereaved.

Too often contracts are awarded to national rather than local firms based on the lowest tender price. A culture develops where the level of service from the contractor depends on the quality of the specification and whether it is open to interpretation by the contractor to their own advantage. The reduced specification also tends to exclude stitch in time work, and contractor staff are not required to develop any meaningful relationship with the bereaved.

The message here to anybody thinking of choosing natural burial is to ask whether contractors are involved and, if so, why? If it is because the work is only seasonal and does not justify full-time staff, then this may be acceptable. Ideally, the contract should be designed to use small local firms to keep the work in the community. If national firms are utilised based on the lowest tender price then buyer beware!

Where an in-house permanent staff is not an option, an alternative is to contract grounds work to a charity such as the Shaw Trust. I introduced this at Croydon before retirement and it continues to attract compliments from the bereaved. The Shaw Trust provides training to people with a disability, or recovering from illness, addictions, etc. They normally employ highly skilled supervisors, who provide training to a recognised and transferable grounds or horticultural qualification. The charity may also have access to government grants to part-fund this work.

1.1.4   Gratuities

Gratuities have greased many palms in the funeral industry, perhaps for all time. I was aware of them being paid during my 45 years of work, and of staff being dismissed for accepting them. Both the bereaved and those planning to open a natural burial site need to be aware of this practice.

Gratuities are defined as a gift or reward, usually of money, for services rendered or perhaps to solicit business or favours. The historical basis for gratuities might be blamed on the mythical Greek, Charon, who had to be paid a coin for being ferried over the river Styx to access Elysium. Alternatively, perhaps it arose because the disposal of bodies was originally a job for 'untouchables' who may leave a curse on you if not placated by coinage.

People working in the bereavement industry are generally well remunerated and therefore gratuities are inappropriate. Small sums are paid by many funeral directors to burial and cremation staff when arriving at a funeral. These are patronising and also buy the acquiescence of the staff involved. Apart from being a serious misconduct issue subject to dismissal in local authorities, it compromises their position and makes it more difficult to oppose unacceptable practices by the funeral director or to act as advocates for the bereaved. For instance, where the funeral director constantly arrives late for services, or takes no care about what goes into a coffin for cremation (i.e. rubber boots that cause smoke) then they may not be censured. Staff compromised by gratuities may also be unwilling to support the bereaved through pertinent advice on using biodegradable coffins, refusing embalming or other actions contrary to the commercial objectives of mainstream funeral directing.

These gratuities have extended to nursing home and hospital staff. In some hospitals the practice of declared gratuities has been introduced to formalise this practice. This declares a set fee payable by the funeral director to the staff member for activities such as helping to move a body to a collection vehicle prior to the funeral. A similar approach should be taken at natural burial sites, cemeteries and crematoria in levying a set fee for the use of a staff member as a coffin bearer.

Finally, gratuities need to be separated from gifts. The bereaved sometimes wish to give a token gift of money to the person who dug the grave and Christmas presents are often given to cemetery or crematorium staff by regular cemetery visitors and funeral directors.

Provided that they are declared and shared between staff it has never been considered a gratuity.

1.1.5   Mortality rates – 'babyboomers' and 'burgerboomers'

History proves that death rates vary to reflect the prevailing social conditions, so they cannot be ignored. In Victorian times, death rates were often highest in summer (now it is in winter), when water-borne infections were rife. Women also lived shorter lives due to death during pregnancy and childbirth or, as women were at home for long periods, from absorbing lead from paint and arsenic from wallpaper and clothing dyes. We have been progressively extending our lives since Victorian times with improved water, sanitation, housing and medicine. Since the 1950s the increase has been remarkable and we now live the longest lives in recorded history. During my life, 1 to 1.5 years per decade has been added to our life span.

Understanding aspects of our mortality is always interesting, but might be considered essential for those contemplating opening a natural burial site. The current death rate is 9.4 per 1,000 population per year. This means that if the population of an area is 50,000, the total number of deaths for the year will be 470 (50 x 9.4). Although the mortality rate is 9.4 per 1000 head of population, it is necessary to analyse such crude averages. Where a high number of elderly people reside, then more deaths will occur. Bournemouth is the ideal spot for a natural burial site, although they already have two in that area. Choosing new town locations or other areas where families and young people predominate is not ideal if a high number of deaths is an important consideration.

Current statistics suggest that deaths will increase by 17% from 2012–2030 due to the baby boomer impact. The bereavement industry is heading for a halcyon period, as the baby boomers (those high numbers of births between 1945 and the early 1960s) reach the end of their extended lives. It will be a big party potentially spoiled only by some miracle drug that extends our lives even further. The party though, might be bigger than we expected, due to the burgerboomers, which is why this section is titled the way it is.

I coined the term 'burgerboomers' during one of my addresses on death when in Carlisle. Although I have joked about how we in the death business appreciate the effects of smoking, drinking and fornication, I have never dared mention the increasing obesity. It is a fact that the four coffin bearers of the past is increasingly six, and the funeral director often assists with the first lift to the shoulders because the coffin is now so heavy.

Medics are now stating that the obese will often not reach 50 years of age! If true and no miracle drug is developed to solve this problem, a mass of deaths will occur around the same time as the baby boomers. If we assume that the burgerboomer period began in 1980, then the deaths will begin in 2030. This would, of course, be reflected in the first reduction in our longevity for perhaps 200 years. If you are planning to open a natural burial site or be a funeral director, now is the time!

Another significant change over my lifetime is the reduction in deaths in the January to March period each year. Previously, deaths were very high and the work stress often led to errors. This was often made worse because of extended Christmas and New Year closures which delayed funerals for some weeks and upset the bereaved. This seasonal spike has definitely reduced, and deaths are now much more evenly balanced over the twelve months of the year, but why? A reduction in hypothermia due to better housing, winter flu injections for the elderly, warmer winters and medication that controls the real killers like pneumonia and bronchitis are thought to be some of the reasons.

As a person who has worked with bereavement for 45 years, I recognise that I can hardly be normal in my approach to death. Nonetheless, I found that people could talk to me, a death professional, about their demise more readily than they could with their children or partners. Some elderly people would tell me that, with their peer group dead, and their bodies tired out, they were ready for death, that it held no fears. Their greatest stress was not being able to discuss this with their children and settle matters that were troubling them.

1.2   WHY DO GRAVE COSTS VARY SO MUCH?

Staff at the Natural Death Centre, as well as the general public, have commented to me about the very low prices for graves in churchyards and parishes compared to local authority cemeteries. Understandably, they have accepted these at face value and considered them good value. Similar comments have been made about some private, natural burial sites which offer very low fees, which I comment about elsewhere as examples of poor pricing (see Chapter 9). These natural burial sites are potentially heading for bankruptcy. It is important to understand why and how fees have been created over the years, and the ethos behind their compilation. For any operator of a cemetery or natural burial site, these prices can be a major competitive challenge and one that needs to be recognised.

1.2.1 Churchyards

As the established Church, the Church of England has the power to provide churchyards for burial, and register burials. The Parochial Fees Order sets out the fees and these apply to all churchyards throughout England. The fees go to the central church authority and are not retained individually by each parish church or the incumbent. The parochial fees are low when compared to principal municipal cemeteries. In part this reflects the uncertain standards the bereaved must accept in a churchyard, such as grass mowing by volunteers as and when possible and no facilities such as toilets. Neither can grave rights be purchased comparable to a local authority cemetery.

The real cost of burial is the use of land, but the church never had to embrace this because they simply re-used graves over and over again and rarely extended the churchyard. Also, in not retaining the fees payable for previous burials, the church has no money to purchase new burial space when the churchyard becomes full. If the churchyard is extended, it is usually because ground is donated by an adjacent landowner, or a landowner elsewhere in the parish. If the cost of maintaining the old churchyard after new graves run out becomes onerous, they can transfer the responsibility for maintenance to a local authority by closing the churchyard by Order in Council (arranged through the Ministry of Justice). A level of maintenance can then be specified by the local authority and whatever this costs is then charged to local council taxpayers. The entire process is severely distorted financially and the low fees reflect this.

The Ministry of Justice Burial Grounds Survey 2007 suggests that between 16,000 and 18,000 Church of England burial grounds exist, with a further 2,000 under the Church of Wales. The survey found that 80% of land available for burials was already occupied by graves, and that the existing unused space will suffice for a further 25 years.

1.2.2 Parish burial grounds

Parish councils are empowered to provide burial grounds. These are usually small, sometimes maintained by in-house staff, or perhaps a local contractor. Often they were set up because the local churchyard closed due to lack of new graves. The parish council is empowered to charge fees, but because of the immediate and more personal contact with local people through parish councillors, increasing the fees is often a sensitive issue. Consequently, as in the past, it is more a social service than a commercial operation, and fees are often very low.

1.2.3   Local authority cemeteries

Local councils, usually district and borough, manage cemeteries often first opened under the earliest Burial Acts in the period 1850–1870. Until recent decades, the cemetery was seen as a social service and generally operated at a heavy financial deficit. From the 1950s burial and cremation fees were often kept equal so that the bereaved paid approximately the same whichever they chose. However, in the 1990s the Audit Commission stated that as cemeteries and crematoria were competing with the private sector, they should, and could, charge market fees. Precisely what constitutes market fees, and how these should be devised, was not outlined. As a consequence, such fees have increased dramatically in recent years, more as a means of helping declining local authority finances, rather than as a response to meaningful pricing policies. It is, then, profoundly difficult to ascertain what represents good value when comparing one authority with another.

Local authorities cannot reuse graves so every grave sold is rather like selling the family silver. Once the land is used, a sum of money equal to the land cost of each grave used should be laid aside to purchase replacement land, which does not happen. Similarly, the maintenance cost for each and every year that maintenance has been agreed should be set aside in a sinking fund. This money is then drawn down each year for maintenance. This was done to some degree in the UK up to the 1970s, but then government decided this prudent action meant that the sinking fund was idle money. They introduced policies that ensured that local authorities used the funds, or were penalised.

The local authority can set fees for burial, for purchasing grave rights (buying a grave) for periods up to 100 years, for caring for graves, and for placing memorials. They specifically cannot trade commercially so selling coffins, caskets, and actual memorials is prohibited (*ultra vires*) with the possible exception where they are defined as essential commodity items. Few, if any, local authorities define a standard of maintenance for graves, so consumer rights are still rather vague.

Local authority budgets are publicly available so whether the local cemetery is subsidised or not can, in theory, be assessed. In practice, as most cemeteries are combined with a crematorium, most of which are profitable, then cremation profits can subsidise burial deficits, a fact which might be hidden within the combined budget.

Burial fees in county towns and rural areas tend to be lower than in cities, especially London. The purchase of a grave right plus the interment fee might average £3,000.00 in London, reducing to below £1000.00 in rural areas (2009).

Local authority cemeteries are often managed in a social service culture and with no commercial strategy. This is often democratically acceptable whilst a labour group leads but, if, for instance, the Tories come to power, the extensive cemetery deficit may be looked upon as incompetent management. This may drive precipitate actions such as a demand for privatising or contracting out the service.

Local authority burial strategies can also be incredibly short-sighted. Take a typical scenario where a district council will propose a new, often huge and extremely expensive conventional cemetery close to its urban centre. Each and every subsequent year the maintenance costs will create a deficit, most of it for mowing land that will not be interred in for perhaps 50 years.

Meanwhile, in the local authority's rural hinterland there might be perhaps 50 churchyards and dozens of these might be running short of land. As stated earlier, with no money or resources they close down and the responsibility for burial now falls to the local parish council. They often manage one small cemetery to accept the burials from perhaps a dozen closed churchyards. Ultimately the parish cemetery runs out of land and, with such low fees, no money exists for an extension. Consequently, the new burials from this parish cemetery and all the churchyards are directed to the new district council cemetery and add to the yearly operational deficit. This illustrates how an inexpensive community burial process spread over many churchyards collapses without anyone noticing. Local authorities should consider funding churchyards and parish cemeteries to maintain a local burial option, although government support would be necessary.

The Ministry of Justice Burial Grounds Survey 2007 was unable to state how many local authority cemeteries, including parish provision, exist in the UK. The survey found that 80% of local authority land available for burials was already occupied by graves, and that the existing unused space will suffice for only 30 years.

1.2.4 Comparison with cremation

Although not a burial subject, the cost of cremation is relevant as a comparison. The UK has 260 crematoria, with 66 (25%) privately owned. This private influence has probably made all crematoria more market-conscious. Few operate at a loss and most are extremely profitable. Cremation capacity may be too small in some areas, a fact exhibited if service times have reduced to around 20 minutes to increase capacity.

For new crematoria, the financial break-even point is somewhere between 600–800 cremations per year. Cremation fees vary, with the highest in cities such as London. Consumers can expect to pay up to £600.00 for the cremation fee including the medical certificates in London, down to perhaps £350.00 in rural areas (2009).

1.3 HOW IMPORTANT IS THE ENVIRONMENT?

1.3.1 Is natural burial better than the alternatives?

I am often asked if, and why, natural burial is a better alternative to cremation. Too many people assume that a universal service like cremation must have been researched and approved, but that is not the case. There is also a disinclination to adversely criticise cremation and potentially upset those who have chosen the process. With conventional burial moribund, a significant number of cremationists now recognise that natural burial is the first real threat to cremation, and take every opportunity to oppose it.

With cremation, the first misconception is that it destroys the body. In fact, it vaporises the water content, soft tissue and organs and converts them into polluting gases. This supports international concern that incineration *per se* is harmful to the environment and best avoided. The hue and cry is usually related to waste incineration only and cremation, perversely, attracts not a whimper!

If an average of two cremators are operated at the 260 UK crematoria during each working day, then every 90 minutes, the average time taken to complete a cremation, 520 bodies are incinerated together with 520 chipboard coffins, 520 plastic nameplates and coffin liners and 2,080 plastic handles plus the gas used. Add to this an assumed six amalgam-filled teeth per body, a total of 3,120 mercury fillings, the emissions of which will drift on westerly winds and deposit through precipitation in the North Sea. The cod, plaice and other fish absorb this mercury through the food chain, which we ultimately eat.

Approximately 400,000 cremations will take place each year in the UK. Many of these crematoria, especially the larger, busier operations are situated in densely populated areas. They are releasing albeit small quantities of harmful emissions such as nitrogen oxides, carbon monoxide, hydrogen chloride, sulphur dioxide, dioxins, furans, formaldehyde and mercury, as well as tiny portions of dust, called particulates. A further concern is the current trend to open crematoria with small population catchments, with such low cremation numbers that their gas usage must be high and their emissions efficiency very low.

The combination of emissions and particulates are adding to those from industrial processes, vehicles and central heating boilers. This air pollution exceeds prescribed EU levels in many UK cities and contributes to many deaths from respiratory problems. It can be stated unequivocally that the disposal of the dead by cremation actually kills people!

The government has accepted that mercury emissions pose a threat to human health and, by agreement with the Federation of British Cremation Authorities (FBCA), at least 50% of cremations (not cremators) will be abated by the end of 2012. The few newly fitted abated cremators are impressive engineering, and with their filters recycled, there is no longer a need to send hazardous waste to landfill. But the abated cremators border on the absurd with their sheer mass of technological equipment, carbon expensive both to manufacture and operate. This fuel-hungry process is also reliant on an uninterrupted gas and electric supply, which is not assured in the future. Crematoria also maintain quite extensive Gardens of Remembrance which are intensively maintained and carry a high carbon footprint.

Some metal residue remains after each cremation, hitherto interred in the crematorium grounds and a potential ground water pollution threat. Of the 260 crematoria, only 160 (62%) recycled this waste by 2009.

If cremation is environmentally poor, then conventional cemeteries are little better. A massive number of graves contain chipboard/MDF coffins with plastic handles and cremfilm coffin liners. Research increasingly suggests that buried plastic is a long-term pollution threat. Finally, it is the intensive mowing with unsophisticated engines consuming finite fuel and spewing emissions that really damage the environment.

At Centennial Park, South Australia, research suggested that a conventional burial created 39kgs of carbon compared to unabated cremation at 160kgs. Uncorroborated internet data suggests the cremation figure is as high as 400kgs, perhaps where abatement is included. Centennial Park concluded that, overall, burial with decades of mowing, irrigation and concrete memorial supports, had a higher carbon footprint than cremation.

Natural burial does not carry the carbon costs of conventional burial and potentially creates a sustainable process that is implicitly low tech. No matter what happens the process can continue insofar as there are people to carry out the work. If the gravedigging is done manually then it might be considered as a virtuous process with no emissions.

The Achilles' heel for burial in all forms is considered to be groundwater pollution. Historically, cremationists have always accused burial of polluting water. During my 45 years' work there were anecdotal comments about water pollution incidents but I never saw or had evidence of a single proven case.

1.3.2   Decomposition – good or bad?

The definition of decomposition reads: 'to break down organic matter into constituent elements by bacterial or fungal action'.

As a student member of the Institute of Burial and Cremation Administration (now ICCM) in the 1960s I visited Witton cemetery, Birmingham. We were shown 21' (7 metres) deep graves in sand and told that after 20 years, only brass handles and teeth remained. This was unusually fast for graves and my later experience showed me that the reduction to friable bone fragments took about 40 years in general, but graves in clay, invariably wet, could retain soft body tissue for much longer periods. My interest in decay rates then was purely related to the need, should it arise, to exhume a body. Exhumations after 40 years were relatively free of odour and fluid but as the burial period reduced, so concern increased. Exhumation of a body after just a few years of burial, especially in wet soils, could be attended by a mass of bloody fluids and a malodorous smell that clung to one's own body for the rest of the day.

Decay rates have not been particularly important in the UK because graves in cemeteries, whether sold in perpetuity or for set periods, cannot be re-used so experience of decay is very low.

In Victorian times, unmemorialised churchyard graves were re-used for further burials because deaths from cholera and other diseases overwhelmed the supply of graves. Body parts were routinely disinterred and were almost certainly visible in the soil mound on the surface. The overwhelming smell of part decomposed body tissue was recorded at that time, a reason why cemeteries were created to replace them from the 1850s. Churchyard unmemorialised graves have been discreetly re-used for centuries, perhaps because they involved small numbers. With the decline in churchyard burials, few have an appointed sexton to dig and manage graves, and this expertise is lost. These duties, such as they are, are now performed by contractors and expertise does not build up as it did with appointed individuals.

The Europeans have much more awareness of burial decay rates, as most catholic countries have maintained their preference for burial over cremation. They also manage graves by reusing them after fairly short lease periods, and the cemeteries are kept small and manageable. In Germany, graves are often refilled with sand after the first burial so that more aerobic conditions are created. This quickly reduces the mass and weight of the body so little remains when the grave is re-used, say after 20 years. The Italians and Spanish place coffins in chambers, often above ground, where the body is quickly dehydrated and becomes a leathery mass. Their experience of decay is of little benefit in the UK.

Although decay rates are not foremost in the mind when considering natural burial, the issue constantly arises. In part this is because most natural burial sites ought to be sustainable over the longer term, by utilising grave re-use, unless, that is, they are creating permanent habitat such as forest. As efficient decomposition may also avoid all possibility of tissue polluting watercourses, this is a further benefit.

The composting of bodies, perhaps as a type of natural burial, was discussed in the 1990s but was quickly closed down by the traditional British reserve, in which decomposition is somehow dirty and malodorous. The fact that it is a natural process, subtly complex and fascinating, was not a consideration. In recent years, the West murders (no relative!) and their deposition of bodies within an occupied house has influenced this issue. There was no odour, neither did any occupant in the house die of noxious disease whilst the bodies decomposed within a few feet. Attitudes and misconceptions to decomposition have been favourably influenced by the American body farms. They monitor the rate and effect of decay by placing donated bodies in a variety of aerobic and anaerobic conditions above and below ground. Their main aim is to assess the decomposition of bodies following a murder or death by exposure to the elements. They have proven that the bodies do not always smell, and even where they do, there is no health threat to the living. They have also confirmed that an uncovered body could be reduced to a few bones within four weeks if left on the surface.

These findings highlight some important issues. The first is that the deep burial we have performed in the past in the UK was based on custom and practice, and has no scientific base. The second is that a body, although it may have an offensive odour, is not a health hazard to us individually, or to the public in general. This is also relevant if you wish to keep a body at home prior to burial, and perhaps to handle it in preparation for a funeral. Finally, there is the fact that to be natural, the body should decompose in an aerobic state rather than rot in an anaerobic one, a topic that we should consider a little more deeply.

Understanding decomposition is complex, and I have little more than a basic understanding of the science. There are few people studying the issue and as decomposition is specific to soil, climate and other factors, I would also be sceptical of anyone stating they were an expert on the subject. Burial decay rates need to be scientifically studied related to human bodies and might be influenced by weight, sex, body fat, cause of death and the effect of drugs taken prior to death. A potential impact on decomposition might be the amount of herbage on the surface, because this maintains a constant temperature and moisture level, perhaps ideal for the soil web to maintain its optimum level of decomposition. Trees like oak can also root at least 3' (92cm) deep and might be an influence on decay.

Any study would need to be carried out with the body enclosed in a standard chipboard/MDF coffin, with the usual, and indestructible, 'cremfilm' plastic liner. Exhumation experience proves that the lid of these coffins collapses within one or two months at best. This then allows percolating soil rainwater to collect inside the 'cremfilm' liner, and pools it around the body. This clearly inhibits natural decay and the body thereby rots in anaerobic conditions, which might take many decades. Some gravediggers have reported finding the body mummified in a dry state, wrapped in the 'cremfilm' liner of standard chipboard/ MDF coffins, after it has punctured at some stage and allowed the water to drain off. This interference with the natural decay process is unpleasant and to be avoided. It is conceivable that a rotting body, where the tissue is not locked up by a natural decay process, allows percolating rainfall to mechanically move tiny amounts of body tissue into the water table.

The study would have to include bodies contained in various biodegradable coffins, most of which do not contain a plastic liner, this being replaced with tightly woven cotton or other materials said to retain body fluids, at least over the days preceding the interment. Biodegradable coffins made of wicker or bamboo have an open mesh and fairly rigid construction, which will resist soil weight and retain air spaces for some time after burial. This should aid decomposition a little better than cardboard which can collapse around the body under the weight of the soil backfilled into the grave. The absence of plastic, resins, formaldehyde, etc. and whatever else is currently used in the construction of standard chipboard/MDF coffins ought to assist in creating improved conditions for natural decay. This not only validates the use of a biodegradable type coffin, it also ensures we leave no legacy in the soil from these unnatural materials.

The scientific study would need to inter these coffins and bodies at varying depths, and disinter them periodically to study precisely what changes are occurring. This is because the decay process is reliant upon aerobic conditions, that is, oxygen being available at all times. The anaerobic burial in peat bog, saturated with water and highly acidic, is the best preserver of human bodies, perhaps only bettered by the Otzi man incarcerated in an anaerobic glacier on the Austrian/ Italian border and only mildly decayed after 5,300 years.

Assuming our ideal natural burial site had a focus on natural decay, then this is most rapid where oxygen exists in the greatest quantity, which is on the surface. An exposed body would also be blown by flies and hatching maggots would remove the soft tissue within a few weeks. The existence of swarms of flies, though ideal prey for other insects and birds, as well as odour, suggests that this is not a way forward.

Burial just below the surface, in a shallow grave, does appear to offer ideal conditions for decomposition, and might be socially acceptable. The first 12" (30cm) of depth contains oxygen and the soil web which includes varying percentages of bacteria, fungi, protozoa and nematodes. There must be a balance between these groups such that one does not out-compete the others in order to host the full range of decomposers. Experts using a microscope can readily count these colonies in a linear sampling and then grade microbial health based on the balance of the four groups, to reflect soil health. The soil health of much of the UK is good, proven by the fact that decomposition of leaves and other plant material is rapid. This organic material is identified as the humus content in soil, and the higher this is, the more fertile the soil is considered to be. Conversely, repeated use of artificial fertilisers, which destroy the soil web, reduces the soil to dust, increases compaction and thereby reduces oxygen levels.

The question that arises is just how deep can we descend before the soil web is impoverished and body decomposition is compromised? This is impossible to answer with scientific certainty, but a depth of perhaps 20" (51cm) is the consensus. Without doubt, this can be deeper in light sandy soil, and shallower in silty, clay soils. These assumptions are always based on open ground and not soil under growing trees, which may or may not be better.

Concern has always existed regarding burial at shallow depth, most often regarding odour. Clay soils in the UK harden and crack during drought periods and if these were deep enough to reach a body then odour is assumed. This might be avoided if sand, leaf mould, garden and municipal compost, etc. were placed over the coffin as a seal. Composted material potentially offers further benefits in being an ideal medium for bacteria and fungi, and perhaps other components in the soil web. An American expert has already suggested that he can select fungi suited to aid decomposition and, in a suitable medium, this can be placed on and around a coffin after burial. It remains to be proved whether this technique could be effective and at what depths.

For ideal decomposition, the conclusion must be to select a site containing fertile soil and to inter as shallow as possible. The legislation on grave depth is set out in a Ministry of Justice publication called *Natural Burial Grounds – Guidance for Operators* published on their website in 2009, and this states:

'Grave Depth

Burials in a municipal cemetery must normally be a minimum depth of three feet from the top of the coffin to the natural soil level. Where the soil is considered to be of suitable character, however, coffins of perishable materials may be placed at a reduced depth, though never less than two feet below the level of any ground adjoining the grave.

> *Natural burial ground operators are recommended to follow this regulation.'*

The legislation only applies to local authorities, within which it has become a convention to work to 36" (91cm) of soil over the final coffin. In part this is an acceptance that the soil over a typical lawned grave does crack in drought periods, and more shallow burial might release effluvium (that is, unpleasant smell or exhalation). If the reduced depth is preferred, the question is what is meant by 'soil of a suitable character'. This description is related back to an undated Memorandum of Ministry of Health printed in 1926, which states:

> *"The soil of a burial ground should be preferably of an open porous nature, with numerous close interstices (crevices or spaces), through which air and moisture may pass in a finely divided state freely in every direction. In such a soil decay proceeds rapidly, and the products of decomposition are absorbed and oxidised. The soil should be easily worked, yet not so loose as to render the work of excavation dangerous through the liability to falls of earth..."*

It is apparent that this advice was directed at rapid decomposition, in contrast to current Environment Agency requirements which lock bodies into anaerobic clay cells (see section 5.6). Natural burial sites should support rapid decomposition, so ought to work to 24" (61cm) depth of soil over the final coffin. This assumes they are not on clay soils, and ideally suit those sites that avoid routine mowing and have extensive ground cover, which will prevent soil cracking in droughts. The cost of gravedigging, backfilling and reinstating graves is also considerably reduced by this decision.

Dr. Ian Hussein of the City of London cemetery suggested at an address in Westminster in 2008 that a body interred only 24" (61cm) deep would decompose in just one year. It must be hoped that shallow burial will be researched in the future so that the advice on depth can be based on science.

Grave disturbance

Another issue with shallow burial is grave disturbance by wild animals, seemingly more of an issue in America and Australia where burrowing animals proliferate. I never experienced human remains being disturbed during my career. This may be less due to the physical effort of digging, and more to the fact that any body odour would not be detectable at typical burial depths. I am aware that in one London cemetery (2008) bones from Victorian graves have been brought to the surface in badger sets. This is probably due to the bones impeding progress below ground, and certainly not related to human bodies as a food source.

Foxes utilise many food sources and may, given the opportunity, consume human remains. If this was assumed, placing a sheet of rabbit wire just below the surface would prevent burrowing. Rodents are shallow burrowers although the presence of an owl would imply some control.

1.3.3   Embalming

Should embalmed bodies be accepted for natural burial? The process was almost unknown in the UK in the 1960s when I began work. Body storage fridges were very rare and, consequently, in hot summer weather it was a given to receive decomposing bodies that exuded a bad smell. This was masked by spray deodorisers, the smell of which could be worse than the actual one from putrefaction.

Embalming has progressively increased, especially in urban areas where large funeral concerns have promoted the same approach as in the USA and Canada, where it is routine. The Europeans never adopted the process and hence the EU is said to be considering prohibiting it because of the formaldehyde used in the process. British funeral directing, at times owned by American companies, introduced embalming to support the viewing of the body, and it also became a new income source.

The process of embalming can often bring out the poetic muse in funeral directors. Their marketing enjoys alliteration with terms like 'restful repose' and other marketing sound bites such as 'experience a beautiful memory picture'. Embalming is the ultimate death denial ritual, where the body can often look healthier dead than it ever did whilst alive!

The process of embalming is completely unlike anything the Egyptians perfected so it does not bare comparison with this ancient practice. In fact modern embalming only preserves the body for a few days to a few weeks. Michael Dunn describes the process in his book *The Good Death Guide* printed in 2000, part of which reads:

> *A two inch incision is made in the leg, the arm or, more usually, the neck. The femoral artery and vein (in the arm), the axillary artery*

and vein (in the armpit) or the carotid artery and vein (the neck) are pulled to the surface. A metal tube is inserted in (usually) the carotid artery – pointing towards the feet – and the other end is hooked up to an embalming machine. A drain tube is inserted in the jugular vein, again pointing towards the feet; this tube drains into a waste sink.

To summarise the rest of the process, an electric pump is used to force a formaldehyde solution through the carotid artery pushing the blood through the circulatory system and expelling it through the tube exiting from the jugular vein. The expelled blood is said by embalmers to be disinfected and discharged down the public sewers. A trocar, a sharpened vacuum tube is forced through the abdominal wall into the heart, lungs, stomach, liver, bladder, intestines and other organs. This is used to suck out blood, urine, fæces, etc. A colouring agent might be added to the embalming fluid to pink up the skin and give it a warm lifelike colour.

This intrusive, process has such a crudity attached to it that the funeral directors prefer to use the term 'hygienic treatment'. They use technical language by suggesting that the process is 'the scientific treatment of a body' and that it 'restores a natural appearance to the body'. They encourage the fear of the dead body by stating that 'certain bacteria' could be released which could be a 'danger to health'. This implies incorrectly, that the process is necessary for public health with a clear medical association to health and cleanliness; a neat marketing opportunity as the Americans would say.

In 1980, my mother's body was embalmed. At that time I relied on the funeral director's advice and had no understanding of what it entailed. When I viewed her body at the funeral directors I did not recognise her. Her pre-death sunken cheeks were filled out and her white pallor replaced by glowing pink cheeks. I did not internalise this, preferring to dismiss the experience in favour of my vision of her when last seen alive. I have since spoken to a number of people who had exactly the same experience. When I raised this issue with the Institute of Embalmers I was told I had experienced poor quality embalming, and had it been done properly, this would not have occurred. A study on the internet suggests that up to 33% of Americans actually find the viewing of the embalmed body a negative experience so we are not alone.

Arranging to view the body at the funeral director's premises was unusual in the 1960s. This was often because more bodies were at home before the funeral, often because they had died at home. Wakes were held in the home, usually with the lid off the coffin and the body was not embalmed. Other than a person sometimes fainting from emotion there is no recorded incidence of mourners keeling over or dying from such close contact with a body. Currently, most funeral directors retain bodies in a fridge or cool room, where it will not deteriorate in the period up to a funeral regardless of the weather.

As to the need for embalming, in a hot country like Australia where one might imagine the process to be essential, only 20% of bodies are embalmed. Perhaps the most damning indictment of the process is that it is actually prohibited in the UK where the person has died of a notifiable disease. It is also worth noting that in the UK over 20% of bodies are subject to a coroner's post mortem so they cannot be embalmed routinely. This is because large cuts are made and arteries severed so that the embalming fluid could not be retained within the body.

A further concern is that the formaldehyde embalming fluid is carcinogenic. I know of at least one funeral director who blames exposure to this chemical for his unusual cancer. In the US it is said there are high levels of leukæmia, brain and colon cancers in embalmers. There are also warnings of the danger of exposure to pregnant women, when more women are now being employed as embalmers. A website also mentions that British embalming allows between two and seven times more exposure to formaldehyde than in the US. Whatever the level of danger, the fact that a hazard exists is not in doubt and this recognition has lead to funeral directors outsourcing the work. The embalmers in the 1980s were often the funeral director themselves, or a member of staff. As its safety began to be questioned, the work was outsourced to peripatetic, self-employed staff thereby relieving the funeral directors of any health and safety responsibility. This also brought about the type of competitive market changes that may well have reduced the quality and standard of embalming. This arose because, with a choice of embalmers, the funeral director could force down the price charged for individual embalming, a similar market practice as applied to coffin manufacturers. A small number of conventional funeral directors and most green funeral directors oppose embalming and advise the bereaved against it.

When I drafted the Charter for the Bereaved in the late 1990s I raised the issue of poor embalming with the British Institute of Embalming (BIE). They actually stated that as peripatetic staff members were now paid so little for each embalming, they had to work too fast and this lead to poor work. I think that the word 'poor' can be taken to mean over-pressurising the fluid pumped into the body so that sunken cheeks over-fill and recognisable features are lost. A further problem is that the embalming fluid percolates through skin and this excess can seep into the plastic coffin liner, where it collects. On a number of occasions during cremation services I have noticed that where bearers perhaps struggled to lift a coffin, or excessively tilted it when lifting out of the hearse, a clear fluid leaked over the foot end and soaked the bearer's shoulders. The clear fluid was not blood and the odour suggested it could only be excessive embalming fluid.

With regard to embalming it is easy to focus on the hazardous chemicals and forget that the waste blood is discharged in the public sewer. Assuming 75% of bodies are embalmed in the UK that could amount to 1.8 million litres of blood each year! This must then be handled by the sewage process, an expense and presumably a potential hazard in itself. It always seems perverse that in a hospital, formal permission is needed to remove miniscule portions of tissue, yet the entire blood can be tipped into the sewer from embalming. New and less hazardous embalming chemicals are being sought and developed. This includes reducing the formaldehyde content or, for instance, replacing it with products derived from seaweed. I do not consider this to be a solution as the blood is still disposed of as waste.

The real risk is that a few days after embalming, approximately 1.2 million litres of embalming fluid in bodies is cremated and casually distributed in the air above our cities and towns, another toxic ingredient in the air pollution cocktail. Embalming is not acceptable within the ethos of natural burial.

1.3.4 Coffins and burial shrouds

When natural burial started in 1993, biodegradable coffins were not in use and neither was a need for them recognised. The veneered chipboard/MDF coffin was accepted as a commodity item with little thought to its content. As time passed enquiries from people opposed to chipboard increased and so a manufacturer produced the flatpack cardboard Brighton Casket. This was the first evidence of how the natural burial movement was to change the moribund funeral process. It attracted artistic and technical innovation and not only created a wide range of biodegradable coffins, but also elevated its status to that of a funeral icon. This has influenced all funerals, not least those choosing cremation where these coffins have potentially reduced emissions. The problem has been, and remains, the lack of meaningful data to prove that biodegradable coffins actually do emit fewer, and less harmful emissions and that overall, using one reduces the total carbon impact.

I wrote to government in 1995 bemoaning the fact that although the Environmental Protection Act 1990 included provisions to utilise low emission materials, funeral directors continued using chipboard/MDF and had no interest in the growing range of biodegradable coffins. They requested more data and I submitted information regarding the cardboard 'Ecology' coffin that Carlisle City Council then sold. The complex emissions data provided with this coffin was evidence of the varied methodology used by different coffin manufacturers which made comparison difficult. Nonetheless, it appeared that overall emissions from biodegradable coffins were 75% lower. The nitrogen oxide emissions for the 'Ecology' coffin were just one seventh of those from a chipboard coffin, and that the 'Ecology' emitted no formaldehyde, unlike the chipboard coffins. There was also the further benefit that none of the biodegradable coffins were fitted with polluting plastics. The government was disinterested and noted:

> *"... the resistance you have come across from funeral directors to the use of cardboard coffins, and I am not sure that evidence of environmental benefits would necessarily, by itself, overcome this".*

That was true, as without government support to produce valid and comparable emissions data the council was unable to take a meaningful stance on the matter.

It is worth reflecting here why funeral directors were so opposed to the cardboard coffin. I had been in contact on several occasions with a manufacturer of veneered chipboard coffins. He explained that his coffins were purchased by funeral directors at about £30.00 each. This was a surprisingly low price as I was aware they were then each retailing at perhaps £200.00 or more (1994) on funeral accounts. He was aware of this and explained that his manufacturing costs had recently risen and he was trying to raise the price by around one pound, as he made little more than a pound profit on each coffin. The response of the funeral directors was to threaten transferring their orders to another manufacturer. The coffins he manufactured looked so like real wood that they could carry a large mark-up without the consumer feeling they had been overcharged.

In contrast, the cardboard coffins at that time could be as much as £60.00 wholesale, as so few were manufactured. The utility appearance of these coffins, and the fact that they were known to be cardboard, made it more difficult for the funeral directors to add-on a significant mark-up. Consequently, a cardboard coffin sale that replaced a chipboard/MDF coffin greatly reduced funeral director margins.

In 1998 I wrote:

> *'I have always been careful not to over emphasise the environmental value of cardboard coffins in comparison to chipboard. This is particularly the case where a funeral director strips all the plastics, including the handles, off a chipboard coffin. If the nameplate is also removed and replaced by card or wood it clearly reduces the harmful emissions significantly. If the chipboard coffin is then made to a FSC standard (Forest Stewardship Council) then it also reduces the potential emissions when used as an alternative to a cardboard coffin.*
>
> *All this, of course, denies the fact that a cardboard coffin is symbolic of care for the environment and therefore has added value to the user. Chipboard is a product manufactured to the detriment of the environment and masquerading as real wood. It epitomises the hollow world of commercialism and is so evidently not a 'green' material.*
>
> *A chipboard coffin also needs a cremfilm liner, which is an extremely strong form of plastic sheeting. There is no doubt in my mind that on balance, even using a stripped down chipboard coffin, the cardboard coffin is the better choice. If we add the liner plus the resins used to bind the chipboard, the glues used to affix the outer veneer and the fact that this might be made of plasticised material, a significant proportion of the coffin is unnatural manufactured product.'*

The objections to the use of cardboard includes whether it contains harmful inks, dyes, etc. from the recycled paper. Added to this is the fact that the production of cardboard is also energy intensive so the overall carbon impact, including transportation, might be higher than imagined. The use of papier-mâché and such products is similar. The more recent introduction of bamboo, wicker, sea grass, etc. are all emission-free organic material but they are often transported across the world and have as yet an unassessed carbon impact. The biodegradable coffin manufacturers have a responsibility to help us all by producing better supportive data.

Conversely, it is almost unbelievable that the manufacturers of the chipboard/MDF coffins produce no similar data, a damning indictment of their ethical commitment. As many of the chipboard/MDF coffin manufacturers appear to be owned by funeral directing concerns, this might be the reason. Neither do the government seem interested that close to 600,000 chipboard/MDF coffins are used each year, and 400,000 of these are cremated and emit pollutants.

A continuing problem with FSC approved or low emission chipboard/MDF coffins is how to recognise them as such, as they have no external mark or stud. This lack of transparency is less of a problem when recommending natural products such as willow, wicker, bamboo and wood from genuine sustainable forests. These cannot pollute with regard to noxious compounds but they do release their organic carbon into the atmosphere. A local, preferably UK-sourced wicker coffin, created by an artisan, is my preferred choice. The beautiful shape of the papier-mâché Ecopod promises such a cosy inhumation that I am also won over. Such coffins are relatively expensive but their manufacture, providing it employs local people, is socially beneficial.

An advantage of cheaper plain white cardboard coffins that was not initially realised was that they are the perfect medium for artistic decoration. Another option if the appearance of cardboard offends is to use a pall, a cloth to drape over the coffin, so that it cannot be seen. In Carlisle we offered the use of a purple velvet pall free of charge for this purpose. The bereaved can also create their own pall if they prefer.

It is also important to reflect that the chipboard/MDF coffin, when buried, soaks up moisture and breaks down very quickly. Although the main side panels might last some months, the corner joints break open within weeks if the soil is wet. The lid will then collapse inside the coffin sides and allow water inside. I feel confident that a cardboard, bamboo or wicker coffin, even a woollen shroud, would actually maintain its integrity for a longer period but I am unable to prove this.

The re-usable coffin

In 1997 Carlisle City Council launched the 'Carlisle Coffin', a beautiful casket constructed of poplar wood, which is hard but much lighter than oak. It was large enough to enclose a basic cardboard coffin, for use by people wanting cremation but not comfortable with mourners seeing cardboard. A fee was charged for the hire of the coffin plus the cost of the inner cardboard coffin. Funeral Directors proved very supportive because the pure wood outer casket looked such high quality. It was beautifully polished and had brass carrying rails along each side in a Victorian style. This was in contrast to the chipboard/ MDF coffins with plastic, fake brass handles which are so weak that they cannot be used to carry the coffin.

The re-usable coffin, now called the coffin cover, works well for cremation because two biers can subsequently be used to slide the inner cardboard coffin out of the outer cover. This is very difficult to achieve at the grave side so I am not aware of coffin covers being used in natural burial grounds.

A coffin is surprisingly heavy, more so as they get larger to contain heavier bodies. Logically, both the emissions and carbon impact can be dramatically lowered if the mass of the coffin can be reduced. Because the coffin cover supports the inner cardboard coffin, this can be made of even lighter cardboard. A funeral director in Bradford now retails a coffin cover and inserts but it is interesting to note how few funeral directors make this available.

Caskets

The word 'casket' is used, in contrast to 'coffin', to describe a rectangular shaped coffin, and not one tapered at head and foot. In view of the often plush interior lining, caskets are much bigger than coffins. Many local authorities charge an extra fee to inter these in view of the increased excavation necessary. The English casket is usually in attractive highly varnished hardwood. American caskets are the real deal and these can be in polished woods and various metals, easily costing tens of thousands of pounds. They are extremely popular in America and with certain ethnic groups in the UK, especially of African descent. Most greens would rather die than use one!

Burial shrouds

The term 'burial shroud' should not be confused with a body shroud used by funeral directors to dress the body, and sometimes included free when a chipboard coffin is purchased. This appallingly garish, backless garment is in rayon. The sadness is that widows have often related to me that the last image of their dead husband was of his body clasped in just such a garment. It is certainly not green!

Fashion victims – what the best-dressed corpses are wearing this season

I designed the Carlisle Burial Shroud after enquiries from people interested in burial without a coffin. In considering this I was aware of the ancient 'Burial in Wool' legislation which once applied in the UK. I was also aware of the crude reusable pauper coffin where, after it was lowered into a grave, the bottom unhinged and the body was ejected onto the grave base covered only in a light cloth shroud. I also noted in the research published in 2004 by Julie Rugg of the University of York on 'Civilian War Deaths in Yorkshire' that the government required local authorities to inter Second World War casualties in shrouds and avoid the use of wood. This was not welcomed and so the Home Office suggested that 'it might be best to take the bodies to the cemetery and lower them into the grave before the relatives came to take part in the burial service'. It was also noted with approval that some local authorities had taken the step of dyeing shrouds black or purple, in what was clearly a vain attempt to dignify their use and disguise their bloodied condition.

In view of this history of opposition to shrouds I felt that a more decorous design was needed, and that it had to be totally biodegradable. I approached a local mill with the largest loom in the UK and they supplied me with ten foot squares of natural undyed wool in a variety of weaves. I sourced natural cotton ropes from Kendal and a wood board for the body. The three carrying ropes are laid on the ground about 2' (61cm) apart, the blanket placed over them and stitched around the ropes to secure them together. The board is placed over the blanket and the body laid on the board prior to being wrapped in the blanket. The body board has to be a few inches less than the width of the body and about the same length, to enable bearers to lift easily on the ropes. As the ropes are forced out and around the body, the friction on the wool gives great stability. The whole package makes a cigar shape and is much lighter and more manoeuvrable than a coffin. The first purpose designed burial shroud was born!

Funeral directors were uncomfortable with the appearance and potential leakage of a shroud so its use was not promoted by them. Where a family insisted on its use, it was placed inside a standard coffin by the funeral directors, and the shrouded body removed at the grave side and lowered into the grave on the ropes. It proved light and efficient and sold surprisingly well over the UK as a whole. Parents losing a child, for instance, much preferred the body in a shroud, as many detested the cold starkness of a coffin. Baby and infant coffins are usually white, which reinforces the starkness. Some years later I was told that in advancing the use of a shroud by white Anglo Saxon people, we destroyed the prejudice and opposition to ethnic requests for shroud burial in conventional cemeteries elsewhere in the UK. It appears that the ethnic groups simply quoted the Carlisle scenario and opposition folded.

The title of this section appeared in the Benetton Colors magazine for January 1998. The whole magazine was dedicated to '*Mort – un guide pratique*' ('*Death – a user's manual*'). Because of this article, Benetton had asked me to send one of our burial shrouds, made in Carlisle, to their offices in Italy. They photographed it and returned it to our Carlisle offices very quickly and efficiently. Months later I received a copy of the magazine and there it was, our shroud neatly draping a very live, and lithe, Italian model! This visual evidence now gave Carlisle Bereavement Services the finest marketing slogan in the UK – 'We send shrouds to Turin'.

Caveat emptor (buyer beware)

It remains buyer beware when choosing a biodegradable coffin! New products come to market and it is essential to inspect these as some cardboard coffins have plastic handles and perhaps conceal a plastic lining. It is essential to ask how any body fluid leakage is prevented. There are some excellent waterproof cotton linings in bamboo coffins, and many cardboard coffins have an inside waterproof gel finish. Handles and nameplates should be inspected. Handles are not necessary as the coffin can be carried from beneath. If the coffin is to be ordered over the internet or by telephone, then full information should be obtained before the order is placed.

1.3.5   Wreaths and floral tributes

My predecessor managing cemeteries and crematoria at Wolverhampton was Ray Stew, sadly now deceased, and when it came to flowers he was no shrinking violet. At some stage in the 1960s he made a statement to the press about the sheer waste of money spent on flowers and wreaths at funerals. Over the next few days he had dozens of telephone calls and one, perhaps two of these, were death threats. He had offended the florists!

He, like so many of us in the death business, was adversely influenced by the massive labour cost of that weekly truckload of dead wreaths and flowers sent off to landfill. Add to this the plethora of telephone calls about whether wreaths had arrived; whether they were still on the grave; could they be taken to a retirement home; when do you throw them away; and the one we all hated, somebody has stolen my flowers! Professionals in the bereavement sphere see floral tributes as emblematic of the consumer society and not as items of organic beauty.

The flower, the token of love for many when benignly sitting in a grave vase, is so often an incendiary device for other grave visitors. Every day, hatred explodes at a thousand graves in the UK! A complex social scenario unfolds, for instance: A mother arrives to see flowers left by the disliked daughter-in-law; a second wife, now the widow, sees the flowers left by the children of the first marriage; a single mother sees flowers left by the father and his new girlfriend on the grave of a stillbirth or baby. Be assured, this is a reflection of modern relationships in Britain, and something that was extremely rare when I started work in the 1960s.

The repeated theft of flowers and wreaths from a grave will also become a periodic complaint at natural burial sites. The family will blame the indolent, thieving, modern youth; the poor cemetery security; or the staff who could not give a damn. It takes a strong and subtle manager to even suggest that there might, just might, be a problem within the family. Repeated assurances will be given that no such thing is possible but I can say with confidence that real theft is rare. All too often, that festering, sibling rivalry will be the cause, or some other deeply offended and remote family member. Death brings out the worst in families, as they say.

In the past the herb Rosemary was a token for remembrance. Holly and ivy, so often seen carved on Victorian memorials, symbolise everlasting life and love. Yew also has a number of powerful associations with death and churchyards. I mention the association of these plants with funerals only to reinforce the fact that the use of actual flowers at funerals is recent, almost certainly a very successful Victorian marketing project.

Flowers are now expected at funerals, and the market for wreaths and tributes is massive business. If it is assumed that there are 10 wreaths or tributes at each funeral multiplied by 600,000 funerals each year, at an average of £25.00 each we have a starting figure of £150 million. Add at least two wreaths or tributes per grave or cremation per year multiplied by 75% of deaths in year one, 60% in year two, 50% in year three, 40% in year four, 30% in year five, and a further £75 million is added. I have no desire to calculate the cost of flowers at Mothers Day and Fathers Day, and the perhaps 15% of all graves and cremations that have the benefit of a holly wreath at Christmas. Rest assured that it is a large and ever-growing figure.

I have two further problems with modern hothouse flowers, one as a horticulturalist and one as a person married to an ex-midwife. As a horticulturalist I detest and abhor the hybridising of flowers so that they have the right form and colour for market. The long-stemmed garish rose in a tube of plastic film is the ultimate horror. The fact that there is no scent from this rose adds insult to injury. The fact that bees and other pollinating insects cannot use these altered or sterile flowers is a further insult.

Secondly, the midwifery profession has reported that in some countries such as South America, pregnant women employed in greenhouses growing carnations were spontaneously aborting and having babies with deformities. This was because they were forced back into the greenhouses too soon after toxic nicotine smokes had been used to control white fly and other pests. Too often, flower production is reliant on intensive chemical use. Consider also the carbon cost of daily flying these flowers to the UK, and the fact that it appears such flowers are the main smuggling resource for illicit drugs.

I have seen recently buried graves overlaid with as much as £18,000 worth of wreaths and flowers. The local authority subsequently has to pay to send them to landfill, where they will poison the air for decades with methane. It is my belief that the £18,000 would have been better spent keeping the local hospice operating for a few days. Conversely, many people feel that the comfort that flowers give the bereaved make all other issues irrelevant!

Wreaths

When I discuss wreaths I refer to those rigid, framed, floral tributes delivered at funerals. In fact, the wreath frame, the part that is constructed to display the flowers, is the major environmental consideration. In the 1960s, the frames were made of dried grass bound with wire. Each flower was attached to a short semi flexible wire and this was pushed through the grass and wound around, holding the flower head erect and facing the viewer. Once all the flowers were placed, the wreath would be entirely plunged in water, and well soaked, could survive a few days. This was labour-intensive work and the wreath, a mass of wire, was heavy and impossible to compost so had to go to landfill. The wires immediately oxidised because they had been in water and rust would often cover the skin when handled. Worse was the fact that if these were left on white marble memorials, a rust stain could develop and might never be removed.

A period followed when moss, often stolen from moors and wild damp places, was used instead of grass. The revolution for florists was when artificial 'oasis' was introduced that could be shaped and fitted into plastic frames. This removed the need for wires, as the flower stems were placed in a medium that allowed them to draw water and they lasted much longer. Little of the plastic, and none of the oasis, was recyclable, a situation that still exists. Added to this, the sodden oasis greatly increases the weight and cost of handling the waste.

In addition, florists have added ribbon, plastic cardholders and even plastic berries on holly wreaths! I have no idea whether these berries kill the birds, but I have certainly seen blackbirds try to eat them.

The pertinent reflection here is that when it suited florists to commercially change the entire construction process to plastics, then they did so, with no discussion or consultation about the increased environmental and financial burden on cemeteries and crematoria. The challenge now is for these poor ethical practices to be reversed.

Flowers

I refer here to flowers left on graves and those other than wreaths which arrive at funerals. The floristry trade appears to see flowers as naked and exposed unless packaged in cellophane and suchlike.

In the 1960s a huge proportion of the flower market was local, often grown in smallholdings and family-run commercial horticultural units. Carnations, pinks and freesias had an intoxicating scent. Dahlias, chrysanthemums and Sweet William were naturally grown with short but inconvenient stems, lasted only a few days and were not cellophane packaged. These local producers are virtually extinct and the flowers on the High Street, many exotic, are now flown in from countries where low wages hold down production costs.

It is disconcerting that the floristry trade takes no interest in where the flowers come from, their carbon impact, or the destruction of local flower production. Consequently, local jobs have been lost together with the opportunity to train youngsters in horticulture.

The wreath and flower strategy

The first issue for a natural burial site is to develop a strategy from the outset regarding flowers and wreaths. The issue seems fairly minor in the early years when just a few funerals have occurred but as funerals increase, and more graves are being visited, the wreath and flower topic will become a major labour and waste issue. There are two principal strategies, the environmental and the commercial:

Environmental strategy

The policy of the site with regard to wreaths and flowers must be transparent. The fact that compostable wreaths are almost impossible to obtain suggests that non-compostable wreaths must be accepted over the short term. Over time, a policy to encourage locally produced, totally compostable wreaths is essential and as soon as this is feasible, then the supplier can be recommended to the funeral director and bereaved. An alternative approach is to allow, or perhaps promote, only garden flowers or collections for a local charity in lieu of wreaths and flowers.

At natural burial sites where memorials are prohibited, few flowers will be placed. A culture in which the placing of flowers is not de rigueur may be feasible and such a purist strategy will exhibit itself through relatively empty waste bins, no cellophane blowing about, less staff needed and low water usage. Some may suggest that the number of customers will also be proportionately reduced!

Commercial strategy

If the commercial strategy is adopted at a natural burial site, it must be assumed that memorials will be allowed, as discussed in section 5.12. Some natural burial site owners have actually told me that my purist approach at Carlisle was commercial suicide so this is not conjecture. If the memorials do not include a vase at the outset, then these will be added by the bereaved over time, as happens in conventional cemeteries.

As in conventional cemeteries, visits to the grave will be overtly welcomed but covertly despaired over. Dead flowers protrude from vases, those poorly designed aluminum vases associated with memorials will blow away in the wind, cellophane and ribbon will abound, much of it plastered against fences after a storm, the bins will be full, waste will pile high and the water meter will never stop revolving. Studies have shown that after five years these problems will lessen as grave visits reduce, and after 15 years very few graves will be visited. The flower issue, like a wave, transfers from the old graves to the new.

Even with a flexible strategy, it may be possible to mitigate the problems to some degree. Regulations and marketing might be used to educate grave owners and visitors to reduce the plastics, ribbons, etc. Also, if a waste recycling centre is provided, most people will separate the waste into types, although much plastic waste, including plastic pots, cannot be recycled. Pot plants will be placed on graves and peat-based compost will arise and need separation. Visitors will do some grave maintenance so soil, soil with weeds, mown grass and green waste will arise, but can be composted.

Composting wreaths and floral tributes

A prominent crematorium manager, in conjunction with the ICCM, has compiled data on the amount of waste arising through floral tributes at cremation funerals. In 2009, he set up a recycling scheme using a part-time special needs employee. This person manually strips the wreaths, composting the organic material and placing the waste plastic frames in a skip, this being recycled as land drainage pipes. The cellophane, ribbons, oasis and other plastic waste still has to be landfilled. To reduce the weight of the saturated oasis they are experimenting with crushing in order to accelerate drying out.

The market urgently requires organic wreath frames that could be entirely shredded and composted without further work. A limited number of these are now produced but there is no evidence the floristry trade will adopt these.

1.4   HAS A DEAD BODY ANY RIGHTS?

Can any binding instructions be left to ensure that your body, your funeral and your final resting place is how you want it to be?

Legally, there is 'no property in a dead body'. In other words, you cannot own your body after death, so you cannot leave binding instructions about its disposal to those who survive, or deal with your funeral. This is quite unlike your estate, which you can dispose of as you instruct providing your will is proved.

It is rather disconcerting not to own your own body. Even the phrase 'own body' now appears to be an oxymoron! The reality is that in the event of your body being stolen after death, the only potential crime is the theft of the clothes, or the shroud, you might be wearing at the time!

This issue of not being able to leave binding instructions mostly influences the funeral service. For instance I recall an Irish Catholic man who became a Mormon, but in leaving no will, his sister arrived from Ireland and took control by saying, "He came into the world a Catholic, and he will go out a Catholic." I have not personally experienced, but have heard of cases where cremation was changed to conventional burial, which was the preference of the survivors.

Natural burial is not conventional and this can create a dilemma. I recall an elderly lady, a passionate advocate of natural burial and cardboard coffins. When she died, her son came to see me because his uncle had made a disparaging remark about her being sent off in a cardboard shoebox, and her children had now lost their confidence. To support them I suggested that they had to be comfortable with their decision even if they had to go against their mother's wishes. This serves to remind us that a funeral does not occur in isolation but involves other people with needs and concerns.

To ensure that a natural burial does take place, it is essential to be able to rely on the support of those who will arrange the funeral. A will must be completed and executors appointed who will carry out the wishes expressed. Although executors are not legally bound by the instructions in the will, and can do otherwise, it is rare for them not to follow the deceased's wishes.

1.5   THE DEAD CITIZENS CHARTER

Lord Michael Young of Dartington 1915–2002 experienced a poor funeral when his wife died. He subsequently created The National Funerals College, which issued a draft Dead Citizens Charter. This was primarily concerned with changing the law so that a person had greater control over their body after death. It also highlighted many other issues related to procuring funerals, mostly on the influence of commercial funeral directing.

The Dead Citizens Charter was shelved following a meeting with representatives of national funeral director organisations. They had strong objections to two radical proposals: first, that a funeral advocate should be appointed to procure and manage the funeral, and second, that this should be in accordance with an advance funeral directive. The advocate was to be well known or associated with the deceased, but not such that they would be too distressed to robustly procure and manage the funeral, and costs. When this point arose, the atmosphere in the room changed from cordial to hostile. Perhaps the funeral directors recognised that a distressed close relative was more easily influenced by current funeral salesmanship? It appears that prior to the meeting they had identified this proposal and agreed to jointly oppose it.

Their opposition was on the grounds that it was ill thought out, and I have some sympathy for that observation. Precisely who this person is, who is close to the deceased, yet not greatly distressed by their death, is a difficult call. Perhaps the answer is a friend, or a workmate. There is then the potential for conflict between this advocate and with the widow, partner, or close kin of the deceased. Nonetheless, this was no reason to oppose the advocate proposal, as the decision as to whether it would work for them could be left to the individual. Conversely, the reason may have been that the funeral directing profession did not want a disinterested, perhaps assertive, individual dealing with them. It would also reduce the crisis purchase aspect so typical of current funeral arrangements. The advocate would be more immune to salesmanship and less likely to be patronised.

The second proposal was the need for each person to complete an advance funeral directive, as well as a will, because the will is often not read until after the funeral. An advance funeral directive was already available to enquirers through the Natural Death Centre, based on a draft I introduced for our council service in Carlisle. This is an extensive questionnaire completed prior to death specific to the body, funeral and final resting place. Because the deceased answers questions which they would not otherwise think of, they can specify a non-traditional funeral such as natural burial, or perhaps request a low cost approach which conflicts with funeral commercialism. This gives the survivors the advocacy and confidence to demand a funeral concordant with these wishes, which they may also find therapeutic.

It is important not to confuse the Dead Citizens Charter with the Charter for the Bereaved, which relates to burial and cremation service standards, and does not influence the rights of a dead body.

Chapter 2

WHAT IS NATURAL BURIAL?

2.1 THE DEFINITION

The *Collins English Dictionary* defines the word 'natural' as 'of, existing in, or produced by nature'.

The immediate conflict with the term 'natural burial' is that burial itself is not found in, or produced by nature, and is wholly a human concept. Without doubt, to be truly natural, bodies would need to be left exposed on the surface and take their chances along with all other creatures which daily die and decompose in that way.

When I first devised the concept I used the words 'woodland burial' and I believe it was the Natural Death Centre that redefined this to natural burial sometime during the 1990s. This was because it embraced new schemes being introduced that created natural habitats other than woodland. It might be assumed that 'natural burial' is a term used to describe human burial when associated with a funeral that seeks to minimise environmental impact, and where the burial area creates valuable habitat. It is a more meaningful term than 'green burial' or 'green funeral', terms often used but too often ill-defined and unclear to the bereaved. The actual name of a site may incorporate words which better reflect their aims such as woodland, downland or wildflower.

Although not considered at the outset, it might have been defined as:

> *'Natural burial' is a term used to describe the burial of human remains where the burial area creates habitat for wildlife.*

It might be assumed that natural burial is always associated with a funeral that takes account of environmental and carbon concerns. Although generally true, it is important to appreciate that some people arrange natural burial without actually arranging a funeral and send the body direct to the site. To accommodate this, the definition could be expanded to read:

> *'Natural burial' is a term used to describe the burial of human remains where the burial area creates habitat for wildlife. Where a funeral precedes such burial, it would seek to minimise environmental impact.*

As new forms of natural burial have been introduced that protect rather than create habitat, the definition could be expanded further to read:

'Natural burial' is a term used to describe the burial of human remains where the burial area creates habitat for wildlife or preserves existing habitat (woodland, species rich meadows, orchards, etc.), which are rich in flora and fauna. Where a funeral precedes such burial, it would seek to minimise environmental impact

Since the millennium natural burial sites have opened as part of sustainable farm management and, in 2008, it was suggested that water features ought to be included as an important habitat, so the definition could further be expanded to read:

'Natural burial' is a term used to describe the burial of human remains where the burial area creates habitat for wildlife or preserves existing habitat (woodland, species rich meadows, orchards, aquatic, sustainably managed farmland, etc.) which are rich in flora and fauna. Where a funeral precedes such burial, it would seek to minimise environmental impact.

This journey from a simple definition to what we might now consider to be the definitive version occurred between 1990 and 2008. It is evident that it will change further as more innovative ideas are introduced. What is apparent with this definition is the ever stronger focus on habitats yet with no change to the funeral reference, which now appears somewhat casual. In effect, as it stands it allows the natural burial site to accept funerals with a body polluted by embalming fluid and/or using coffins made of non-biodegradable materials. Clearly, it is not acceptable to create habitats and then allow polluting substances to be placed in the soil. The definition of a funeral which will minimise environmental impact is challenging and is discussed later in this book. The final definition could now read:

'Natural burial' is a term used to describe the burial of human remains where the burial area creates habitat for wildlife or preserves existing habitat (woodland, species rich meadows, orchards, aquatic, sustainably managed farmland, etc.) which are rich in flora and fauna. Where a funeral precedes such burial, it would seek to minimise environmental impact by prohibiting embalming and where a coffin is used, ensuring that this be made of natural biodegradable materials.

This definition ignores what actually happens to the body after burial. The decomposition is influenced by the depth of burial, and this, and perhaps the social impact, especially the cost of funerals, may need consideration in the future.

This extensive review of the definition illustrates the importance of considering carefully the desired outcomes. A site that does not fit within this definition offers no assurance regarding the environment or sustainability.

Chapter 3

IS THERE A STANDARD
FOR NATURAL BURIAL?

3.1 THE NEED FOR STANDARDS

Having created a definition of natural burial, the next stage is to develop standards. I have been involved in this for at least a decade, and yet there are still no standards in place by 2009. For the bereaved person, it is extremely difficult to understand the differences, not least in law, between the many natural burial sites on offer and their comparison with conventional cemeteries and crematoria.

It is important to define what is meant by standards. Most people assume that the law rigidly controls the sensitive activity associated with the disposal of human bodies, but that is not the case. Provided a private individual obtains planning permission, anybody can open and operate a natural burial site.

The government approves the opening of new crematoria but does not routinely inspect or certify any natural burial site, cemetery or crematorium in the UK, although they have been known to set up investigations regarding activities that might not be lawful; for instance, the practice of reselling graves originally sold in perpetuity or even of disinterring human remains without lawful authority. In fact the government does not even possess a list of all cemeteries and natural burial sites in the UK.

When Carlisle Council started natural burial in 1993 the private sector immediately recognised that the concept could be profitable, as it avoided the high costs of intensive maintenance which routinely bankrupted conventional private cemeteries. This highlights the fact that ecological standards, principally related to the level of mowing, cannot be separated from the sustainability issue. Because of this reduced risk private natural burial grounds started to open up and reversed the decline in burial over the previous 100 years. This was not anticipated by government who had rescinded the legislation that previously applied to private sector cemeteries. This effectively puts these new private sites outside burial law. Neither is there any legislation to ensure the continuity of a private site, in contrast to the process that protects local authority cemeteries and crematoria.

Present governments show no inclination to legislate so any proposed sites will also exist in this vacuum. This is disconcerting because in 2008 it appears a private cemetery owner in financial difficulty abandoned the site and left the country. It also appears that a number of existing private natural burial sites do not have robust financial policies, and might ultimately fail. The main concern is long-term sustainability because many of these still utilise intensive maintenance procedures. Whatever happens to these sites will influence the bereaved to a greater or lesser degree, and there will be consequences that could not have occurred if the sites had been municipally operated.

It is a concern that when private cemeteries get into financial difficulties, the local authority is expected to intervene. This is because the cemetery users are residents of the area and the local authority has a mandate to support them. Conventional, private cemeteries in both Sheffield and Bristol have been taken back into municipal ownership in the past few decades. In neither case were any funds recovered, and all the early profits went to directors and shareholders.

The local authority opens and manages cemeteries within regulations drafted under a raft of Burial Acts. This framework generally ensures that the cemetery will survive perpetually under public control, perhaps excepting in Westminster, where a cemetery was sold and then had to be recovered after a great furore from local residents. What the law does not do is set any standards of management or maintenance. Consequently, the maintenance is often good when it opens and is in use, but declines as the ongoing sustainability of the site becomes a constant annual drain on council taxpayers. Cemeteries are often then de-staffed and gradually decline in condition, causing great distress to those who have burials on the site.

The consequence of all this is that the government chooses to leave the maintenance and service provision standards to those involved in the industry.

3.1.1   Charter for the Bereaved

Both private and municipal sites can adopt the Charter for the Bereaved operated by the ICCM, the first and only standard devised for UK burial and cremation. It sets out a minimum number of rights, standards and targets to ensure that the service moves forward, and includes a complaints and appeals process. A Charter Assessment Process can also be used to create a score against these rights and targets, to develop a national ranking of burial providers. However, the Charter is not specific to natural burial and consequently is not an effective way to rank sites based on ecological, environmental and sustainability issues.

3.1.2   ECOLOGICAL CHALLENGES

The natural burial site at Carlisle did not compromise on the environment as there was no intensive maintenance or individual grave memorials. Nonetheless, I accept that natural burial can be developed under various guises. Provided it creates habitat, and gives people the opportunity to avoid energy intensive cremation, then it has merit. Schemes should not be accepted at face value, and need to be assessed against standards. For instance, burial within a Japanese themed garden, with flowering cherries and a surface of gravel that needs no mowing, would probably be extremely popular. Such a scheme would lock carbon into trees, and if the graves were hand dug, have a fairly low energy impact. A closer analysis would show that cherries are non-native, a poor habitat for wildlife, and that road hauled chippings are hardly sustainable or ecologically sound. It is essential that natural burial sites are transparent about their commitment to the environment, sustainability and the short and long-term management of the site. It is only through defined standards that these can be assessed.

When I stated at the beginning of this section that I have been involved in trying to set standards but failed, perhaps I can explain why. Around 2000 I created an ecological classification scheme to identify sites that were ecologically sound, as class A, and all the others relegated to class B. This classification was sent to the Natural Death Centre (NDC), a charity who had organised an Association of Natural Burial Grounds (ANBG). The report was considered but not adopted because they were aware that some of their commercially successful members were regularly mowing grass, planting non-native trees, accepting chipboard coffins and embalming. The NDC were aware from complaints that people were using natural burial sites for an interment and, perhaps some months later were finding that an embalmed body was interred just a few feet from the one they had buried. The fact is that these sites had not clearly declared their standards regarding these issues, nor conveyed this to users.

As natural burial developed, some private site owners stated that the ecological principles established at Carlisle were commercial suicide. I am also aware that the Environment Agency and other planning authorities might have accepted green burial as a defined term, assuming it to prohibit embalming fluids and MDF coffins, which is not the case. These points suggest that there is a need for standards to be defined.

3.2   NATURAL BURIAL STANDARDS

This section defines the management standards required at a natural burial site to achieve a high level of commitment to the environment and sustainability. As a number of existing sites do not meet these standards, it is followed by a sustainability index which could be used to determine what standard is actually achieved.

3.2.1   Site reference

- The term 'natural burial' will only be used to encompass sites offered within this standard. This does not prevent site owners using names incorporating the terms 'woodland', 'wildflower' or other preferred description.

3.2.2   Size of the site

- The site shall have a minimum total area (including reserved burial space) of no less than 2 hectares.

Comment: Some local authorities were paying lip service to Local Agenda 21 by opening token sites. Some of these were just woodland strips around existing cemeteries. Such schemes could never offer real benefits to the environment being either too small or incapable of meaningful expansion. Neither could they be used to educate people in this new concept as they lacked a variety of habitats.

3.2.3   Planting material

- All planting will be native species, indigenous to the area.

- All trees, shrubs, wildflowers and seed will be of local provenance (unless such supply is shown to be unobtainable).

Comment: It is recognised that any scheme that leads to an increase in habitats and diversity is beneficial to the environment. Even a non-native cherry tree locks up carbon and provides succulent shoots for woodpigeons. Nonetheless, ecological value must be measured by diversity and must include insects, birds, mammals and wildflowers.

*To create diverse habitats, native trees and plants **must** be used and these ought to be of local provenance wherever possible. The design and planting should mimic the **local** flora and not conflict with it. An ecologically sound natural burial scheme cannot compromise on these issues. If it compromises too far, it becomes a cemetery with trees and is not a natural burial site!*

3.2.4   Habitat creation

- The planting on or around graves must create at least two habitats. This can include native woodland, an understory, woodland margin, woodland glade, wildflower/hay meadow, sustainable farmland, etc.

Comment: Habitats increase, and the potential for groundwater pollution decreases, as the diversity and amount of surface vegetation becomes greater. Native trees with understory and ground cover are the ideal.

3.2.5   Design

- Paths in grave areas should be constructed of gravel, bark or other substance conducive to a natural setting, which absorb rather than reflect the sun's heat, and allow precipitation to drain into the soil. Concrete slabs, kerbs and similar materials should not be used except on entrance roads, around buildings, etc.

- Paths should be suitable for disabled access subject to the foregoing clause.

Comment: Access to each and every grave can create excessive surfacing and, in inviting people to visit the grave, increases human intrusion which will also tread out habitats.

3.2.6   Graves and grave maintenance

- Grave rights can be sold for a defined period not exceeding 100 years.

Comment: The grave right gives the grave purchaser control over the grave for the defined period subject to conditions set by the site owner at the time of purchase. The land always remains in the ownership of the land owner. In local authority cemeteries this period cannot exceed 100 years, but 50 years is common. After the right expires, the grave continues undisturbed and the land owner has no authority to disturb or remove the human remains.

- The coffin, shroud or body container shall be covered by a minimum 24" (61cm) of soil.

- Gravedigging shall ideally be performed by hand, but if mechanical means are preferred, this should be clearly stated in leaflets.

- All burials shall be contained in earth friendly material, which might include cardboard, bamboo, wicker, pure wood from sustainable sources, wool burial shroud and any other natural material including recycled products. Chipboard, MDF, particle board and non-biodegradable material shall be prohibited. The use of metal fixings, screws, etc. on these products shall be acceptable, but should be phased out wherever possible.

  Comment: Particle board, chipboard or MDF coffins are all harmful to manufacture and because they do not biodegrade, are at the very least alien to the earth and might also be polluting in other ways.

3.2.7   Memorials and memorabilia

- No permanent memorials will be placed on individual graves.

  Comment: As part of the original concept, the marking of graves using an inscribed memorial was deliberately avoided. This was because the presence of a memorial was seen as an invitation to tend the grave thereby damaging ground flora as well as leaving artificial flowers, etc. which are not compatible with a natural setting. One of the perceived benefits of this memorial-free concept was that anonymity was seen as a benefit with a tree or shrub replacing a stone memorial. They were also donating the body to nature or sustainability as evidence of their commitment to a new approach. Individual memorials as part of a communal memorial placed within the site might be an alternative, such as a sheepfold with plaques inside, which does not invite people to attend the actual grave.

- No vases or memorabilia will be allowed on graves.

3.2.8   Embalming

- Bodies shall not be embalmed prior to burial. The term 'embalming' might be described as hygienic or cosmetic treatment by funeral directors. Where a body is embalmed abroad prior to a flight home, and refusal would prevent a couple being interred together, this requirement may be waived at the discretion of the site owner.

3.2.9   Sustainability

- Seats and other features should be constructed of natural materials, locally sourced if possible. No rainforest timber or timber from unsustainable sources should be used on site, or tanalised or other chemically treated wood.

- Grass cutting will not exceed two cuts each year. These will be anticipated in summer and autumn. Native meadow indicator species such as meadow brown butterfly, crickets, voles, etc. will be used as targets for meadow or glade, and progress should be monitored and reported periodically to grave owners and in promotional material.

  Comment: Natural burial was specifically designed to remove the aspects of conventional burial that had several disbenefits on the environment. For instance, intensive mowing (more than twice each year) destroys all habitats and wastes finite fuels from which harmful emissions are created.

- The routine use of chemicals, slug baits, fertilisers or other potentially polluting products shall be prohibited on the site. The only exception is the spot weeding of noxious weeds, to a recognised standard, in the manner of the Woodland Trust (see www.woodlandtrust.org.uk).

- After any grass cutting, clippings should be removed to reduce fertility and thereby increase wildflower diversity.

- All clippings and green waste must be disposed of sustainably, e.g. composted on site or municipally, used as hay, etc. and not sent to landfill.

- Tree bases must not show evidence of damage due to mowing operations.

- All trees must be inspected each year, and replaced, staked or protected as required for the first five years and periodically thereafter.

3.2.10 Management

- A register of burials and a register of purchased graves shall be maintained in book or electronic form.

- All graves must be individually locatable using a grave plan or other permanent means.

- A site representative will supervise every funeral, taking responsibility while they are on site and ensuring that bodies and cremated remains are identified and correctly interred.

- An environmental management plan must be created, including development of the site over at least the next 100 years. If the support and advice of Local Wildlife Trusts, or other agencies involved in ecology and conservation has been obtained, this should be indicated. Waste and water management must be included.

- Has the site adopted external standards, e.g. Charter for the Bereaved?

- The site will accept independent funerals and will facilitate these wherever possible.

3.2.11 Promotional information

- A copy of these standards must be displayed on site and/or given to every purchaser of a grave right.

- Promotional information outlining the objectives of the site must be available to potential users of the site.

3.3 SUSTAINABILITY INDEX

If these standards were universal, a number of existing natural burial sites could not use the term 'natural burial' in their advertising as they fail to meet a number of the points. Apart from the divisive influence this might have, I am also conscious that this purist approach only appears acceptable to a small percentage of users. If the standards were readily identifiable against a sustainability index, this transparency would enable everyone to assess and compare natural burial sites and conventional cemeteries using a simple score.

A national sustainability index would consider the five fundamental factors of mowing, memorials, coffins, embalming and site management. The score could be included in leaflets and websites to enable comparison with alternative options.

To illustrate two opposing burial options, I have scored a sustainable natural burial site as (a) with a top score of 25, and a unsustainable conventional lawn cemetery as (b) with the lowest score of 5. The surprise is that some natural burial sites would score just 7 points, bettering the conventional cemetery in only replacing memorials with stone plaques and slightly less mowing. I managed so-called conventional cemeteries in Wolverha. Croydon where only plaques could be placed, so they wo   ᴜre identically to some existing natural burial sites.

Burial Ground Sustainability Index	Index Score	Site (a)	Site (b)
Mowing			
Mowing once/twice per year	High = 5	5	
Mowing fortnightly (16 x p.a.)	2		
Mowing weekly (32 x p.a.)	Low = 1		1
Memorials			
No individual memorials	High = 5	5	
Biodegradable memorials	3		
Stone plaques	2		
Conventional stone memorials	Low = 1		1
Coffins			
Green coffins or shrouds only	High = 5	5	
Green coffins & shrouds promoted	3		
Particle board/MDF coffins only	Low = 1		1
Embalming			
Embalming prohibited	High = 5	5	
Embalming discouraged	3		
Embalming accepted	Low = 1		1
Management			
Environmental management plan in use	High = 5	5	
Environmental management plan not in use	Low = 1		1
Score		25	5

This index could also to be incorporated into the Charter for the Bereaved by the ICCM, and all UK cemeteries could be required to indicate their own index score. In conventional local authority cemeteries that offer a variety of burial options, such as lawn graves, traditional graves and natural burial graves, it would be essential to highlight the sustainability index for each grave type, and not for the site overall. The consumer will then be educated on the issues, and understand why charges might vary. As a risk management technique for site managers the score correlates with the risk factors highlighted below:

Sustainability – Low score correlates to:

- High financial risk to the continuity of the service posed by potential pollution, long-term mowing, care and disposal of memorials (need for sinking fund).

- High risk to diversity and habitats.

- High risk to social benefit through need to charge increased fees.

- High risk of groundwater pollution.

Sustainability – High score correlates to:

- Low risk to the financial continuity of the service.

- Low risk to diversity and habitats.

- Low risk to social benefit through reduced fees to the bereaved.

- Low risk of groundwater pollution.

3.3.1 Conclusion

There is a general view within the burial profession that too little inspection is carried out to ascertain standards. The only inspections at present are a limited number of those who adopt the Charter for the Bereaved. The government takes no responsibility for inspections and prefers to leave this to self regulation. There is the risk that the matrix is abused and it would be preferable if some form of policing, especially involving contact with site users, and monitoring of complaints could be instigated. These are expensive activities and it is doubtful that they will be introduced in the short term.

Chapter 4

WHAT IS A NATURAL BURIAL SITE?

4.1   INTRODUCTION

It is perhaps necessary to consider here the final definition of natural burial from Chapter 2, which read:

> *'Natural burial' is a term used to describe sustainable human burial where the burial area preserves existing habitat (woodland, species rich meadows, orchards, aquatic, sustainably managed farmland, etc.) which are rich in flora and fauna. Where a funeral precedes such burial, it would seek to minimise environmental impact by prohibiting embalming and where a coffin is used, ensuring that this be made of natural biodegradable materials.*

In illustrating the various types of natural burial, it is not intended to be an exhaustive list and many sites exhibit a combination of types. It is important that site owners are transparent and ideally agree national definitions related to the type or types of habitat they are creating in order to be able to correctly manage and market their site.

Whatever the type of site the aim should be to blend it seamlessly into the adjacent countryside and ensure that it ecologically complements the surrounding area and any nearby native features. The County Wildlife Trust may advise on this, but payment may be required. Such advice might also forestall any objections made by Natural England or other ecological body to a planning application. In planning to unify the site with the locality, or recreating habitat it is vital not to destroy any existing valuable habitat. If the site is used by badgers, bats, newts and other threatened species, or the destruction of valuable or rare plants might occur then advice must be obtained.

It is essential to know which indicator species can be expected as evidence that a habitat has been created over time. Whatever type of habitat is offered, excellence can only be achieved if there is also adherence to the environmental and sustainability standards as set out under Chapter 3.

4.2   TYPES OF NATURAL BURIAL SITE

4.2.1   Glade burial

'Glade burial' could just as easily be called 'woodland edge burial'. This type of natural burial site is usually surrounded by a buffer zone of native trees, with groups of trees planted within the site and open glade areas between the trees. The trees can be planted in advance, or as the site develops. Trees planted in advance cannot be disturbed to inter a coffin so only those along the edges, with a clear adjacent grave, can be sold as tree graves. By planting in advance a site matures more quickly but it denies the bereaved the opportunity to plant the tree themselves. If planted incrementally, graves can be used over the year and a tree planted in the autumn. This also means that on a large site used over many years there is a mix of unused graves, young trees and maturing trees. It can look a little unbalanced but it is a valuable habitat.

The environmental benefit is that native woodland edge is the finest habitat for wildlife. The trees abutting onto understory shrubs surrounded by wildflowers supports the greatest range of insects and wildlife. It also potentially allows three grave types to be offered, tree graves, understory graves and meadow/wildflower graves in the glades. For sites that want to be permanently sustainable, the glade graves can be re-used in, say, 75–100 years assuming legislation is introduced. The trees will mature over this period and potentially create heritage trees. Depending on the area, oak on clays or beech on chalk would be suitable. Oak is deeper rooted and allows more ground cover, especially bluebells. Beech is more surface rooting and can make it more difficult to encourage vegetation. It is also a tree native only south of a line from the Wash to the Severn Estuary. More woodland information is included under section 4.2.2 and should be read in combination with this section.

The glades could be sufficiently extensive to enable heritage trees to be sited individually within the glades. These individual trees could be part of a more gradual and feathered edge to the trees so that there is not an abrupt change from woodland to glade, a feature that experts now say improves the wildlife value. Mown paths weaving through the glades could provide pedestrian access.

4.2.2   Woodland burial

It is my experience that where a tree is included as a component of the grave sale, the appeal to grave owners is increased. For many people trees have a romantic connotation. Certainly, the forests and woodlands of Britain have played an integral role in people's lives since ancient times. Perhaps because of this people's perception of what constitutes a woodland can vary. It could be a vision of great oaks set amidst meadow or of dense woodland with little sun, or of trees under planted with bluebells and ramsons (wood garlic). This indicates the importance of planning carefully and defining precisely what habitat is being created.

The one important aspect of trees is that they should be considered as permanent, and these graves cannot be readily re-used, as in glade burial. The word 'cannot' is a little strong in that given time, the trees could be logged, but the roots are expensive to remove and will make grave excavation hazardous, so this approach is best discounted.

Commercial woodland practice is not a useful guide because it involves mass tree planting, using small transplants or whips, and the routine application of herbicides. The trees can hardly be seen in the first few years, but it works well, if not ecologically, in creating timber. In a woodland burial operation, finance is available to buy larger containerised trees and create a more immediate impact. Conversely, horticultural practice suggests that the smaller whips or transplants set better roots, grow faster, and catch up over some years with larger, more expensive plants. If containerised trees are used, the standard 'lollipop' tree, i.e. where the trunk is clear of branches up to a certain height, ought to be avoided as it does not look natural and is often unstable. The more natural looking feathered tree, i.e. with stems growing up the trunk, is preferred.

The tree planting can only be done in advance if the grave is sufficiently large to allow a burial without disturbing the growing tree and its roots. Otherwise, as occurs at the natural burial site at Carlisle, the tree is subsequently planted over the coffin in autumn, the most suitable time. What is essential here is to consider the value of giving each grave an individual tree, and the symbolic involvement of the bereaved when planting the tree. Both of these aspects can have an influence on the success of this type of natural burial.

When visiting a natural burial site I am often dismayed by examples of poor tree care, especially when trees are competing with grasses and wildflowers. Mulch mats and/or mulch mediums can be placed around the tree base to reduce the competition. Rabbit damage is also easy to control using plastic planting tubes and/or spiral protectors.

If deer are a local problem then a deer-proof fence is necessary, but expensive. The problem with deer is that they might appear just once, in spring, yet cause permanent damage with their browsing of shoot tips. Strimmer nylon line damage or any form of mower damage is inexcusable, and once the bark is stripped in full or part, the tree is ruined. If a mulch or clear zone is maintained around the tree base then mowing is not necessary near the tree. If contractors or casual staff are employed, vigilance is essential.

I have also visited many sites where native and non-native (exotic) trees have been planted together. If the site is parkland, this is acceptable horticultural practice, but it is not sound on ecological sites. A choice of specified trees is fine if they are compatible. Groves of silver birch (*Betula species*) with mountain ash (*Sorbus aucuparia*) are found naturally on heaths and so work well together. It is far more difficult if the bereaved are allowed to choose the species of tree. They will favour familiar trees such as cherries, magnolias and other flowering garden species rather than trees more suited to the site. Apart from not being native, these trees may require different soil types and specific horticultural care programmes.

Sourcing native trees and other plant material can be difficult. It is essential to identify a supplier, preferably local, to confirm the plant's provenance and obtain stock as and when needed. This is especially important if the bereaved are to attend tree plantings by appointment, which should never be cancelled or changed by the site manager unless unavoidable. Care must be taken not to use trees of a single provenance, such as oak whips derived from acorns collected from a single tree. With a small genetic base they are more likely to succumb to a specific disease.

The indicator species for a woodland grave is restricted by the reduced habitats when compared to glade burial. The tawny owl is the most obvious together with the orange tip butterfly on the margins. This assumes that dense woodland is intended. If more open woodland is sought then the glade burial indicator species can be expected. The marketing approach to the woodland type grave might emphasise the carbon benefits of trees rather more than the habitat benefits, a marketing approach that is the reverse of the glade burial.

The Carlisle Woodland Burial site specified oak trees in order to recreate Cumbrian oak forest, a declining local habitat. This was partly because the oak (*Quercus robur*) was suited to the site, soil and climate and is a known tree to local people, unlike lime or beech. Local RSPB research also showed that the oak was the most valuable tree to birds because it can sustain over 300 insect species. For these reasons, the Carlisle scheme emphasised the environmental benefits far more than it did the locking up of carbon in the trees.

4.2.3   Conservation burial

This type of burial conserves existing valuable habitats rather than specifically creating them. The definition of natural burial suggests that these might include established woodland, meadow, orchard and aquatic habitats. Such schemes have much to commend them in that the perceived wildlife value is immediately visible, unlike those that create new habitat; no imagination is required as to their long-term appearance or ecological value. Planning permission for such a site might only be obtained by phasing the burials so that they do not damage the habitat being conserved. If parts of the site are not valuable habitat, these might be managed so that they further enhance the conservation value.

As with all sites, the income from the burials can be used to fund improvements to the environment. This is often enhanced if public access is allowed and would create community green space.

The presence of old or neglected trees might depress the purchase price of the land. A conservation burial scheme would gradually improve the habitat, referred to as restoration ecology in the US. This needs to be integrated into a comprehensive environmental management plan, integrating burials into preferred habitats and perhaps phased over decades.

Conservation often requires a need to reduce competition from what might be considered undesirable species, often self-set trees like sycamore. As this work can leave the area looking devastated and generate complaints, it is vital to keep the grave purchasers and the community aware of the proposals. This selective removal is very necessary if specimen plants are to thrive (such as orchids) or heritage trees are proposed. Usually, the plan begins with identifying the existing valuable flora and fauna and structuring everything around these protected zones.

The burials must enhance and not damage the ecology of the site. If the burial need is subservient to the ecological requirements, then this must be understood by all parties. As a significant part of the site might have some immediate ecological value, the burials must be fitted into the site with great care. For instance too many burials around a growing tree will potentially upset the delicate water balance, as well as severing many fine roots. Phasing burial over a period of years and within a radial grid around the tree will limit such damage. Phasing burials around the whole site will have similar benefits and disperses the graves giving bereaved people more choice. This has a financial cost in that burial density will be low so a larger area is necessary for an equivalent number of graves. It is also more financially onerous to maintain an extensive site in good order and within it manage a large number of burial locations. This requires the construction of more roads and tracks, and staff will spend more time moving around the site. This is in direct contrast to what occurs with most new cemetery sites, which is to open up a small area near the entrance, with dense burial in perhaps one or two adjacent plots, and leave the remaining space relatively unmanaged until needed in the future.

I am not aware of any natural burial sites that conserve hazel coppice, a rich habitat which supports the appealing, furry dormouse, a marketer's dream as a target species for a natural burial site! Hazel plants are cheap, easy to grow and big enough to have visual impact. They are easily planted over a grave and the poles can be cropped about every seven years, with the potential for income from the crop for hurdles. The timber is ideal biomass fuel so if this technology can be used, the crop could have a perpetual local market. A further advantage is that hazel stools, unlike trees, could be stripped out in a phased way at say 75–100 years and the graves re-used, assuming that the legislation for grave re-use will have been introduced by then. The site would be perpetually sustainable and the biomass potential could make the site carbon neutral. Such a proposal would ideally fit within a project that includes an ecology or environmental centre.

The conservation type is potentially so variable it is impossible to specify indicator species. As it is likely to include habitats within the glade and woodland types then the indicator species for both might apply.

4.2.4   Orchard burial

Some years ago, I visited and advised the owners of a potential natural burial site that was to be integrated with their organic apple orchard. Sadly, one of the partners died prematurely and so the scheme foundered. This was an inspiring idea and had the added benefit of already having the infrastructure of office, toilets and barns that could be used for services. In comparison, I visited a natural burial site in the style of an orchard that was situated in an old churchyard. The graves were planted with threatened old apple species but these were poor-looking specimens. It was remote, along narrow lanes, with no toilets on site, no site signage and was difficult to contact by telephone.

The environmental benefits of an orchard type site are difficult to quantify. In the two schemes I outline, the organic orchard burial would have been on a separate native woodland area within the orchard grounds. That area would potentially be as environmentally sound as either glade or woodland burial above. The second scheme placed the burial beneath an apple tree, but the site was not ecologically managed.

In addition, fruit trees are notoriously difficult to manage without chemical pest controls. Typically, herbicides are used to control grass and weed growth between the trees. Organic orchards might use grazing sheep, known as land maggots in Cumbria, as an environmental and sustainable alternative. An environmental compromise might be valid here if the scheme generates interest in local organic food production.

I have not specified any target indicator species, but with open grassland between fruit trees, the glade indicator species might well be cited. Apple trees are excellent lichen hosts, especially mature trees, and an existing orchard might be more suited to being a conservation type. Any scheme that supports lichens is to be commended, and specialist advice may be sought from the British Lichen Society. Such a site could only exist in clean air regions of the UK, mostly the West Coast and especially in Wales and Scotland.

If the income from natural burial could support an otherwise uneconomic orchard, it would validate its placement on prime agricultural land and would provide a local community with a burial facility.

4.2.5   Farmland burial

The definition of natural burial includes the phrase 'or preserves sustainably managed farmland'. This type of burial utilises existing pasture and meadowland on farms and is a recent and inspiring use of the concept. The burials occur on land which is actively farmed, and a proportion of the income supports the farm. Currently, a management company maintains a separate and centralised administrative office and manages the burial bookings and activities. This relieves the farmer of the practicable problems of operating a burial facility. The land remains part of the estate; the landowner retains a large degree of control and continues the practical stewardship of the land with the support of the income from the natural burial scheme.

In considering this innovative approach, it is necessary to realise that the mixed farming that was commonplace up to the 1950s is now considered to be uneconomic. Economies of scale now demand a single focus such as dairy or grain production and this has contributed to a serious decline in habitats and diversity on farmland. One of the benefits of mixed farming was that manure from the animals was used to nutrify the fields used for grazing or crops and artificial fertilisers were not needed. This farming practice has recently been termed a virtuous circle, because the farm provides for its own needs and is thereby sustainable. If the income from natural burial could support an otherwise uneconomic mixed farm, it would sustain the virtuous circle whilst also providing a local burial option to the community.

This virtuous circle is being reintroduced at Sissinghurst Farm, an integral part of Sissinghurst Garden, a National Trust property. The project is called 'From Plot to Plate' whereby all food for the on-site restaurant is grown in adjacent fields, and the vegetables and fruit manured by on-site farm stock. It appears that where chickens are given free range, as in the mixed farms, they seemingly delight in heading straight to old cow pats in order to eat the larvæ of dung beetles! A mixed farm is also the perfect habitat for swallows and a range of insect eating birds and a valuable habitat for the disappearing sparrow. This virtuous circle can, as at Sissinghurst, be guaranteed organic but it is a mistake to assume that it is necessarily sustainable. Fossil fuel is essential for tractors and other forms of transport, as the heavy work involved in such farming could not justifiably be done manually.

Farms are also sold periodically so some assurances, such as long ground leases, might support the promise of sustainably managed farmland in the event of a sale. Farms and farming practice are also notoriously susceptible to the EU, government interference, grant conditions, etc. and potential users would need to be comfortable about this. Farmland schemes should also make it clear whether they are organic or not. Any natural burial proposal on a farm might qualify for farm or rural enterprise grants.

To conclude, farmland burial, preferably associated with the preservation of old farm buildings, and a historical perspective related to the locality, is an attractive proposition. It protects the existing pasture, and economically supports sustainable farming. Users would need to assure themselves that the word 'sustainable' includes the preservation of hedges, woodlands, wildflowers indigenous to the area, and the diversity and habitats once evident on farms. The opportunity also exists to educate people on the unsustainability of modern farming and the benefits of local food production. A farm shop associated with the site would offer considerable promotional opportunities.

A further attraction is that such schemes can be anticipated to be situated in attractive rural areas. There is also a defensive element in this type of scheme, as covered in section 4.2.8, whereby users might feel their burial will prevent farms being bought for undesired development. Promotional material should also make it clear about the limitations on visiting graves, and the situation regarding site visits and any restrictions on memorabilia.

If farmland burial is measured against the sustainability index, see section 3.3, it potentially scores very high. The prohibition of embalming, use of biodegradable coffins, the anonymity of the unmemorialised grave and absence of associated grieving waste, and the fact that unsustainable mowing is replaced by grazing animals, are all commendable features.

4.2.6 Wilderness burial

There is no wilderness in England or Wales, but perhaps Scotland could claim some in the Caledonian Forest. This type of burial is being offered in the US and is marketed as the only true representation of natural burial. This contrasts with natural burial in the British landscape, where all land is influenced by human use. In Britain we treat Victorian hay meadow as if it was natural even though this is an artificial, managed habitat, which coincidentally has ecological value.

I have my own doubts about any type of burial that intrudes into a pristine wilderness environment, especially if prior to death the body was treated with medication or was embalmed. However, I am not aware of any scientific evidence to prove whether these treatments in sufficient quantity would pose a threat to the environment. Whatever the findings, human intrusion into a wilderness is best avoided. Secondly, natural burial assumes sustainability by using local facilities and thereby reducing the need to travel and waste fossil fuel. Logically, as most wilderness is remote and by definition lacks public transport, such a scheme validates personal travel and fossil fuel dependency. Anecdotal evidence suggests that in the US some bodies are actually flown to wilderness sites for burial!

In order to limit the intrusion, it must be assumed that the funeral would occur where the person dies, and then only the body with perhaps one or two close family would travel to the site. A prohibition on grieving visits, annual memorial visits and placing floral tributes must be expected, so the bereaved need to understand what is expected of them. To conclude, if the natural burials are being used defensively, to prevent development, as in section 4.2.8, then support for wilderness burial might be environmentally sound.

4.2.7 Church of England natural burial

The Times reported on 20th June 2009 that "The Bishop of London, the Right Rev. Richard Chartres, is emphatic – environmentalism is not about the fashionable concern for polar bears or about saving money on light bulbs, but is a matter of religious duty". For Christians, at least, a concern for the environment can counteract the futility of consumerism, which includes modern funerals, and perhaps the need to hold down funeral costs because they have a massive impact on the poor.

The uniqueness of the two Church of England managed sites is that they were created to ensure that consecrated graves (see section 5.5) and natural burial, were brought together to benefit the environment. The sites at present are based on the woodland type and can be used by anyone, whether religious or secular. This support by the established church gave the natural burial movement enhanced credibility in the 1990s, when its adoption by atheists, pagans and wicca was such that it was close to being identified as anti-religious.

The support of the established church could be fostered by creating 'Living Churchyard Natural Burial'.

Living Churchyard Natural Burial

One of the adverse criticisms of natural burial suggests it destroys the national heritage of the English churchyard memorial. In truth, responsibility for that lies with modern masonry using machine-cut memorials and inscriptions, and stone quarried in China. In the 1990s I was an ardent supporter of the Living Churchyard scheme, which is funded by the Church of England, so I prefer to be cited as a defender of the churchyard. This scheme was intended to highlight the heritage of churchyards as the local repository of native wildflowers and grasses, voles and the omnipresent barn owls and bats. The scheme opposed the desire to routinely mow the churchyard to the detriment of the habitat.

A natural burial site, whether private, municipal or church owned, could be opened as an extension to an existing churchyard. The grounds management could accord with sections 4.2.12 and section 5.2, to create a living churchyard habitat. Scything twice a year, to produce hay, would be the ideal and is low cost. Hand-carved stone memorials could be permitted, preferably rough-hewn free standing with no concrete foundations or metal pins and, unlike modern memorials, they would not be polished. The stone would need to be in the vernacular avoiding foreign granites and marbles incompatible with the churchyard. A low cost oak cross manufactured in sustainable local timber could be specified, which would biodegrade over 30–50 years.

With limited mowing or scything, the memorial would be visible over autumn, winter and spring and only obscured by vegetation for perhaps two of the five strong growing summer months. What I describe here is a true Living Churchyard, a modern take on an old theme. The poet Thomas Gray would still be able to stand within it and write his elegy, as the droning beetle and moping owl would return. If the church agreed to the re-use of those graves free of trees after 75–100 years, it would ensure sustainability. Such schemes have the potential to raise much-needed income for the church, as would the similar re-use of old churchyard graves.

4.2.8 Defensive natural burial

The idea of defensive natural burial was devised by activists' intent on protecting natural areas from building development or road building. This approach assumes, quite rightly, that the exhumation of bodies is so sensitive and expensive to carry out that, at the very least, it would deter any public authority or private firm from proceeding with development. The activists and supporters use their bodies after death for burial around the perimeters of valuable habitat, or at other strategic points. There is something essentially British about such schemes and the passion and organisation can only be admired. I am not aware that defensive natural burial is available to paying members of the public.

4.2.9   Natural burial with pets

I visited an attractive natural burial site in Cornwall in 2008 which offered pet burial plots as well as plots for humans in which pets could also be included. A completely separate, designated plot was available for the burial of horses. This owner recognised that pet death can be as significant as that of a human. A number of other natural burial sites in Britain offer similar options.

In the 1990s I proposed a burial plot at Carlisle cemetery called Companions Graves. This was a separate plot of human graves with a pet grave alongside. This would have allowed people to inter a number of pets for some decades prior to their own death, and to then be buried alongside the pets. The council felt that the scheme could be seen as insensitive as there was ill feeling about dogs being walked in the cemetery at that time. Cemeteries in Bath and Haltwhistle stepped into the breach but only insofar as to create a separate pet burial plot within a municipal cemetery. I am not aware of any municipal cemetery that combines pet with human bodies.

The burial of pets is a potential marketing niche for natural burial sites. I would suggest that, if provided, the grave plot is segregated from human only burial areas, as a number of people are not pet lovers. I assume only private pet burial by families, and not the bulk disposal of pet bodies collected from veterinary facilities.

It is necessary to consider that many pets belong to, or are shared by, children. The death of a pet is a valuable experience for children in understanding loss and grief, and a pet funeral gives children the opportunity to mourn. The opportunity for children to coffin their pet, perhaps just a cardboard box, and to create and perhaps participate in a ceremony in any celebrant's hall on the site, or at the grave side, and then to see the pet buried, is potentially therapeutic.

I hesitate to support an overtly commercial approach to pet funerals, especially where the needs of children are involved, but that is, of course, the prerogative of site owners. I am aware that many conventional funeral directors are conducting pet funerals using miniature human coffins, conveyed in a hearse normally used on human funerals and with a plethora of wreaths and flowers. Such funerals are expensive and commercial marketing can be expected to encourage such funeral excesses, which I deplore.

It is important to note that, unlike human burial, pet burial is considered waste disposal and a Waste Disposal Licence is required from the Environment Agency. Likewise, if the pets are to be collected or otherwise transferred by road, a Waste Transfer Licence is also required. Restrictions apply regarding the amount of waste that can be buried, and the distance of the burials from water courses and boreholes.

4.2.10 Garden burial

A number of people choosing to inter in their own garden, farm or parkland do so in the sense that it is a natural burial, so I have included this as a type of burial.

Garden burial has existed for centuries on large estates and farms. This expanded in the 1990s with interments in small gardens and even under the patio behind terraced houses. This was in response to media coverage of what became known as the 'Independent' or 'DIY' funeral. The driving force of this movement was the Natural Death Centre led by its founder, the late Nicholas Albery. Nicholas focused on expensive funeral directing and the fact that local authorities did little to help people carry out DIY funerals at cemeteries and crematoria. To avoid the use of both funeral directors and local authorities, he supported those people who wished to be interred in their own garden.

Advisors to the NDC highlighted the absence of legal restrictions on garden burial and also clarified the otherwise complex planning situation. It was advised that planning permission was not required because a small number of unmarked and unfenced graves would not represent a change of use. Neither could small memorials be considered any form of development. The NDC recommended that the burial details should be entered on the property deeds in order to meet requirements to register the burial. Other concerns were expressed on grave excavation, especially the dangers of hitting electricity cables, the burial depth and distance from watercourses, most of which are covered elsewhere in this book.

It is also important to note that the graves cannot be sold and that the burials will be restricted to family and close associates. A small number of such burials could go on indefinitely over later generations.

A garden cannot be consecrated but there is no reason why a minister of religion could not take the ceremony.

Time has proven that there are negatives to garden burials. In one instance a woman interred her child's body on her estate, which she was later forced to sell and was then denied access to the grave. Other access problems were reported and to counteract this, it was suggested that the body be interred next to a path or other public access, or the burial plot be isolated in some way within a protective Trust.

As the property must ultimately be sold, the new owner can exhume the remains providing they obtain a Home Office Licence. There was reportedly a case in mid Wales where an elderly lady had asked to be interred in her orchard. This occurred but the new owner had the body removed and placed in a conventional cemetery. The new owner was then ostracised by the residents of the village for this act. In truth, the removal of a body because it offends the feelings of the new owners is not a valid reason to apply for an exhumation licence, but it appears to have been approved in this case. I would suggest that the longer the burial remains in place the less likely this is to happen, as the remains will be decomposed. In addition, if the grave is unmarked and the garden large, the new owners might consider the search cost too great. The problem with unmarked graves, of course, is that if the burial is uncovered at some stage it might be treated as a potential crime.

Some burials have occurred where the grave is readily seen from upstairs windows of neighbouring houses, which has caused upset. The burial details on the property deeds are certain to complicate any sale of the property, deter many buyers and reduce the sale price. Although the death will be registered with the Registrar of Births, Deaths and Marriages, the actual place of burial is not recorded so future generations, who can only assume that the conventional choice of burial within local churchyards and cemeteries was made, will fail to find the grave.

4.2.11 Arboricultural burial

There are no arboricultural natural burial sites available at the current time. I use the term 'arboriculture' to describe a tree park on similar lines to Westonbirt Arboretum. The idea for this type of burial was proposed in the 1990s but not adopted. It anticipated burials clustered around single specimen trees or groves, the park progressively extending over decades. The memorials would be small and unobtrusive, or of the communal type, perhaps as art features.

Native and non-native trees would be planted and mowing perhaps restricted to meandering paths. Access would be restricted to prevent people walking up to and around individual trees, which creates soil compaction. With a high level of environmental management, perhaps coppicing and preferably crafts utilising the various woods, it would have a unique marketing potential. The educational opportunity, in making natural burial an integral component of a populist park, would be invaluable. Burials and admission of the public could be on separate, designated days of the week, or burials restricted to closed sections until full.

4.2.12 Wildflower burial

Although many natural burial schemes include wildflower graves as an integral part of their project, I am not aware of any that specifically focus on wildflowers alone. This could ideally be part of butterfly conservation, as well as the conservation of specific wildflowers, e.g. native orchids on chalk downland. As wild rabbits maintain a valuable sward, to see them as a virtue after hundreds of years of persecution would be pleasing. There would be no benefit in using existing valuable habitat so it would ideally be part of a proposal to purchase degraded land adjacent to existing quality habitats, and then use restoration ecology practice to create the desired habitats. Wildflower meadow can give an exceptional display in spring and early summer, but can look washed out in late summer.

I do not propose to outline in detail how to create wildflower meadow from seed, which is complex, generally not advised, and entails expensive groundworks. If taking this course, the seed ought to be obtained locally, perhaps through the County Wildlife Trust rather than buying it in from a distant specialist supplier. The second problem is that degraded habitats are usually such because they have been ploughed or seeded to create pasture, usually using non-native grass species. Whatever, either approach will have seen the application of artificial fertilisers and a raised level of nitrogen in the soil. Soil rich in nitrogen is ideal for vigorous grasses and when the wildflower seed mix is applied, grass flourishes and quickly shades out any preferred wildflowers. Wildflowers prefer nutrient poor soil and can be very difficult to establish. Reducing the nutrient levels is relatively simple, but can take many years. I describe this process in more detail in section 5.2.

It is interesting to note that when photographs of natural burial graves are taken over the year as a whole, some grave shapes are picked out by specific plants in flower at that time. It might just be a rectangle of daffodils planted by the family, or forget-me-knots, or some other plant not evident within the herbage until the time of flowering. This is not a recommended planting proposal as it can look somewhat artificial. It reminds us that grave visitors impose their own personality on graves and potentially introduce plants which are not native varieties, and which might prove invasive.

In the Victorian grave conservation areas at Carlisle cemetery, when I first changed the mowing regime to encourage wildflowers, I realised that we had been preventing many interesting plants from flowering and increasing. The plants were almost certainly placed by grave visitors from as far back as the 1860s. These included martigon lilies (*Lilium martagon*) and dog's tooth violet (*Erythronium dens-canis*), both of which flourished and spread as soon as mowing was reduced. I saw these as typical of a Victorian cemetery flora, and as visitors also appreciated them, I had no wish to destroy them. The spring crocus (*Crocus tommasinianus* and *Crocus vernus*), snowdrops (*Galanthus nivalis*), Spanish bluebell (*Endymion hispanicus*, sometimes called *Hyacinthoides hispanica*) and pheasant's eye narcissus (*Narcissus poeticus*) were also established because they were well into growth by Spring and so staff had avoided mowing them. Unfortunately, the bulbils (small new bulbs) that spread out into the grass are difficult to see so had been mowed off and the areas of naturalised bulbs restricted in their expansion. These spread rapidly as soon as mowing was restricted. The advantage is that these non-native plants then sheltered attractive native species such as wood anemone and primrose, and the spring was an amazing floral show of diverse species. This display was appreciated by cemetery visitors and gave vital support to conservation.

Because this Victorian grave meadow, a small amount of the total, was a mix of native and non-native, I had no compunction in enhancing it horticulturally as opposed to environmentally. This was done by introducing a Memorial Bulb Planting donation scheme to create a half-mile bulb walk with wheelchair access alongside old paths off the main cemetery drive. This walk was signed between March and May each year in conjunction with a leaflet describing the varieties of bulbs, and the wildflowers to be seen. Once the bulbs were over, a succession of wildflowers proliferated until July, when the grass turned into hay, the crickets performed their noisy mating and new anthills sprung up ready for the woodpeckers to feed on.

I describe these actions in some detail because the beautifying of the site, if I can call it this, was an important element in gaining public support for a more environmentally sensitive approach to cemetery management. The Victorian grave areas were essentially native meadow and the bulb planting an example of human interference in the habitat. Environmentalists can, understandably, abhor such an approach.

To remain native, the wild daffodil (*Narcissus pseudonarcissus*) or Tenby daffodil (*Narcissus obvallaris*) is preferred to the larger blousy hybrids. No crocus are native yet they offer nectar to insects in sunny locations. Native bluebell (*Endymion non-scriptus*) and snowdrop are more suited to dappled shade. Native wildflower plants (plugs) can be sourced including primrose, cowslip, knapweeds and oxeye daisy so that a display is assured in year one at least. Subsequently, the plants will suffer and potentially die if the soil, moisture and/or sunlight level are unsuitable, and the potentially less showy local grasses and wildflowers will exert their domination. The process of introducing bulbs and plants may have to go on for a long period, and it is expensive. The Spanish bluebell hybridises with the English bluebell and should not be planted. The bulbs must be reliably sourced and not collected from the wild.

I leave the decision on whether such plants should be brought in to site owners. I have no doubt that I would utilise such a policy if I was creating a site on an otherwise degraded location, i.e. fields ploughed and/or artificially fertilised for many years. I would not use this approach if it risked damaging an otherwise ideal habitat, or if opposition was evident from County Wildlife Trust or other such group from which I preferred to obtain support. Neither would I buy in plants that already existed on the site, for instance bluebells or wood garlic, as their seed can be harvested and used. If in doubt on these issues, it is essential to commission a full environmental and ecological survey by a qualified ecologist, e.g. a member of the Institute of Ecology and Environmental Management (IEEM).

Grasses are wildflowers!

Some people assume that an absence of wildflowers like primroses suggests a poor meadow. Grasses are an attractive and valuable habitat but are more difficult to identify and specialist surveys may be necessary to assess their habitat value.

In Carlisle cemetery the conservation zones on Victorian graves realised a wealth of attractive wildflowers and few grasses. In contrast the natural burial area was developed on land reserved for future cemetery extensions, but leased for farming. This land had been annually treated with artificial fertilisers for some decades. Once mowing stopped, nitrogen-loving grasses like cocksfoot grew rapidly up to a metre and soon dominated the sward. Broad-leaved docks (*Rumex obtusifolius*) and curled dock (*Rumex crispus*) proliferated in some parts and had to be treated individually with chemical controls, a policy recommended by the Woodland Trust. Within ten years, the oak trees shaded the grass and probably aided by our denutrification mowing regime, the strong growing grasses slowly died away. Smaller softer grasses like Yorkshire fog gained the ascendancy, and bluebells soon increased creating the habitat promoted in our natural burial marketing.

The wildflowers I knew at Shrewsbury in 1961 were exceptional (judged only by my memory of the butterflies and insects, as no specialist surveys were carried out then). Although I now have experience, I am aware that creating wildflower meadow is not an easy science. In the case of new sites, the existence of past records related to the natural history will be extremely rare as will the history of usage regarding ploughing or cropping. It is quite possible that the entire site may have been killed with an herbicide prior to being re-seeded, so no native species of grass or wildflowers will be present. This, combined with a range of soil types, varying fertility levels and the potential existence of a seed bank in the soil make it impossible to say what will happen. When I moved to manage Cardiff Bereavement Services I assumed that my conservation experience at Carlisle could be replicated, but this did not happen. Few wildflowers appeared and strong grasses dominated. Nonetheless, an incredible number of voles existed within these grasses together with slow worms proving that this was a rare and valuable habitat.

When I moved on to Croydon, a London Borough, I suspected that the Shrewsbury policy of applying herbicides had been used there in the 1960s. I designated a number of conservation zones and grasses again dominated, but to varying degrees. Some plots were extremely strong growing, others less so. Oxeye daisy (*Leucanthemum vulgare*) was present in small quantities all over but the specialist plant proved to be large areas of meadow saxifrage (*Saxifraga granulata*), a beautiful small plant with attractive leaves and white flowers. In the second year around 30 pignut (*Conopodium majus*) plants were found in one cemetery, almost certainly evidence that this plot was managed as hay meadow in Victorian times. Pignut is fairly unobtrusive and is best spotted when it flowers in May and before it slowly recedes into its tuber. As it does this so early, the hay cut in June is no detriment to it, which is why it proliferates in such a regime and qualifies as an 'indicator' species for hay meadow. This highlights the important need to routinely survey the entire site at various times of the year.

At all times I would encourage managers to be patient with sites that have a poor flora, especially those that have been farmed in recent times. A conservation grass regime, see section 5.2, will reduce fertility and slowly improve the variety of species, especially if wildflowers exist locally. If the site is covered in ragwort, docks and thistles then control is necessary.

4.2.13 Heath and moor burial

I am not aware of any sites specifically conserving heath or moor habitats, but these would possess ideal promotional advantages. Heath and moor habitat has declined rapidly in the UK over the past 50 years, yet there is a strong desire to both maintain what remains, and perhaps to restore previous heath and moor areas. Whilst the heaths stretching from Surrey to Hampshire tend to be dry and potentially suitable for burial, the Pennine moor is typically peaty and often very wet. Although the Environment Agency might not be keen to approve the use of peat land, the marketing sales pitch relating back to the bog people and 'preserving the body for eternity' might prove successful.

Both heath and moor are at least green all year, and do not have dormant periods similar to the end of summer appearance of wildflower meadow. Both heather (*Calluna vulgaris*), typically on moors, and Erica (*Erica cinerea*), on heaths, are recognisable to the public. The New Forest heaths and the Pennine moorlands are both well-known habitats and yet pock marked with re-seeded grazing land which would be ideal for restoration through natural burial.

4.2.14 Urban natural burial with reclaimed graves

It is wasteful that so many urban graves are filled and cannot be re-used. If natural burial is to become mainstream, its introduction into these urban, rather than rural, locations would represent a significant sustainability initiative. The economy of scale in a city enables a transport and utilities system to function with a vastly lower carbon footprint per head of the population. If intensive mowing can be reduced and wild habitat recreated, an assessment of what constitutes a green funeral (see section 9.7) would prove that cities like London could offer the lowest funeral carbon footprint in the UK. The future is living in the city, not the countryside!

London authorities have the powers to reclaim graves which contain burial space, and suitably large blocks of these graves could be used for urban natural burial. Authorities outside London and London authorities whose graves are full must wait and see whether the government approves grave re-use, called lift and deepen.

Apart from potentially creating an improved habitat, this approach has two important social benefits. The first is that constant and expensive mowing can be stopped or greatly reduced; the second that it uses existing land already owned and maintained by the local authority. Churchyards could be similarly used. This creates the conditions to offer a local and low cost burial option that is affordable to all. The fact that it is local also reduces the funeral director input in both time and travelling, so reducing funeral costs. It is an entirely win win situation for the bereaved and the environment!

The layout would be based on a 3' (91cm) wide slab path laid along the foot of two rows of existing graves, leaving an 18" (46cm) strip along each side, in turf or gravel. This would be reserved for the memorial, preferably a small free-standing lump design that would never present a safety hazard. The path and memorial line on either side will use 3' (91cm) from each grave, leaving a 7' (214cm) conservation strip behind the memorial. This, added to the 7' (214cm) allocated from the next grave, will give a 14' (428cm) wide conservation strip enclosed on both sides by memorial rows. No visitor would need to step into this or otherwise use it, so it can be entirely left to wildflowers, grasses and nature, with perhaps one mowing each year. The design would look as opposite

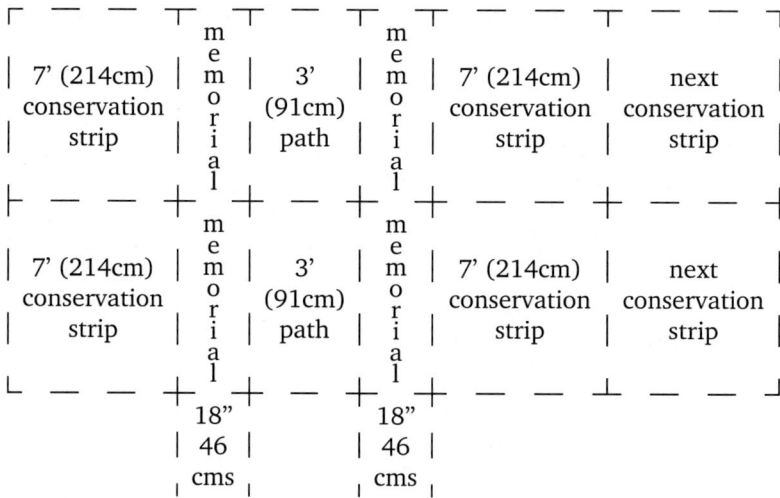

The conservation strip could be planted with native hazel (*Corylus Avellana*) and this could be coppiced to develop a large shrub rather than a small tree. After 75 to 100 years the hazel stools could be grubbed out when the grave is re-used, and could be replaced at low cost. With just a few months growth, visitors would hardly notice that the old shrub had gone. A hazel planted on every fifth grave would be suitable, and if much closer would create a hedge effect.

It can be seen that this design allows easy access, including wheelchairs, to grave rows via a 6' (1.8m) strip with a central 3' (90cm) wide slab path. Every memorial is easily accessible and 70% of the grave is conservation.

If this mix of horticultural and conservation skills sounds too unusual then a visit to the famous Sissinghurst gardens would suggest otherwise. They have a hazel coppice garden underplanted with bulbs and other decorative plants. This grave type would have a very high sustainability index score, see section 3.3, will enhance biodiversity actions plans and may score well in the Britain in Bloom competition!

4.2.15 Cremated remains natural burial

There is at least one site that accepts only cremated remains. Although this may appear to support cremation, there may be advantages. It can provide a cremated remains grave in a natural habitat, unlike the intensively maintained locations typical at crematoria and conventional cemeteries.

4.2.16 Other potential options

It is extremely difficult to categorise many existing sites. I have visited sites which include trees, yet the owners do not identify them as woodland, and because they are mown, they are not wildflower sites. If the mowing is mentioned, the owner will suggest that this will reduce over time. There is often a desire to maintain distant views, so the trees will not be allowed to dominate. I find the management of such sites, confusing and unfocused, and so must the bereaved. Neither is such an approach marketable or transparent.

Many new and innovative proposals can be expected in the future. For instance, vineyard natural burial sites have been considered and in 2009 a farmer in Cleeve, Somerset proposed to sell 'burial' allotments on his land. These would be intended for growing vegetables, beneath which the allotment holder's family members could be interred.

Chapter 5

HOW DOES LAYOUT AND INFRASTRUCTURE AFFECT THE SERVICE?

5.1   LANDSCAPE DESIGN

The first principle in creating a natural burial site is to work with nature by setting design criteria that complements the local environment. To achieve this it is essential to survey the existing habitat, and recognise how this can be used to create the type of site that it is intended to market. It may be necessary to employ an ecologist or at least seek advice from the County Wildlife Trust. The destruction of existing valuable habitat to create another is not an acceptable approach.

In achieving this desired natural environment, the question is whether an expert in landscape design is necessary? I recall a site owner touring their potential natural burial site with a landscape architect, when they realised that the site already had the natural features they needed, and that redesign was unnecessary. This, of course, may reflect the fact that they had the skills necessary to work with the existing site but the knowledge base of others may be very different.

The ideal natural burial site is one where no buildings or vehicles intrude visually on grave areas and mourners have a sense of peace and solitude within a natural setting. It is that sense of being spiritually subsumed within nature, and for many it is the planting and nurture of trees which is a prime motivator.

So many sites I have visited display little skill in the use of trees and plants, but my real dismay is the evident lack of historical awareness concerning maintenance costs. Mowing caused the virtual collapse of the once burgeoning private cemeteries in Victorian times. The design of the site can influence the long-term maintenance liability and must be a major influence not just in the initial planning but as an ongoing consideration. Once a maintenance standard is established it is difficult to change or discontinue. In fact, a natural burial site with an intensive mowing regime is misnamed; it is a just a cemetery carrying the same financial burden that will one day cause its demise!

For those proposing a natural burial site that includes regular mowing I would urge them to consider employing a skilled cemetery consultant. They will understand the historic background and may prove invaluable in specifying maintenance standards and genuinely costing these to cover extended periods of time. Such consultants advertise in the ICCM periodical *The Journal* on a regular basis.

Who to use in designing a natural burial site requires some consideration. Ecologists can recognise and work with native plants, but they are rarely landscape architects. That said, the latter may lack native plant skills and be too attuned to modern design and less to creating a natural and sympathetic landscape for burial. As a regular reader of the RHS periodical *The Garden*, it is evident that more garden designers are utilising native plants, but such skills are rare. Rather too many plant exotic species and support this by stating that global warming is moving us towards a Mediterranean climate!

I am not a landscape architect but would suggest the following:

- Relate the site to its surroundings both ecologically and historically.

- Screen ugly features, and buildings, from sight.

- Appreciate that all noise, especially road noise, intrudes on funeral services so use gabions, banks and trees to reduce this where possible.

- Use native trees and hedges to frame and structure the site and create calm, quiet zones.

- Highlight and frame attractive views using trees and hedges.

- Embrace grazing animals as they prove calming and an ideal displacement for mourners.

- Ensure the best features (e.g. bluebell drifts, views, mature trees, etc.) are actually seen and perhaps walked through by visitors and mourners.

- Ensure the entrance is open, wide and attractive.

- Keep intensive maintenance, i.e. lawns, to the minimum. Perhaps limit to the entrance, chapel, etc. (what you might call the shop window).

- Consider creating points of interest throughout the year, e.g. spring flowers, summer flowers, late summer herbaceous butterfly border, etc.

- Increase wildlife habitats especially natural ponds filled from clean catchments (no farm fertilisers or run-offs), water features generally, habitat piles, bird and bat boxes, etc.

- Ensure the habitat is created to meet any indicator species specified for the site such as owls, crickets, etc.

- Protect and where possible enhance plants such as ivy and nettles as these are valuable habitats.

- Add artistic features in natural materials. For instance, do not fell trees without considering whether the boles can be carved into art features.

- Plant trees early to mature on plots to be used in the future.

- Think carefully about how much land is opened into immediate use, as maintenance costs are reduced by keeping land in reserve.

- Erect signs to explain the breadth of environmental and ecological value on the site.

- Design to have visual impact.

- Design all buildings and paths, etc. to enable the disabled and funeral cortège's ease of access and movement.

I have always found with landscaping that new features, when completed, tend to look much smaller than anticipated, so design on a scale that will have impact. This is especially true of ponds and water features. A single tree can look very solitary, but a grove of trees can dominate the eye. Talk to as many people as possible about the proposals and listen to their views. Look with a new eye at the area around the site and try to replicate attractive planting and design.

The design has maintenance, ecological and financial implications. It is essential to create confidence through the development of an environmental management plan. Such plans often appear frightening and consequently are avoided, but they can be quite straightforward. People using or proposing to use the site will ask many questions and this is the document which should contain the answers to these assumed questions. The way to start is to write down a definition of the site, its financial and environmental objectives in the short term, and long term, and how it will be managed to attain those objectives. If development is to be phased, indicate the proposed phases over the whole site and the estimated timescales involved. Specify the regime with regard to maintenance, e.g. mowing, chemicals and herbicides, and the ecological objectives of this. State how graves will be set out and over what period.

Once this has been completed, a vision of how the site will potentially look in 50 and 100 years ought to be possible. This is vital if the site is a clean slate with lots of planned tree planting and development to take place perhaps over decades. The average person is not a landscape designer and few can visualise what an undeveloped site can look like in the future. The grave purchasers will feel more confident if you can say what will happen if the site owner dies, or if the site is sold. Long leases or a Trust to protect the site for at least 100 years might answer this question, especially if details of the fund to support the Trust for this period are also given.

5.1.1 Disability legislation

Site users can be expected to be old and infirm. Their needs are similar to those of a funeral cortège composed of closely packed, often distracted, weeping mourners, following bearers struggling to carry an increasingly heavier coffin. It makes sense to grade paths carefully and to avoid all steps, so meeting the Disability Discrimination Acts is less onerous if implemented from the start.

Under the Disability Discrimination Acts of 1995 and 2005, it is unlawful for service providers to treat disabled people less favourably than other people for a reason related to their disability, and they must make reasonable adjustments to the way they deliver their services so that disabled people can use them. It is therefore legally required to carry out an access audit and make reasonable alterations to remove any physical barriers to the service from people with disabilities. In this context, disability includes people who have hearing or sight impairments and people with certain illnesses.

With regard to wheelchair users, paths in the burial ground need not have a hard surface but they must not have unmanageable bumps or holes, etc. More information can be found at: www. equalityhumanrights.com

5.2   THE DEMON MOWER

It is valuable for natural burial site managers to consider how local authorities have maintained their green spaces, including cemeteries, and to gain from their experience. Local authorities tend to employ practicable people, most often working up to management from manual posts. I recall how every year a period of mowing stress was anticipated, often a few weeks in June, or much longer as growth reflected the perfidious temperature and rainfall balance. Hours were spent at management meetings giving updates on mowing schedules, on mower reliability and staff sickness. It was always difficult and failure led to cemeteries, parks and verges having acres of untidy grass, and the complaints flooding in. Falling behind cutting schedules was serious because this meant that the grass was then taller and heavier, so each cut became more onerous.

I recall a park manager in the 1990s becoming despondent about the absurdity of grass mowing. The sheer futility of cutting a plant that has a biological urge to flower, and when denied this, increases its growth rate. It was not just a vicious circle, it was a very expensive vicious circle. With an air of resigned desperation he wondered whether all grass mowing could be abandoned until after the plant had seeded in June, and exhausted itself. It fell on deaf ears!

Global warming results in grass growing earlier and later, so mowing starts in March instead of April and finishes in November instead of October. Growth can occur in mild spells during winter, and contributes to the fact that the first mowing in March can be the hardest and therefore the most expensive. The grass is often long and stringy, and if there have been hard frosts, dead stems are often hidden within the green stems, all damp and heavy. Grass growth varies throughout the UK. With the west being wetter and milder, grass grows thicker and faster than in the east.

Even if the cost and the pollution of mowing are ignored, it is difficult to ignore the fact that mowed lawn is a green desert. All flowering is denied, insects starve or are annihilated by a steel blade and the soil is impoverished. The English striped lawn has become a modern day icon representing the sheer absurdity of our relationship with nature.

My work experience beginning at Shrewsbury cemetery in 1961 reflects this absurdity. The older half of the cemetery was an exceptional wildlife habitat, in effect, a hay meadow for 100 years.

Three old men cycled in each day and hand scythed using the large and heavy English scythe, cutting from one side of the cemetery to the other over about 3 months. In between the cuts, the wildflowers grew at various stages and the cemetery was teeming with voles, butterflies and crickets. A barn owl fed on the voles and resided in the church steeple on site. There was no understanding of habitat and complaints were constant about the long grass and unkempt appearance.

This was also a period of burgeoning technology and I joined the team who chemically sprayed this area with grass growth retarders (*maleic hydrazide*) and herbicides (2,4,5-T) developed in the US. The managers were enthused with this new horticultural science and over a few years the herbage was tamed, memorials were levelled and we introduced rotary motor mowers, which were then a relatively new technology. The scythers were dismissed!

Consequently, the wildflowers, butterflies, crickets, voles and inevitably the barn owl disappeared, but with tidiness, the complaints stopped. Today, some 45 years later the cemetery is still neat and tidy, and remains as dead as the dodo! What is astounding is not so much that I participated in the destruction but that neither I nor anyone else noticed, or cared. Shrewsbury was not an isolated instance and in the 1960s this culture of mowing and chemical usage swept through the UK. Even when so-called garden towns like Welwyn Garden City were planned around the mower, people were duped into thinking that grass mowing was sustainable. Even now, those planning and managing our green spaces rarely understand their responsibility and the environmental implications.

Shrewsbury cemetery was previously farmed native hay meadow, so the scything had continued unchanged. This low intervention by humans did not affect the wildlife, which flourished. The maintenance was relatively low cost, no finite fossil fuel was used, no carbon emitted, and even the hay was sold each year for fodder. This was eco-friendly and incredibly efficient as a form of management, efficient but not effective! It did not suggest progress; long grass and wildflowers were untidy; untidy graves equated to lack of respect for the dead; petrol was cheap.

We are no longer as ignorant as we were in the 1960s. By reflecting back it is evident that as mowing increases, so habitat diversity decreases. My original concept of natural burial was to recreate the association of burial with the diverse and rich habitats I experienced at Shrewsbury cemetery.

The purpose of this section is to consider the impact of mowing. The section needs to be considered in conjunction with information in Chapter 4 and especially section 4.2.12.

The schedules set out below illustrate how different mowing and management regimes will result in specific outcomes.

5.2.1   Schedule 1 – feature lawns

32 x weekly cuts per annum

Sustainability index = 1 (low)

This grass will rarely exceed 1" (2.5cms) in height, and routine feeding using artificial fertiliser, constant chemical weeding and much irrigation for the green lush look, can be anticipated. Such high interventions do not make lawns bio-healthy so they rarely have ants, leatherjackets, or crickets. If this feeding, weeding and irrigation is stopped, the lawn declines in appearance. This would only be noticed by the most ardent gardeners but can increase wildlife diversity. The lawn will be green when it rains, go brown during droughts, but can maintain some ants and leatherjackets. Sure evidence of this is if a green woodpecker regularly feeds on the yellow ants and starlings feed on the leatherjackets.

With this schedule the grass clippings are always removed, often called 'boxing off' in order to avoid them dying into the surface and creating a 'thatch'. The removal of the grass is labour intensive and equally as expensive as the mowing but less so if composted on site and not transported to a recycling centre. The finest cut will be achieved using expensive cylinder machines, with a cylinder manufactured with a high blade count.

5.2.2   Schedule 2 – standard lawns

16 x fortnightly cuts per annum

Sustainability index = 2 (low)

This is the average conventional cemetery mowing regime with grass cut to 2–3" (5–8cms) in height. The height is not crucial in that providing the grass is relatively even in height it appears neat and tidy. A higher cut is also much easier if the ground is rough or stony. With this schedule, dandelions, daises, mouse ear, etc. can flower by the second week after the cut, which can appear untidy to those inclined to complain. The flowers are, of course, a habitat for a period of one week before the next cut!

To suggest a cut every two weeks is slightly misleading. This average ignores the fact that in spring, when grass growth is rapid, a cut or two will have to be advanced by a few days based on local experience. This is always counterbalanced by expanding the two weeks when dry spells arise, perhaps omitting a cut or two altogether.

No fertiliser, chemical treatments or thatch removal would be anticipated on such grass, and the clippings will be left to recycle into the surface. This can create a thatch which might also increases moisture and encourage moss. If the soil is biologically rich, worms can be highly active in pulling the clippings and leaves into the soil, not a problem in itself, but worm casts will appear on the surface. These can attach to shoes and foul up vehicles which might upset funeral directors. The grass clippings dry out quickly in warm weather, but in long wet periods accumulate on the surface and often generate complaints. Mulch mowers shred the grass more efficiently and can reduce this problem. In prolonged wet periods it is not unusual to have to manually rake off all wet grass, and clean off any memorials in order to maintain customer satisfaction.

General mowing is completed using pedestrian rotary mowers, replaced by ride-on machines where space exists with few obstructions. Sometimes, the grave areas are mown but the grass around the memorial left uncut on every second occasion, to reduce costs. For the best appearance, these two activities must be completed in unison. General mowing should always be done first and taken as close to obstructions as possible so that the more onerous strimming is reduced. Banks and dangerous slopes can be strimmed or mown with Flymo machines, but preferably should remain uncut.

Where memorials exist, these are usually mown using nylon strimmers that are handheld using a harness. Strimming is physically arduous, possibly a cause of an occupational injury called white finger, and expensive. When the grass is wet, the strimmer plasters the clippings over memorials and plaques, where they can adhere to the surface. On plaques and tablets it mixes with dust, soil and leaves to obscure inscriptions and create complaints. The strimmer ejects the cut grass at an angle so if the operator is correctly positioned, the grass can be directed to memorial free areas, if they exist.

Strimming, or at least the person operating the strimmer can also potentially damage the surface of memorials, and the bark on trees and shrubs. Once the bark is removed, even partially, then the plant is ruined. The repeated impact of a nylon line, especially on heavy duty strimmers, erodes sandstone and marble, and removes the polish off harder stones. Mulching the base of trees and obstructions can reduce the need for strimming entirely, but is labour intensive. Broken pieces of nylon line left on grass surfaces is also evidence of a lack of care.

Many sites leave an extensive grave mound after each burial, whether deliberately or due to unfamiliarity with grave excavation. The mound should only be large enough to settle back to level ground over perhaps two years. The mound can be useful for locating the grave but are often so large that they have to be mown using strimmers, which is onerous.

With regard to the environment, this mowing schedule is a graduated improvement on Schedule 1. It allows a few wildflowers to appear, but not seed. The ants will have more to forage, but their rising anthills will be periodically truncated by the mower. It is still a labour-intensive regime using expensive petrol machines, with a negative carbon impact and low ecological value.

5.2.3 Schedule 3 – spring meadow

11 x fortnightly cuts, June – November

Sustainability index = 2 (medium)

I have personally never implemented this regime but the principle is to leave the grass uncut from March to June. In theory this allows spring flowers such as primroses and bluebells to flourish, and when the vigorous grasses develop, to start mowing fortnightly from say mid June to November. This mowing immediately removes all wildflowers, nectar and pollen for insects, so it is preferable if alternative wildflower areas exist nearby.

The first cut will be challenging and might need a specialist reciprocating blade mower, or progressively lower cuts by a more modest machine. The mown surface will look bleached for a few days. Ideally, the first cut will be as a hay cut, which is described under Schedule 4.

The ecological value varies with a wide range of wildflowers early in the spring, but few later. Insect lifecycles are potentially interrupted by the sudden resumption of mowing, any developing anthills will be truncated and voles will not find the mown period tolerable.

5.2.4   Schedule 4 – conservation grass

2 cuts per annum

Sustainability index = 5 (high)

The principle in Schedules 2 and 3 is to maintain a minimum consecutive fortnightly cut. Reducing this to three or four weeks makes the mowing onerous and the finish untidy, with no benefits to the bereaved or to the environment. Operationally, the real danger is that the mowing is too difficult for the average machine, and a specialist reciprocating mower is required.

The Schedule 4 mowing will be the choice where the environment is given priority over grave access. Mowing is restricted to that which creates and maintains the richest habitat. This is the original concept of natural burial, the twice yearly hay cut using a reciprocating mower.

It is a mistake to assume that reduced mowing is comparatively less expensive. The actual cost per cut is lowest in Schedule 1 because, with so many cuts, very little grass needs to be removed on each occasion. However, because the cost of each cut in Schedule 1 is multiplied by 32 it becomes overall the most expensive over the course of a full year. As the frequency reduces the actual cost of the individual cut becomes more expensive, but the annual cost is lower because a smaller number of cuts are completed. The increased cost per cut arises because the grass is longer and heavier, and needs to be physically removed to prevent it rotting on the surface.

Schedule 4 requires mowing in June and then late October. It results in relatively short tidy grass from January to April and as the temperature rises, the grass will be perhaps 18" to 24" (46cm to 61cm) high in early June depending on grass species. As a dry warm weather spell approaches, a reciprocating type mower is used to cut the grass, which is left lying on the surface to dry out, releasing any ripened seeds. Hay rakes are then used to remove it for composting, or to a fodder haystack. The grass surface looks bleached for some days until the newly emerging green shoots appear.

In late October, the grass is often drier, weaker and lighter. The heads often contain more ripened seed at this time of year and these must be allowed to dissipate, which the raking assists.

The choice of mower

The mower used to cut for hay must cut the grass just once and at the required height. A reciprocating mower achieves this because the blade protrudes out at the front rather like a mass of scissors laid side by side. Under power the blades slide sideways across each other as it surges forward, the grass is cut and falls to the side in neat rows. Unlike all conventional mowers, no suction is created which in itself kills many insects and creatures. The blades can be set high, say at 4" (10cms) so that most small mammals and amphibians are passed over, and sufficient grass cover for voles remains. I always advise a demonstration of any new mower before purchase to ensure it meets these criteria, and that it is powerful enough to handle the grass on any specific site.

Mowing and habitats

The denutrification (see item below) usual with this regime reduces vigorous grasses in favour of wildflowers. Often crickets exist somewhere in the vicinity of a new site and, given this habitat, they will rapidly increase. They establish a territory in native grasses by creating a burrow in the soil, out of which they appear to deliver the typical rasping buzz to attract females. Once established and able to complete their lifecycle, they will never disappear provided this schedule is followed. The undisturbed habitat of native grasses in various degrees of growth will also attract the meadow brown butterfly, an ideal indicator species of native meadow. Ant hills can be bypassed with the mower to some extent and all forms of insects can flourish. Nectar and pollen sources are good, but the first cut reduces these to zero for a spell, which Schedule 5 addresses.

5.2.5 Schedule 5 – conservation grass

1 occasion per annum

Sustainability index = 5 (high)

My original intention at Carlisle cemetery and natural burial site was to follow Schedule 4 but the first cut potentially removed all the nectar and pollen. Because of this, some plots were only cut once in late October. Surprisingly, there seemed little more grass arisings in late October even though the first cut had been missed. It was also half the cost! The disbenefit was that it failed to denutrify the soil as rapidly as two cuts, although there was no way of measuring this.

The single cut creates perhaps a richer insect and vole habitat than in Schedule 4 because the impact of intervention is halved. I posed this point to a panel of bumblebee and green gardening experts at the Science Festival at Surrey University in 2009. The consensus was that mowing, especially strimming, was harmful and they preferred cutting once, and as late as possible, preferably towards November.

The disbenefit in cemeteries rather than nature reserves, is in the poorer appearance and reduced access to graves for site visitors. With Schedule 4, the site is mowed in June, the appearance relatively neat and access to all graves possible for at least a further month or two, after which the second cut occurs. With Schedule 5 no clearance of graves occurs in June so the matured grasses and wildflowers seed, then decline in appearance, often looking very dry and unkempt if a hot spell occurs in August. If other wildflowers such as black knapweed receive ample rain and warmth, they may flourish and obscure the fact that other plants, especially grasses, had declined. As always, it is a balance that has to be considered by the site owner based on the objectives marketed by the site.

It should be noted that on larger sites, Schedules 3, 4 and 5 can be tried in different areas, and the timing of the cuts varied so that pollen and nectar sources always exist on the site. The use of various schedules would create the greatest number of habitats, and thereby increase the variety of wildflower and grasses. This will take many years and require a consistent programme of plant surveys to identify what appears, and potentially what disappears, as a consequence of different mowing schedules.

5.2.6   Schedule 6 – scrub

No mowing

Sustainability index = 5 (high)

At Carlisle cemetery I left two areas completely uncut to demonstrate what happens. The first experimental area proved that within three years, oak saplings appeared at one or two per square metre. There were no oak trees in the immediate vicinity, and the culprit was a jay secreting acorns beneath the surface. Without mowing, this plot would have reverted to oak forest within ten years and actually bypassed the anticipated scrub stage. The oaks had to be cut down periodically to prevent this happening.

The second experimental grassed area remained that way and no scrub or trees appeared. Each year the grass grew higher and overlay a mass of dead grass beneath. It was extremely difficult to walk across, and only strong growing wildflowers such as black knapweed made any headway. This became a very active vole nursery. The long-term aim was that having bred under this protective grass canopy safe from kestrels and owls, they might spread into the adjacent conservation plots and provide a food source for owls. It will take a few decades to prove whether this is effective or not.

5.2.7 Reducing grass density – denutrifying the soil

Most strong growing meadow grasses prefer a high level of nitrogen in the soil, hence the need to feed lawns in Schedule 1. The grass in Schedules 2 and 3 will not be routinely fertilised, but because the grass clippings recycle into the soil, their nutrients return via the nitrogen cycle. Even if the herbage is grazed, the nutrients return through any animal excreta. Whilst these processes continue, the grass will always outgrow and out-compete wildflowers.

In Schedules 4 and 5 the long cut grass must be physically removed in the form of hay. Without these nutrients or any other form of fertiliser, the grasses progressively weaken and many other flowering plants become more dominant. This is hay meadow, mostly restricted to uplands, like the Yorkshire Dales and Swiss Alps, where even if dung is used to manure the fields, the high rainfall leaches out nitrogen. Many of the wildflowers such as the clovers create their own nitrogen supply through nodules on their roots. Mycorrhizal relationships also develop that provide nutrients to plants in these conditions.

Reaching the necessary level of denutrification that will enable wildflowers to flourish is a slow process and may take decades. Even so, in glade, wildflower and some other types of natural burial at least 100 years of management is anticipated so time is available. As the wildflowers increase, the bulk and weight of the grass can be expected to reduce.

The wildflower, yellow rattle (*Rhinanthus minor* and variants) was once common in hay meadow, but has seriously declined in recent decades. It is semi-parasitic on grasses and in taking their nutrients, can greatly reduce their vigour. If seed or plants can be obtained these might establish over time and reduce grass density.

5.2.8 Hastening denutrification

There is a theory that if topsoil and subsoil are mixed to specific ratios then denutrification to encourage wildflowers can be achieved fairly immediately. Such labour-intensive work would be financially discounted in most scenarios but because natural burial grounds routinely remove and replace soil, grave by grave, over an entire site, it could be considered. The danger is that this activity changes the local ecology which creates conditions alien to local flora and fauna. The subsoil might also be particularly heavy clay containing mineral compounds. If this idea appeals, specialist advice ought to be sought before proceeding.

All natural burial sites remove top soil as part of excavating graves, and this must be carefully managed. As the wild seed bank, and biological life, is in the topsoil it must not be buried beneath subsoil when graves are backfilled. In conventional cemeteries, the topsoil is seen as a resource, and separately stored. When excavated graves are periodically topped up after sinkage, subsoil is used in the earlier stages. When the principal sinkage is complete, say after 3 months, or a period of heavy rain, the topsoil can be replaced where it belongs, on the top of the grave. It is feasible, when this final topping up is completed, that topsoil and subsoil could be mixed 50/50.

5.2.9   The dipping lawns

Burial grounds are unusual habitats because cavities, in the form of graves, are excavated across the entire surface. I recall a mower demonstration by a young salesman familiar with conventional lawns. As he operated the mower he immediately asked, "Why is the ground full of dips?" The lesson here is that regular, skilled reinstatement of graves is important to maintain even surfaces which are safer for pedestrians and the cheapest to mow. Even as conservation meadow, the mowed appearance will look worse if it occurs over dips and rises.

5.2.10 Mowing paths

Where grass is allowed to grow relatively unchecked, sinuous paths can be cut using a conventional mower every two weeks as in Schedule 2. Such paths become relatively firm and easy to walk, albeit more of a struggle for the less able and those with a manual wheelchair. The paths also allow people to observe the growing vegetation, butterflies and crickets.

5.2.11 Leaves on grass

The feature grass in Schedule 1 and grass in Schedules 2 and 3 are usually raked free of leaves arising from trees on the site. If left on the surface they deny light to the grass and can kill extensive areas from November onwards. Leaves on all other listed grass schedules are allowed to remain and rot down, or get drawn into the soil by worms. This rotting leaf mulch is also a valuable forage habitat for birds over winter, as it rarely freezes solid and harbours many insects and worms.

The degree of raking depends on the number of trees, the leaf growth (especially high in warm wet summers) and the degree of wind moving the leaves around. Most contract specifications allow for two rakings, one in November after all leaf fall has completed, and perhaps one in early December if leaves are missed or blow in from surrounding areas. Leaves on paths are potentially dangerous for pedestrians, and leaves over drains cause blockages, so both must be cleared regularly.

5.2.12 Disposal of green waste

It is useful to consider that the traditional haymaking process occurred on mixed farms, the hay moving from the field to feeding stock, perhaps a distance of a few hundred metres. This was a virtuous circle in which the carbon impact was close to zero. This is a reminder that if hay has to be treated as waste, the carbon impact becomes a consideration. If the hay can be sold, or given away, as local fodder then the virtuous circle is replicated. I am told by horse owners that native meadow hay, free of dog fæces and ragwort, is an outstanding feed full of nutrients not found in commercial fodder. If sold or given away locally, and it replaces road-hauled fodder travelling some distance, it would represent a carbon credit for a natural burial site.

Alternatively, hay might also be used as pet fodder or bedding. The default option is to compost the hay on site, which I consider below. Otherwise, the hay must be hauled, a carbon negative, to a municipal green waste site and composted. This appears to provoke conflicting experiences in that some sites find this no problem, whilst others find the municipal sites opposed to accepting hay. The problem appears to be the type of mechanical shredder at the municipal site, whereby some cut the hay easily, others find the long dry stems bind the cutters and can prevent them working. My experience was that the green waste facility accepted the hay, but only in small amounts. They then mixed the hay with other materials before shredding.

If hay is a problem, rough-cut mowers could be used that shred the grass. This is likely to be more acceptable to a recycling centre, as it would be similar to household mown grass. Such grass would be more difficult to rake up, and a percentage would remain behind to nutrify the soil. The final carbon issue is the distance required to transport the grass for recycling. If the distance is too great, the answer is to abandon collecting any cut grass and allow it to return to the soil.

5.2.13 Composting waste

This book is not a treatise on composting, but some consideration is necessary. If the boxed-off grass in Schedule 1 covers an extensive area, the resultant bulk of grass is considerable. If tipped in a corner it will rapidly heat up, rot and create an oozing black fluid that kills nearby plants and can severely pollute a watercourse. Ideally, it should be composted in boxed units suitably layered with brown waste such as hay, leaves and prunings. Cold composting works, but if the heap warms up, the compost is ready sooner. Compost heaps on concrete rafts are easiest to handle mechanically but, when placed on soil, decompose more rapidly.

No green waste arises with Schedules 2 and 3. With Schedule 4 and 5, the hay is preferably used as fodder. To compost this it needs to be mixed with green material such as grass from Schedule 1. If there is no green material, the piled hay may throw off most rainfall and remain as a rotting dry mound. This can contain dust and fungal spores which, if disturbed, can be highly irritating to the lungs. It is also a favoured habitat for nesting rats.

Although leaves are often mixed with grass, they can decompose perfectly well in their own boxed units. They do not form polluting fluids and tend to take 18 months to create good leaf mould depending on the type of leaves. It can be used as surface mulch around trees, shrubs and obstructions. In theory at least, all compost heaps should be turned at least once. This is heavy manual work and mechanical turning is preferable. If the amount of compost increases such that it cannot be composted on the small scale described, larger scale windrow techniques must be considered, and advice sought.

5.2.14 Sheep

The demon mower was not intended as a reference to sheep, often suggested as an alternative to petrol mowers. Goats could well be included, and rabbits are good grazers if the short fine grasses that they prefer form the sward.

Sheep and goats are fine for periodic grazing, but if permanent they degrade most habitats. New trees will require robust protection and voles do not flourish under such a regime. In addition, anyone who has ever visited a sheep-grazed churchyard will recall the pungent odour on warm days, and the gumming up of shoes. They are also indiscriminate feeders so any flowers will be eaten and the surface of any horizontal memorial tablets will be fouled by the droppings. I do not feel that sheep and grave visitors complement each other. Exceptions to this are where a semi-natural environment needs grazing periodically, and where grave owners have accepted such activities as an integral part of the site, e.g. permanent grazing of stock on a farm.

5.2.15 Contractors or permanent staff?

Private natural burial sites may need to use contractors for completing grounds work and gravedigging. This is especially true at small sites with too little work for full-time staff. In addition, those sites that utilise mowing Schedules 4 or 5 do not need staff over a full year. If it is a site that does not allow memorials, very little waste will arise and it may be possible to manage without permanent grounds staff, at least in the first few years, assuming a contracted gravedigger can be utilised.

The majority of local authority natural burial sites will use contractors, as mentioned previously in section 1.1.3. If the contractors are local family firms, they will appreciate consistent and known work through the year and may submit competitive quotes. They may also work through inclement weather, often necessary to meet funeral bookings.

Long term, permanent, in-house staff are a better option than contractors. Higher work standards are achieved and knowledge is gained of how the site operates. This can be invaluable where they have day to day contact with site visitors and grave owners. When the site owner is off site or on holiday, they can work without supervision, and can be empowered to help grave owners beyond anything that might be written into a specification for contracting. The bereaved always appreciate pleasant, helpful and recognised staff, qualities rarely possible through contracting. In addition, in-house staff can mow as required, and not to a set regime. This can be at times that avoid creating noise when funerals are on site, which is often a problem for contractors. Gravedigging capacity is also more manageable with in-house staff, as obtaining contractors at short notice, and to fit within funeral demand, can prove difficult.

5.2.16 Work specification

It is anticipated that there is sufficient detail in this section to compile a basic work specification. Most permanent staff in conventional cemeteries are utilised over a full year by balancing summer mowing over say 32 weeks with a winter work programme over the remaining 20 weeks. Where the summer mowing was insufficient, the staff would supplement the gravedigging staff. Usually, the gravediggers were separate from this work regime, being fully employed on that task and only assisting other staff when grave orders were low.

The winter work programme was always organised to include tree planting, hedge cutting and remedial works, such as creating easier mowing conditions for the following summer. This included levelling graves, filling hollows and turfing, edging paths and roads, and laying mulch around trees and obstructions, and against solid walls to reduce strimming needs. If this work is neglected for some years, the mowing gets progressively more difficult and costs escalate by degrees.

5.3   FACILITIES FOR SERVICES AND INFRASTRUCTURE

Natural burial sites vary greatly in their infrastructure. Some are small, remotely situated amidst a thousand acres of farmland and usually with an infrastructure limited to a sign on a gate. Others are in urban settings, with asphalt roads, a chapel or celebrant's hall, toilets and sometimes an office. Between these two extremes are sites without their own infrastructure but using those of an associated business or a local chapel or community hall. This latter situation supports the local community, reduces costs for site owners, and if it gains local favour, might assist with the planning application.

Whatever the infrastructure of the site, the facilities and the objectives of the owner must not be mismatched. If maximum income is the main objective and customer numbers are a priority, a lack of infrastructure is perverse. Conversely, a site where the environment and creating habitat is the main objective, and commercial objectives are secondary, a high quality infrastructure would appear less necessary.

This was an issue at Carlisle, where despite support by the council, there was no funding to create a completely, separate site. It was necessary to use land adjacent to the existing Victorian cemetery and utilise the existing infrastructure, which is what tends to occur at municipal cemeteries throughout the UK.

There was ample parking, a staffed office where leaflets and information were readily available, the choice of two chapels for services, and fully accessible toilets. The attractive, adjacent cemetery was considered by many people to compliment the natural burial site. This was because it had conservation zones, tree carvings and butterfly beds (herbaceous plants). The half-mile entrance drive is lined by flowerbeds and thousands of mature trees including over 100 clipped yews. The disbenefit for some included the urbanisation and traffic noise and the fact that the conventional cemetery and memorials could not be avoided.

At that site there were over 40 funerals a week using conventional burial, natural burial and cremation so approximately 100,000 mourners and grave visitors came onto contact with bereavement services each year. An annual programme of memorial services and guided walks added to these numbers. Consequently, many people became aware of natural burial incidentally and without the need for publicity and promotional expenses.

Whatever the main priority of a site owner, as the numbers of people using the site increases so must the need for customer facilities be reassessed. A lack of facilities might not be missed on a summer's day in June but on a wet freezing day in January the reverse is true. The value of rural remoteness and serenity has to be balanced with the potential discomfort of the funeral experience.

5.3.1 Celebrant's hall

I took care not to use the word 'chapel' as celebrant's hall embraces both religious and secular beliefs. The term 'celebrant's hall' is also more suited to multi-purpose use. Alternatives are possible and at a site built in 2009, the architect described his 'woodland hall' as a sacred non-denominational building.

Cemetery chapels are often considered, wrongly, to be consecrated buildings and assumed as not suitable venues for catering and secular events. In the past, the established religion dominated the infrastructure. For instance, a chapel I managed had a cross picked out in bricks embedded in one wall. Some Hindus, Sikhs and atheists complained, so I arranged for curtains to be fitted. The cross was routinely on display and only obscured by the curtains at the request of someone holding an alternative service, but some Christians felt that this demeaned the established religion. The lesson to be learned is not to place permanent symbols. Crosses and other symbols can be kept aside and displayed as requested.

Most early cemeteries included two chapels, one for Church of England and one for Catholics and/or free churches. The design and building features are often subtly different to reflect the differing faiths, but any symbolism is missed by most people today. Although assumed to be designed just for funeral services prior to the actual grave-side committal service, they were often described on old plans as mortuary chapels. This reflected the fact that a coffined body could be taken to the chapel and kept overnight prior to the funeral service.

The non Church of England chapel was provided to give the minority religions the ability to hold their own funeral services. This aspect is perhaps more important now than in the past with so many atheists or humanists without premises to hold a funeral service. Then there are the myriad people who profess to be Church of England who are embarrassed to hold a ceremony at the local church, which they never attend.

There are some exceptional multi-purpose buildings at natural burial sites. Because of their flexible use it appears to encourage people to alter the present day format of funerals, sometimes returning to some of the historical traditions of the past. For instance, if a body is conveyed to the celebrant's hall early in the day, the family can have private time for a farewell or to decorate the coffin prior to the funeral service. In pre-delivering the body they can use an inexpensive estate car as an alternative to an expensive hearse at the funeral.

Some natural burial sites have very attractive, barn style buildings, constructed in wood. It is essential, the more so if the site has environmental objectives, that the building be made of sustainable, preferably local products, and includes a high level of energy conservation, all valuable promotional aspects. Where all mourners cannot be accommodated inside it is helpful to place speakers and perhaps a video monitor outside so that large congregations can hear and watch the service.

The celebrant's hall at some sites has a room or area used as a contact centre for displaying leaflets, etc. It is essential that everyone coming onto the site has the opportunity to readily obtain information about the site and the services provided. An accessible toilet(s) is also essential and ideally should have external access for when the hall is in use or closed. As a multipurpose building, the hall can be used for the funeral service, and whilst the cortège are walking to the grave side for the committal, a funeral tea can be set out, perhaps brought in by external caterers. The hall is also an invaluable shelter during inclement weather.

When planning and designing buildings it is advisable to consider that extensions may be required in the future, perhaps by leaving one side of the building free from development or burial. It should be appreciated that most crematoria and cemetery chapels are underused throughout the UK. These buildings are heated and maintained but used infrequently during daylight hours, and never in evenings or at weekends. This resource could be utilised for pet funerals, weddings, music events or community meetings, if suitably planned.

Currently, a small number of people leave instructions for burial and cremation without any attendance of mourners. They might include a request for a later memorial service, perhaps over the cremated remains before they are placed in the grave, or perhaps they will request only a wake. This deferred service approach to funerals may develop and a multi-purpose building, especially at natural burial sites, will be perfectly adaptable to meet this need.

It is convenient and makes economic and environmental sense to concentrate as many of the funeral activities on one site as possible. Each year tens of thousands of conventional funerals include a service at the parish church, then a drive to the crematorium for the committal ceremony followed by a further drive to a hotel for a funeral tea. It is time-consuming, expensive, and with a cortège of perhaps 50 cars, has a massive carbon cost. The environmental and financial logic of focusing all these activities on a single site is obvious (see Chapter 10).

5.3.2   Practical considerations

It is important to know what typically happens at a funeral. This is necessary for everyone wanting to arrange or attend a funeral as well as for site managers to recognise their practical, religious, cultural and safety responsibilities. Once the typical service is described, the potential for variations can be considered.

When a funeral arrives, a site representative should be visible at the gate or celebrant's hall to greet the cortège, and any funeral director involved. This person should be prepared for any last-minute requests or changes, such as the need for a wheelchair or special music. A wheeled bier might need to be in position at the entrance to the celebrant's hall or the funeral director might use their own collapsible version from within the hearse. Some funeral directors or local custom might abhor the coffin being supported on a low bier, and shoulder the coffin into the chapel instead. The coffin can then be placed on a small bier, or two wood trestles.

Conventionally the coffin sits feet first in front of the altar, but the celebrant's hall ought to allow it to be placed virtually anywhere. This denies the use of large heavy pews and demands church chairs, which are more flexible because they have fittings to link them together. A circle or arc of chairs around the coffin is increasingly requested.

The site manager should have communicated with all local religious groups and ethnic groups to identify precisely what they would prefer to have available for services. We can assume a small wood altar, or at least a table to represent an altar, a free-standing simple cross in wood for free churches, and a crucifix type cross for Catholics and high churches. A pair of altar candles might be appreciated by some ministers. A table is also useful to display photographs or other artifacts at secular funeral.

The ability to play CDs, tapes and old records is essential, as the elderly often request music from their childhood. An electronic organ is extremely flexible, assuming the organist is skilled, and can create a church atmosphere, render 'The Last Post' for service funerals and extend through to much popular music. Opera and most classical scores are not written for the organ and CDs are infinitely better. The electronic Wesley Music System downloads music through the internet and can very quickly provide a wide choice of artists with a high-quality sound, but might be expensive for a small site.

Musicians or vocal soloists can be requested for funerals and thought given to where they should be placed for best effect. This might dictate the positioning of the seating. If the celebrant's hall is to be used for functions other than funerals, such as concerts or other public performances, then a movable podium might be an advantage and a fairly sophisticated speaker system, but this is dependent on known and relatively fixed seating positions.

A lectern is useful as a support for microphones and a prop for speakers when they are tearful, emotional and perhaps even a little faint. It should be movable around the room but this can be a problem if it includes a microphone servicing a hearing loop. These are placed around the celebrant's hall and enable those with impaired hearing to switch their hearing aid to a specific setting, which greatly improves their experience. A separate radio microphone can be fitted for the speaker's use, and this can be used anywhere in the hall. The ability to video services is increasingly requested, perhaps with internet video link so the service can be watched anywhere in the world. The minister or celebrant must be in agreement if this is proposed. The ability to view photographic slides of the deceased at services might be requested. Video type equipment could be hired for the service and, if so, the arrangements and cost should be formulated at each site.

In local authority facilities the only service book automatically provided is *Funeral Services with Selected Hymns* published by Canterbury Press, and edited by the Churches Funeral Group. The book includes two Anglican services (traditional and modern), the Roman Catholic rite and one for free churches. Some ministers may prefer to use their own service books, so it is necessary to be sensitive to such requests. Secular officiants normally produce their own service sheets, perhaps through the funeral director.

The provision of hassocks (kneelers) may be provided, but few people kneel these days, and often the linked chairs are so close that kneeling is difficult. The site manager may wish to provide a cassock, the black robe that vicars wear, and a surplice, the garment which goes over the top, as these can occasionally be forgotten by the minister.

5.3.3   A typical funeral

Our typical funeral service starts with the playing of the entrance music. The minister or secular officiant then leads in the coffin upon which are any designated wreaths or flowers, followed by the funeral director and then the mourners. The funeral director will attend to the seating of the mourners and then sit with them through the service. Whilst this is being done, the bearers will place the coffin, perhaps stand back and bow to it, and usually quietly disappear outside. At this point, the minister or secular officiant reads the service, and where pre-arranged, it will encompass the wishes of the bereaved. The site manager ought to monitor the service, either by inconspicuously remaining in the celebrant's hall, or from an adjacent room where the music is controlled, a further responsibility of the site manager. At a natural burial site there is rarely a service time limit and perhaps 20–40 minutes later, the service will finish. In Scotland, the only difference is that it is usual for the funeral director to show the mourners to their seats before the coffin is brought in.

At the end of this typical service, the exit music will be played and this will signal the end of the service to the bearers, who re-enter to lift the coffin, and the same procedure will occur on exit as on entry. Depending upon where the grave is situated, and perhaps the weight of the coffin, the bearers might carry it directly to the grave. If there is no road access and the weight is too much, then a bier must be used. If road access exists then the coffin will be replaced in the hearse, the family mourners in the limousines and perhaps other mourners will use their own vehicles. Sometimes the funeral director, family and mourners will walk behind the hearse to the grave side. It is not unusual to lose mourners on a large complex site so at all times, the site manager must ensure that everyone gets to the grave side, especially if the route is complicated. A lack of sufficient toilets is often a cause of delay, so care must be taken not to start the grave-side committal service before all the mourners have arrived.

It is important to consider that at some point during the service the family usually expects to stand together and personally greet everyone attending the ceremony. This rarely happens when leaving the chapel or celebrant's hall but might be considered during inclement weather. The greeting typically occurs after the grave-side service, when the mourners have viewed any floral tributes and prior to them leaving the site. It may be sensible to identify a convenient assembly point at every funeral. A supply of black umbrellas might be appreciated in inclement weather but many funeral directors accept this as their responsibility.

Variations to this typical funeral are highlighted in Chapter 8.

5.3.4   Toilets

Whether a celebrant's hall is provided or not, a toilet should be considered essential. Often, the fact that many parish cemeteries and churchyards have no toilet is used as an excuse to avoid provision. In reality, these sites may experience one funeral every six months; the people attending are from the immediate locality, and used a toilet before they left home. Most people attending funerals are aged and need a toilet. A fully accessible single toilet can cope, but if 100 mourners are attending a funeral, a queue will form. If there is no toilet, some men will be forced by their prostate to urinate in bushes, and some women will be very uncomfortable. I have witnessed a number of funerals where a prominent mourner has had to be taken to a distant toilet by car, whilst the funeral has had to be suspended until they returned.

With remote sites, or sites where no infrastructure is desired, it might be possible to tow a portable toilet unit to each funeral. This could be put in the car park or other suitable place, and removed after the funeral. Such units could be hired on each occasion, or could be purchased specifically for this purpose. Portable toilets are not accessible for the disabled.

5.3.5   Other considerations

If independent funerals are to be accommodated or an integrated funeral directing service is provided, a body storage unit should be available. Purpose-designed free-standing refrigerated units can be purchased to take three or four coffins, or an insulated room with cooling unit might be provided.

The site infrastructure should have as little concrete as possible as its environmental credibility is poor. Asphalt roads are acceptable for access to buildings and car park but beyond that is a compromise with the sites environmental objectives.

A lich gate at the site entrance, or perhaps the entrance to specific burial plots, can be a feature. Such gates were designed to shelter the coffin whilst the bearers rested prior to moving to the grave side. This facility is rarely used today and the gates are more decorative than functional. Some old lich gates have an integrated coffin rest to avoid using coffin trestles placed on the ground.

The perimeter needs to be considered as cemeteries have been traditionally well fenced. Whether this was to keep the dead in, or the living out, was never defined! It is a fact that where vandalism or grave theft occurs, the complainant will highlight any weak boundaries. Hedges blend well with surrounding countryside and would be preferred to the traditional railings or standard fencing. Such hedges could be a habitat in themselves if planted with native species to recreate an ancient hedgerow. Given time they could also be laid as an example of local rural skills.

One or more gates or stiles might be included in the perimeter if access is to be allowed at all times, or perhaps restricted to when the site is open. Access through the site might complement local footpaths or provide a recreational walk in its own right. Creating amenities like this might be a valuable way to gain local support and reduce objections to any planning application.

Facilities for the disabled necessitate an induction loop for those with hearing difficulties in the celebrant's hall and any office reception area. Ramp access is also essential for those in wheelchairs or with mobility problems. Steps are a hazard for the disabled and coffin bearers. The worst hazard is the slight elevation, perhaps only half inch, often preferred when two surfaces, like decorative paving and a tarmac road surface, meet. Aged people cannot see these and inevitably fall over them.

5.3.6   Temporary infrastructure

The placing of temporary shelters at the grave side can enhance the funeral. Inclement weather can mar grave-side services when everyone and everything is wet. Mourners will leave the grave side immediately after the service and often without speaking to the widow or widower. This lack of communication after the service can upset the bereaved and inclement weather is considered a principal reason why cremation has become so popular.

If buildings are not to be provided on the site, whether because of cost or environmental concerns, then perhaps a screened marquee and/or portable toilets could be erected. These could be hired or purchased, and could remain in place for a year or two until such time as the burials cease or move to another part of the site.

5.4   RITUAL WALKING

Walking is no longer a feature of daily life as we become more mechanically mobile and adopt passive interests. One of the most significant losses through this change is that we no longer experience those periods of reflection which typically occur whilst walking, perhaps induced by the rhythmic unstressed movement of the human body. Walking was once an integral aspect of funerals when burial in churchyards and cemeteries was the norm. Reintroducing walking into a funeral can slow the ceremony and offer time to reflect upon the death.

The words 'ritual or processional walking' could be used to describe the actual walking process at funerals in churchyards and Victorian cemeteries. It was usual at both locations for the coffin to be unloaded from the hearse and placed on a wheeled bier. This was waist high and had large carriage wheels or later, large balloon tyres. The bearers would wheel this into the chapel or church for the ceremony, and after this, wheel it to the grave side. In cemetery chapels, the entrance door was opposite the exit door, which discharged directly into the cemetery. The entrance and separate exit formed a processional route that was itself a ritual. No concern was given to reduce the physical effort necessary to get the body to the grave, as this was seen as due regard given to the dead by the living. The current trend of using vehicles to reduce walking has usurped this ritual.

In the early days of municipal cemeteries, say the 1850s, the grave might have been adjacent to the chapel but over time, the nearby graves were filled and new graves were up to half a mile away. The paths were not designed to accept horse-drawn carriages and, subsequently, limousines beyond the chapel. Carriages were certainly noisy and intruded on the ceremony, and the carriages and horses hoofs caused much rutting and damage to gravel surfaces. This may have been the principal reason for excluding them although horse droppings were then also seen as a nuisance, as these had to be removed manually.

The noise of carriages would also have obscured the tolling bell, which was a tradition at cemetery funerals. Silence intermittently permeated by a mournful bell was a potent sound, one guaranteed to exclude the outside world and allow total concentration upon the funeral, especially when walking.

The natural burial movement has re-introduced ritual walking at funerals, perhaps by design although often because there is no road access to the grave side. Added to this, some bereaved families have insisted on keeping vehicles out of sight during the funeral, using them only as far as the celebrant's hall, and then having the cortège walk behind the coffin. Many sites have the type of bier used in municipal cemetery chapels, with small plastic wheels, which vibrate on rough surfaces and are very difficult passing over gravel or soft ground. Funeral directors use a more suitable collapsible bier with small rubber wheels that they are able to store under the deck of a hearse. It is only when a walking funeral is experienced that the typical noise of engines and slamming car doors at conventional funerals is recognised. This discordant noise is replaced by wind in the trees and birds singing.

Compared to Victorian times there is now a considerable increase in the number of old, and perhaps less mobile, mourners. These could be transported at a walking funeral using quiet electric buggies like those used on golf courses.

Neither natural burial sites nor conventional cemeteries specify a time allocation within which the funeral must occur. Even so, it would be prudent for the bereaved to be aware of the time a ritual walk will take and the distance involved. If a processional walk is proposed on the way to the chapel and direct to the grave side, it is sensible for site managers to actually plan the walking route and record the time taken. This is the only way to ensure that the cortège arrives at the chapel or grave side at the agreed time and does not leave any minister or celebrant waiting to take the service, perhaps standing in the cold.

It may be important to highlight the ritual walk in a natural burial site as a meaningful contrast to the slick efficiency of a cremation ceremony. Some funeral directors have recognised this fact and now walk in front of the hearse, what they call paging the funeral, for a short distance from home and on the approach to the crematorium chapel. This, though it slows the ceremony, does not involve the mourners in walking or increase periods for reflection.

5.4.1 Planning the ritual walk

It is important to plan the ritual walk, especially at a new site. This could be seen as a farewell journey from the entrance through to the grave. The vehicle park could be screened off at the entrance, so that vehicles need not be seen at the funeral at all. A ritual walk could then lead to any celebrant's hall and burial area, and could be subtly surfaced so that vehicles could be used in poor weather or to convey the less able.

The walk needs to be as level as possible and graded to accommodate slopes. A soft surface is quieter and more intimate that tarmac or concrete. Woodchip may be possible if compacted although clearing snow and future weed control may be more of a problem.

It is essential to create a ritual walk that gives the best views of the site and the surrounding land. This can be a problem if open views are associated with exposure to wind and inclement weather, so a compromise may be necessary. Wind breaks using native shrubs or hedging can increase protection, but formal evergreen garden hedging is not appropriate. Although views of entrance buildings, residential buildings, farmyards, silage pits, etc. should not be visible, this advice might be ignored if the site is farmland burial or otherwise integrated with farming.

5.5   TO CONSECRATE OR NOT!

Consecration was an essential requirement in the past. Victorian cemeteries usually allocated consecrated areas on half to three quarters of the total cemetery area and within that area would be placed the Church of England chapel. Plans of the consecrated area had to be prepared and marker stones placed at the four corners of the grave area. The mayor and other local dignitaries would join the bishop for the consecration ceremony, and only after this formal ceremony could Church of England burials take place.

The remaining area would be the unconsecrated portion, upon which a second chapel might be built for use by Catholics and the free churches. The size of this area compared to the consecrated would be proportional to the numbers of local people within these two groupings. The non Church of England religions believe that all land is sacred, so no formal consecration ceremony is required, although the Catholic priests might bless each grave as it is used. The secular such as atheists, humanists and pagans should be interred in the unconsecrated portion.

It is anticipated that a public authority will provide consecrated graves for the established church and thereby allocate an exclusive area. Catholics, Free Churches and the secular are usually buried together on one plot, even though their beliefs vary greatly. The Muslims, in view of their lobbying on this point, are also often allocated exclusive plots. If it is preferred not to allocate exclusive areas, even for the Church of England, then all burials can take place on undenominational plots. If these are recognised by Christians as unconsecrated, they might prefer burial elsewhere. A chapel or celebrant's hall intended for general use must not be placed on consecrated land.

The Diocesan Registrar for each bishopric currently manages arrangements to consecrate burial areas. A visit by the bishop is no longer routine, nor consecration markers. The diocesan bishop has jurisdiction over all consecrated ground, even where it exists in a public or private site. These powers extend over the chapels, memorials and inscriptions, and any major work done on these. In practice an assurance might be obtained that these powers will not be exercised.

There are many reasons why consecration of part of a natural burial site might be advisable. First, it provides consecrated graves for those with strong Church of England beliefs; secondly, it might attract the necessary support of a local Church of England minister and congregation, particularly in a recognisable parish locality; and thirdly, if the local consecrated churchyard is closing because grave space is exhausted. Where the site is in a position to meet any, or all, of these needs it may foster support for the planning application.

A natural burial site needs to recognise its impact on the local church at all times, especially its ability to generate opposition in any planning application. The provision of a celebrant's hall on the site might dramatically reduce services in the local parish church and might be objected to as unwanted competition. The feasibility of using local church and chapels for religious services and a community hall for the non-religious ceremonies should always be part of any considerations.

At least one existing natural burial site advertises the consecration of individual graves upon request, which is not possible. This is perhaps confusion with the 'blessing' of the grave, which many ministers will perform as part of a funeral service.

5.6   GRAVES AND WATER

Historically, churchyards in cities and large towns appear to have polluted wells in the immediate vicinity. Consequently, legislation was drafted around the 1850s, to create cemeteries with efficient grave management and reduced burial density, which was the real problem in churchyards. It is now apparent that a properly placed and managed cemetery has a very low impact on the environment. With very light touch planning requirements in the past no evidence of a single pollution incident has come to light in any cemetery in the UK. This was also prior to the cremation boom, when some urban cemeteries carried out a very high number of burials in densely populated areas.

Nonetheless, it is now essential to give an assurance that burials will not contaminate groundwater in order to obtain planning permission.

This is just the beginning, as the developers of a new site, and those already in operation, have a responsibility to ensure that ongoing burials do not contaminate. Also, the bereaved as consumers need to understand what to expect with regard to water in graves, and the kind of questions they need to pose when considering natural burial. There is, after all, no value in organising a green burial, to then find it pollutes local groundwater over a period of decades.

The Environment Agency is a principal consultee regarding every planning application to open a new cemetery, or extend an existing one. Their increasing involvement is in response to the high number of new natural burial applications since the early 1990s. Prior to this, burial was moribund and few new cemeteries were opening. Many existing cemeteries opened before the formal planning process started, and even when planning approval was obtained, it was then a relatively superficial process. The Environment Agency has been sympathetic to this historical perspective, but will undoubtedly act if these cemeteries are found to be polluting. With this in mind, it is worth considering how it was, and indeed, still is, in many municipal cemeteries.

From around 1850 cemeteries were developed outside city and town boundaries by the local authority, often using land they owned. The cemetery was usually situated on land that was least valuable for building, perhaps because it was wet just below the surface. Even good sites included low areas that had wet clay soils. In some eastern parts of the UK the water table is just below the surface, so wet graves are difficult to avoid. My nine years of managing Bushbury cemetery in Wolverhampton, on a hill of clay overlying running sand, was a case in point. Every time a prolonged wet period arose, graves filled with water, the shoring and then the grave walls inevitably collapsed overnight, and completing a contracted burial became a race against time. Staff excavated the soil slop until a crater arose surrounding the 6' deep grave to be used, often with the previously buried coffins in adjacent graves clearly exposed. A timber platform was constructed over the crater, and grass mats hung over the grave edge so that nobody could see that the grave actually had no sides. The funeral took place, the timbers were removed, and a large excavator replaced the grave slop. Often, the grave was taped off until it dried out because anyone stepping on the soil would have sunk the full depth of the grave.

Many of my associates experienced these types of conditions, and they were often difficult for the gravedigging staff. A consensus developed that because burial was often dirty and difficult, cremation was the way forward, until it was recognised as polluting. This increasing denigration of the practicable aspects of burial contributed to its decline. That apart, water is upsetting for the bereaved, as they do not like to think of the deceased's body being placed in a wet grave, and most cemetery authorities are well aware of this. I describe techniques in section 8.1 as to how the presence of water is obscured to avoid complaint.

These are practical problems, but with no evidence of pollution, is the current planning stance too restrictive, and expensive?

5.6.1   Water and the planning application

I am grateful to Justin Smith of Cemetery Development Services for providing me with much of this audit information.

Modern living uses far more water than in the past, and a far greater proportion of this water is treated, which is expensive both financially and in terms of carbon. As the volume of water in aquifers and rivers has reduced, the concentration of pollutants and minerals in the water has increased, so the risk is greater. In view of this, every natural burial and cemetery planning application requires a site audit, in effect, a risk assessment. The very fact that a site is assessed suggests that a specific level of awareness already exists with the land owner. For instance, a site on a known flood plain can expect automatic refusal, so even starting an audit might be pointless. The audit process is to allocate a score in a range between highest and lowest, for:

- Soil type – sand, silt, clay or combination of these.

- Drift thickness – the soil deposited over the surface by glaciation.

- Drains – whether land drains (or others) exist within 10 metres horizontally of the boundary.

- Aquifer – whether such exist below the site.

- WT height – the position of the water table.

- SPZ1 – source protection zones related to abstraction points.

The score is logged and measured against the number of burials per year. Consequently, as the number of burials increases, the requirements get increasingly tighter. In theory, at least, permission to inter a few burials (*de minimis* exemption) might be given even though the site risk assessment is high. Once the risk level is assessed, whether this can be mitigated is then considered, and if this is not financially practicable, the site must be discounted for burial.

Before considering the audit in more detail, it is worth reviewing precisely what the contaminant risks actually are. These are reviewed below.

5.6.2   Water contaminants

The potential contaminants are bacteria – mostly the contents of the human gut – and viruses. There is also very little research on pathogens in soil, or whether they can move away from their concentration around the body, and contaminate groundwater. The limited research suggests movement is restricted and the threat to groundwater is generally low, although this is dependent on soil types and vegetation.

Concern about virus such as hepatitis, and protozoa such as cryptosporidium appears low, whilst the reverse is true of prions such as CJD, as these can move quickly through sandy soils. The principal chemical concerns relate to organic elements, nutrients and heavy metals, which include formaldehyde (if used in embalming), ammonium, sulfides, chlorides and mercury, which remain after the body decomposes. Many of these are very soluble, and also difficult to remove from water.

5.6.3   The audit – soil dynamics

Soils are usually broadly classified in four groups as sand, silt, clay and organic (such as peat). Chalk, limestone and sandstone-based soils are included within those categories. The most significant aspects relate to the texture of the soil, which is the size of the particles, and their structural organisation. The particle variation is immense, with the largest sand particle at 2mm and fine clay less than 0.0002mm in many grading systems. As the soil particles get smaller, the surface area expands dramatically and presents a large area for cationic exchange, which binds up elements, and the rate of water movement declines to no more than 2mm per day.

The site audit will utilise the national soil map to identify the local soil type, and geology maps to identify the base rock. A soil profile will identify the thickness of soil and rock and where the water table is situated. With this understanding, the audit might provide an indication of how fast water is moving, and its direction. The Environment Agency favours clay soils because water movement is restricted. As water movement increases, it is probable that the risk increases on sand and fractured rocks such as sandstone, limestone and chalk.

5.6.4 The audit – risk map

With the soil and rock data mapped, aquifers, rivers, water abstraction points and land drains are considered. No river or stream can be within 30 metres, and boreholes must be at least 200 metres away from the cemetery boundary in general. Land drains, if they exist, are a real problem even within a few metres of potential graves. With regard to groundwater abstraction points, a source protection zone (SPZ) will be designated. An SPZ1 or red zone (inner source protection) will exclude a burial ground, and it is unlikely to be approved in an SPZ2 or green zone (outer source protection). An SPZ3 or blue zone (source catchment) is preferred for a burial ground, although it will still be difficult to obtain approval. The source protection zone will be modelled around the potential site based on groundwater flow, and will be smaller on clay soils and greater on sands, chalk, etc. The number of burials (a large number is considered to be 100 + per annum) and the way these are spread over the site will greatly influence this assessment.

At this stage, the potential risks from the proposed burial site have been audited. If these appear to be so great that the Environment Agency will object, the question is whether the risks can be mitigated (reduced) to some degree.

5.6.5 Mitigation of groundwater pollution

A number of options are possible:

- Reduce burials to below the *de minimis* exemption.

- Do single depth burials rather than double depth.

- Inter only during summer, when groundwater is low.

- Inter only in parts of the site with acceptable conditions.

- Increase the attenuation layer.

- Reduce bottom water (dewatering at the site by reducing the water table).

- Reduce top water through drainage.

The first four options reduce burials and therefore income but may be acceptable, especially if expensive engineering solutions are not feasible. If not, the final three mitigation options above need to be considered, which are potentially expensive. These are very technical issues and considering them in more detail is worthwhile.

5.6.6 Attenuation

The attenuation layer is the depth of undisturbed soil required beneath the lowest coffin, assumed by the Environment Agency to be at least one metre of clay. The clay has a vast slightly charged (re-active) surface area, which binds up potential pollution from the body. An acceptable attenuation layer in non-clay soils is less easy to define. In theory at least, sand and chalk soils can equally absorb pollutants and, provided the attenuation layer is increased in depth *pro rata* the capacity of clay, should be acceptable. This is referred to as 'linear description of absorptive capacity' but is highly technical and complex.

In theory, the attenuation could be enhanced by placing an efficient absorption layer under the coffin. Kitty litter (clinoptilolite) has been considered, but the science is unsound and should not be considered until researched. If the attenuation layer of clay is below one metre, or otherwise is required to be extended, dewatering may be the only feasible solution.

5.6.7 Dewatering

This is intercepting water below the grave, called bottom-water, to prevent it rising to the coffin through the attenuation layer and becoming contaminated. This might be water from spring lines, confined aquifers and lenses (pockets of water). If the grave is 1.8 metres deep, plus a 1 metre attenuation layer, then the dewatering must be 3 metres deep. Costs may be £150,000 per hectare, and it requires constant pumping to a filtration reed bed or outlet. This needs a discharge consent licence, so the water must be monitored before being discharged to ditches.

In existing burial grounds, this bottom-water, which is the real water table, can rise in winter and at times of high rainfall to the point that it covers bodies in graves. The water is then potentially contaminated and, as 'grey water', it cannot be pumped over the surface or released to ditches. Graves excavated into this soil will fill with grey water, and the offensive smell is often noticeable.

5.6.8 Drainage

Correct surface drainage is a matter that has not been given sufficient attention in the past. Drainage involves removing water from the surface soils, called top-water. This is often the only water that causes grave excavation problems, which cemetery staff often erroneously refers to as the water table. The majority of this top-water is retained in the root or thatch zone just below the surface. This layer can be visualised as a sponge into which a grave is excavated, and then water from all sides drains into the hole. This top-water is not polluted, as it lies above any bodies, so can be pumped out, but over the surface so that it can be re-absorbed by the soil.

In existing burial grounds top-water can still get contaminated, especially where graves are excavated on slopes. This is because the surface water permeates the grave down to the coffin, where it is contaminated. This water can seep under pressure caused by the slope into any graves dug on the downside of the slope.

Soil water dynamics have a considerable influence on drainage, which makes this topic extremely complex. For instance, silt or clay soil overlaying good draining soils like gravel does not want to release its water. Technically, this relates to a phenomenon whereby surface tension does not exceed the capillary effect. Consequently, an expensive gravel (French) drain does not work if a thin layer of fine soil seals the surface. This surface tension is broken if the drain opens to the surface. This science is critical in the spacing of drains, which are usually placed about 12 metres apart. Drainage is very expensive work so putting in more drains than necessary is wasted expense.

Drainage is improved on slopes, so graves set on ridge and furrow can benefit. This requires two rows of graves, head to head with the furrow following the head of the graves, and the ridge running between the foot ends. This channels the water to the head of the graves, perhaps to a drain under a row of plaques. This directs the water to undisturbed soil with good absorption characteristics, and reduces the amount seeping down the backfilled fractured soil in the grave and onto the coffin and body.

It is important not to over consolidate backfilled graves, especially clay, as a perched water table can then be retained over the grave. The mounding of the grave after backfilling will also effectively cause water to run off into the undisturbed soil of the midfeathers, rather than infiltrate the ground.

In view of the different meteorology over the UK, and variable annual weather, the monitoring of water on a site may be necessary for at least two years and then it may well be rejected!

5.6.9 Conclusion

Groundwater protection is a statutory requirement, so must be treated seriously. The completion of the audit and any mitigation of the risk might appear quite expensive, but must be kept in perspective. In a worse case scenario, with perhaps £200,000 per hectare spent (1,000 graves), this amounts to £200 per grave. If grave rights are sold for perhaps £2,000–£3,000 or more, this may be considered a perfectly acceptable level of expenditure. If pumping costs arise over the period of the grave rights, these costs must also be factored in. The carbon cost of permanent pumping must also be considered as an environmental and carbon footprint issue.

In conventional cemeteries where mitigation is not feasible, best advice favours sealed concrete chambers, with de-watering if necessary. I do not believe that natural burial and concrete chambers are compatible, because of the carbon cost of the concrete as well as the soil degassing and soil web destruction necessary in placing them.

5.6.10 Is the Environment Agency audit too limited?

The answer appears to be yes! The bureaucracy of the Environment Agency not only increases the difficulty and costs of opening a burial site, it also potentially denies large parts of the UK of any burial option. As clay soils cover perhaps 60%–70% of Britain, those areas predominantly on sand, gravels, chalk, limestone and sandstone may find mitigation impossible. In such areas, once existing burial space has run out, the bereaved can then only turn to cremation, which perversely, might well be environmentally more harmful than burial on unsuitable soils. The Environment Agency places such emphasis on mitigation in burial, yet mitigation in cremation is ignored. The efficient use of cremators, of coffins made of natural materials and a prohibition of embalming could be demanded, but these issues are ignored even though air pollution contributes to human illness and even death.

A further concern is that if new cemeteries and natural burial grounds are refused, the area in question has less resilience with regard to pandemic planning. There will be nowhere in that locality to inter the dead when cremation inevitably becomes overwhelmed by anything other than a mild epidemic! This illustrates the importance of considering body disposal in its entirety as an essential public service, and not piecemeal. The question to pose to the Environment Agency is whether their audit should extend to include the risks posed by the alternatives where their actions deny a burial option?

5.6.11 Is the mitigation of groundwater pollution greater with natural burial?

Assuming our definition of natural burial has a high sustainability index (see section 3.3) then chipboard/MDF coffins and embalming will be prohibited. This is recognised as a valuable mitigation factor by the Environment Agency. Any trees on the site will be retaining water and absorbing harmful substances from the burial such as ammonium. The problem is that these trees are not growing in winter, when water levels are at their highest, so mitigation is seasonal and inconsistent.

What may not be sufficiently researched or understood are the mitigation factors evident where dense vegetation, which may include trees, overlie graves. It can be anticipated that what research exists is focused around conventional cemeteries with lawned surfaces. If this research is from the USA, it might also be distorted by the fact that their cemeteries do not replicate the UK situation. Typically, they contain far more embalmed bodies, the turf surfaces are heavily irrigated, and are treated with far more herbicides and artificial fertilisers than in the UK. It should be noted that intensively mown lawns allow precipitation to immediately penetrate the surface, and rapidly descend through non clay soils to the body.

A ground cover of dense unmown grass, perhaps reinforced with a tree and understory, potentially maintains a far higher proportion of precipitation. Moreover, such soils contain a greater amount of organic material including humus, which supports a far higher microbial population. In other words, the soil web in such natural conditions is denser and far healthier than soil under unnatural lawned surfaces. Dr. Boyd B. Dent, a hydrogeologist in Australia, researched these issues to some degree in the late 1990s but did not publish all of his work. Much of his work is covered by the current Environment Agency guidelines. In 2002 his recommendations added the following:

● Plastic coffin liners, and plastic generally, should be prohibited.

- No burials should lie at the site boundary – buffer zones are needed of at least 10 metres in clay soils, and 20 metres in sandy soils, which varies with topography and hydraulic gradient.

- The best soils in order to favour decomposition and with good decay product attenuation are well-drained clayey sands.

- Develop burial grounds from the outside-in and around the perimeter first.

- Preserve and plant deep-rooting native trees and shrubs, particularly in buffer zones.

- Cremated remains may be scattered in buffer zones, but must be at least 2 metres from any boundary, and must be prevented from washing past the boundary.

It can be seen that Dr. Boyd B. Dent's research emphasises restricting water flow off site using vegetation on undisturbed land. His comments on decomposition are at odds with current Environment Agency thinking, as they favour the body locked anaerobically in fine clay, where it will remain for hundreds of years. Burial in more open soils, with higher levels of oxygen, will accelerate decay (see section 1.3.2). Neither do the Environment Agency favour chalk, yet its high pH actually kills micro-organisms, presumably many of them harmful. That said, an alkaline pH also supports growth of some harmful bacteria like *aerugenosa pseudomonas*, which just shows how complex this topic can be.

I believe the Environment Agency should take a more responsible approach. The relative ease, by which new crematoria obtain planning approval compared to the often subjective opposition to new burial sites is potentially distorted. For instance, the emissions from crematoria contribute to the 60,000 UK deaths each year related to air pollution, yet none are recorded from groundwater pollution. There is a need to organise more research into decay rates and the true potential for contamination of groundwater. In my 45 years working in cemeteries I experienced considerable pungent water from graves, yet staff never contracted any illness nor was there even the remotest damage to flora or fauna, which I would have noted. Conversely, I consistently experience stinking farmland drainage ditches whilst in the countryside, and have reported two cases of significant pollution from one farm. In these cases, the grass and trees around the farm were dead or dying. The danger from human burial and cemeteries needs to be kept in perspective!

5.7   GRAVE TYPES AND DENSITY

It is perhaps easier to understand the types of graves at natural burial sites by first considering what is offered in conventional cemeteries. I have discounted above ground burial techniques, e.g. mausolea, as of no interest to natural burial sites. Imperial measurements are stated as most established sites work to grave plans in imperial, but the metric equivalent is given. The following sections detail what types of graves can be available.

5.7.1   Lawn grave

The universal grave option, approximately 10' x 4' (305cm x 122cm) with the whole surface covered by intensively mown grass. Often a border at the head of the grave, which is usually 2' deep (61cm) and the width of the grave. A stone memorial headstone can be erected within this and usually 3' high, 2'6" wide, 10" deep (92cm x 76cm x 26cm). Many cemeteries since the 1950s and most new grave sections are restricted to this pattern, which mimics war graves. It is not liked by those uncomfortable about walking over a person's grave. This point, together with the fact that grave mounds are prohibited on lawn graves means that it is not acceptable to Muslims.

5.7.2   Traditional grave

This grave is approximately 10' x 4' (305cm x122cm) upon which a wide range of memorials can be erected. Often the memorial covers the entire grave, perhaps using kerbs to form a surround within which gardening can occur. This grave type is disappearing because of the long-term costs of safety inspections and repairs. Pedestrian access is also severely compromised, with perhaps only 9" (23cm) of space between memorials.

5.7.3   Unpurchased grave

This grave size is the same as above. They are owned by the local authority as the grave right is not sold to a private individual as with the above options. The burials are of those who may have been homeless or whose bodies were unidentified, and deaths where nobody will arrange and/or pay for a funeral, perhaps because there are no known relatives. With higher funeral costs and more poverty, it appears that increasing numbers of people in the UK and US are refusing to arrange a funeral for which they should be responsible, and leaving this to public authorities.

In a town of, say, 100,000 residents, perhaps 30 such burials might occur each year. As bodies usually remain in a mortuary for some time before a local authority will accept responsibility, this number would increase if the policy was more accommodating. Burial is usually the default option because cremation is opposed by some religions and not permitted if the deceased had declared opposition to the process. A memorial will not be placed unless sufficient estate exists to pay for this. This pauper or common grave was the most frequently used in Victorian times because it was the least expensive. With fewer of these graves being needed now, they are often just the next grave in line on a typical lawn grave plot, and the absence of a memorial might be the only giveaway. Some authorities do a single burial in such graves, and then allow a period to lapse before further burials occur so that if a relative does appear, or an estate arises, then the grave right can be purchased and a memorial erected. Other authorities do a fairly immediate sequence of unrelated burials in the grave, and because a number of families are involved, they prohibit the sale of the grave right or the placing of a memorial.

5.7.4   Cremated remains grave

These are specific graves sold to allow the burial of cremated remains, usually in a small casket. These graves are often a scaled down lawn grave design, allowing a small headstone at the head end, or perhaps a horizontal tablet. Many other cremated remains schemes exist, including above-ground units in which the casket is put within a small chamber with a plaque on the front. Many cremated remains are either strewn or buried in the Garden of Remembrance at crematoria, upon which a personal memorial is not permitted. Where this happens, a separate plaque can often be placed on a path kerb, memorial wall or similar. A few sites use the ossuary approach, where cremated remains are poured through an aperture, perhaps over a cone shape, to fall and mix into a large underground hole.

CR graves – as they are often called – vary in size but often utilise a quarter of a full grave so they can be fitted neatly into existing grave plans. This will make them 2' wide and 5' long (61cm x 152cm). A mini-headstone is placed at the head end, often back-to-back with the headstone on the next row, and the area in front is turfed. Often up to four caskets can be interred, each in a 12" square (31cm) and with 12" (31cm) of soil over the casket. Although the law accords cremated remains an equivalent status to a full burial with regards to, say, exhumation licences, the usual burial depths are not practicable for a casket.

The cremated remains grave has become a principal income source for local authority cemeteries, as cremation advocates increasingly desire a grave which they can visit whenever they wish. This might be seen as perverse because cremation was intended to dispense with the need for burial and memorials. As a memorial sale might be sought by the funeral director, they can encourage the bereaved to purchase this grave type.

Cremated remains can be placed in full-size graves with the associated higher costs. As this was felt to waste land, the smaller cremated remains grave was introduced. Cremated remains are often added to owned graves otherwise considered full with regard to body burials.

5.7.5   Baby or infant grave

Small graves for babies and infants were often insensitively used to infill small awkward spaces and verges not large enough for adult graves in churchyards and Victorian cemeteries. More recently, specific plots were introduced with the small graves set out in a grid pattern. Stillbirths continued to be placed in adult-size unpurchased graves, and filled to capacity with over 100 small coffins. Such graves were not backfilled after each burial but covered in wood boards. These were moved, perhaps weekly, to add coffins until 2' to 3' (61cm x 92cm) from the surface, when it was backfilled and another adult grave opened to continue the process.

In recent decades a more caring process has developed, usually in the form of a purpose designed Babies Memorial Garden. This allows for the interment of a fetus, stillbirth or a child up to, say, five years of age. These graves are usually 2' x 4' (61cm x 122cm) but the depth might vary according to the size of the coffin. It is extremely difficult for a gravedigger to work inside a small grave, so it will suffice to excavate perhaps 30" deep (76cm). With this depth it is feasible to add a second fetus or baby burial at some future stage. This can be valuable as some women who experience a fetal loss, stillbirth or perinatal death, often experience a second within a few years. It would be insensitive not to place a second body with the first should this occur.

Deaths of children above the age of six years are rare and would normally be placed in an adult grave. If well-advised and they can afford it, parent(s) may prefer to purchase a full grave for themselves and inter the infant below six feet. They then have the satisfaction of knowing that that their body will be reunited with the child when they die. It also enables all family members to have their inscriptions on a single memorial, which is more inclusive and reduces costs. The problem is that to accommodate the parents' bodies the grave must be excavated to the full depth, and adult-size. The benefit is that by excavating the full grave size on this first occasion, the later re-opening is much easier. When excavated to 6' (183cms) depth in this way, it is usual to create a niche at the head end into which the small coffin can be placed. Lowering a small coffin to such a depth is difficult, as it requires long webs or tapes, and having somebody stand in the grave might be preferred. A child's coffin is pitiable when lowered into a gaping grave and some prefer to cover most of the grave with timbers and grass mats to avoid this.

In the past the fees for grave right and excavation varied according to age. As having to explain this to a grieving family was difficult for the funeral director, some local authorities now charge a set fee regardless of age, or make no charge at all, often up to 18 years of age. Some funeral directors reputedly make no charge for their provision of a basic funeral for a baby or child.

In recent years the design of burial areas for fetuses and infants has greatly improved, partly in response to the bereaved and to the Cemetery of the Year competition, which judges such provision. These small garden areas provide privacy and a sense of shared grief with other parents. The gardens will often be hedged, have attractive shrubs and planting, sometimes with small statues of toys or fairytale characters. Organisations like SANDS and Compassionate Friends instigated this process and are an invaluable source of advice and support when such burial areas are being considered.

5.8   ADULT GRAVES

5.8.1   Depths

I have covered grave depths for cremated remains, and baby and child graves in those specific sections. I also comment on the shaping of graves in section 8.1. All that remains is to specify the depth of standard adult graves, often assumed at 6' (183cm). In fact, that depth is for two burials, one above the other. If the first coffin is interred at 6' (183cm) with 15" (38cm) for the coffin depth, and 6" (15cm) of soil left over this coffin, the grave can be re-opened to 4'3" (130cm) depth for the second burial. With the second coffin assumed as 15" (38cm) deep, this leaves 3' (92cm) of soil to the surface. Cremated remains, whether in caskets or not, can still be added within this 3' (92cm) depth.

Where the surface depth can be reduced to 2' (61cm) to assist decomposition, as in section 1.3.2, then the first coffin can be placed at 5' (152cm) and the second at 3'3" (99cm).

The 6" (15cm) of soil left undisturbed over all previously interred coffins is assumed to reduce the danger to the gravedigger of removing soil fouled by body fluids. This is rare where the previous burial was at least ten years earlier, but a real possibility when the last burial was perhaps only weeks or months previously. This happens because after a long relationship between two people, the shock of the first death clearly has an impact on the second, and their fairly immediate death is not unusual. It has always been the practice to bury one body over another, but this fact often comes as a surprise to many.

The combined depth of coffin plus a layer of soil makes a total of 21" (53cm) of depth for every additional burial in a grave. With this depth in mind, any number of burials can occur assuming groundwater is not a restriction, and that shoring can be safely achieved. Graves were routinely dug in the past to 7'9" (236cm) for three burials and 9'6" (289cm) for four burials. In fact, at these depths many cemeteries reduced the 6" depth of soil on the lower two coffins to 3", so that three burials were at 7'6" (229cm) and four burials at 9' (275cm). In many cases these lower burials were old and had often collapsed under the weight of soil, so more depth actually existed and the 3"–6" between coffins was hypothetical.

Some cemeterians will even suggest that all burials should be dug deeply so that more capacity is achieved. This suggests that a grave sold for two burials should initially be interred at 9'6" (1st) (289cm) and 7'9" (2nd) (236cm). Then, after the grave right has expired, say at 50 years, the grave be re-sold for two further burials at 6' (183cm) and 4'3" (130cm). This process does not result in the disturbance of any remains, and it assures two 50-year grave right sales as well as four interment fees per grave. At such anaerobic depths the body will rot rather than decompose.

I have previously mentioned graves dug 21' (640cm) deep, and I have managed churchyard exhumations of that depth. This has occurred because, perhaps after 50 years, grave spoil has been tipped over an earlier burial. As this has accumulated a second burial has taken place in the spoil. Over centuries this process might occur six or seven times.

The assumption that a grave is always for a couple can upset single people, who only need a grave for one. As the number of single people is expected to increase by 31% between 2009–2029, this assumption should be reviewed.

5.8.2 Adult grave widths

As stated above, the standard grave width has been 4' (122cm) for perhaps the last 100 years. With an excavation of up to 36" (92cm), this leaves 12" (31cm) to form a retaining wall between each grave, called the midfeather. This is made up of 6" (15cm) on each side of the grave, plus the 6" (15cm) of the next grave. Where space is restricted, some authorities have reduced the grave width by up to 6" (15cm), but where a large coffin is interred, the midfeather is too thin and prone to collapse. A grave with a collapsed midfeather is extremely difficult to excavate and shore. Grave width is a matter for local determination, the soil type and structure being the main consideration.

In the past, bodies were smaller, coffins were bespoke, constructed tighter to the body, with less lining and often tapered at head and foot. Graves were hand dug and often no shoring was used, or the shoring planks were recessed into the side walls and flush with the sides of the grave. Needless to say, excavations were much smaller than they are today.

This situation has now reversed and with obesity common, body weight and size is increasing yearly. I have had to refuse bodies for cremation because they were too large to go through the cremator door. Now, when a large body is received by a funeral director they sometimes have to advise the use of a specific crematorium with modern cremators with larger doors. A second issue is that coffins are not bespoke but constructed in standard sizes. If a limited range of coffins is stocked then it is all too easy to use a size larger than actually needed. The coffins also have to be stronger to carry the increasing weight. Whatever the cause, the width of coffins is increasing and those in excess of 30" (76cm) are not uncommon. Also, specific ethnic groups are using more caskets for burial, which are generally wider than coffins. The coffin length is rarely an issue. With grave shoring now essential, many cemeteries have moved to 4'6" (137cm) wide graves. This represents a 12% greater use of land, a major cost factor when it is so expensive. Where their soil conditions are less sound, a few cemeteries have moved to 5' (152cm) width.

5.8.3   Density

Grave density in conventional cemeteries is 1,000 graves to the acre based on a grave size no larger than 10' x 4' (305cm x 122cm) including roads and paths. Most natural burial sites utilise larger graves, and often reserve more space for tree planting and foot paths, so grave density of between 500 and 700 graves per acre is usual.

5.9   GRAVE TYPES IN NATURAL BURIAL SITES

Only grave types are covered in this section and all memorialisation on graves is considered in section 5.12. It should be noted that the different grave types relate to individual market segments, so identifying these segments is the key, and discussed in Chapter 9.

5.9.1   Standard grave – purchased

The standard grave available at natural burial sites effectively duplicates the lawn and traditional grave types outlined above with a grave size of at approximately 10' x 4'6" (305cm x 137cm). The grave size will increase to perhaps 10' x 10' (305cm x 305cm) if tree burial is anticipated on the grave. The sale of the grave right will be the principal income source at the site, as discussed in Chapter 9.

Once the grave is full, say two body burials, further burials of cremated remains can be accepted – say, one per square foot – which increases income. This is potentially a large number and a limit is usually set according to the entry spaces available in the register of graves, whether handwritten or computerised. Also, if a grave is full, adding cremated remains is the only way of keeping relatives or partners together. Some of these cremated remains might come from countries where cremation is routine such as Australia, New Zealand or America. Even if tree roots exist, the remains can be scattered on the grave without causing any physical damage to the trees.

5.9.2   Standard grave – unpurchased

I am not aware of any natural burial site offering unpurchased (pauper or common) graves that replicate those offered by local authorities. Despite this there is no reason why private site managers could not ask the local authority to confirm that these funerals are arranged and what interment fees are paid. If these can be undercut or a more sensitive funeral provided, the local authority may transfer the burials to the natural burial site. If such funerals are tendered through a funeral director then it may be possible to make an arrangement with them to carry out the burials. Such a burial will only raise an interment fee, and only worth considering if the fee is sufficiently high to give a realistic profit margin. This might be supplemented by increasing the number of these burials in a single grave.

At natural burial sites where grave rights are not routinely sold, the grave is effectively an unpurchased standard grave. As income is not raised through selling a grave right, the interment fee might need to be increased, or a donation, or a grave maintenance fee, charged so that sufficient income is raised. As the sale of a grave right may complicate the transfer of graves to a Trust or wildlife charity, this approach does avoid that complication.

5.9.3   Cremated remains grave

The cremated remains graves in natural burial can be very similar in size and type to those in conventional cemeteries, but with less mowing and a conventional memorial replaced by a small plaque or tree. I am aware of potential site owners being opposed to cremation and refusing all cremated remains on their site despite the related income. That aside, the provision of cremated remains graves attracts more people to the site, who may then choose natural burial in preference to cremation in the future.

A further benefit of cremated remains is that they require a small excavation, or can be scattered on the surface, which avoids damage to tree roots. Some sites pre-plant and establish trees which can then be individually selected and purchased by the bereaved specifically for cremated remains. Every tree on a natural burial site could be used in this way, whether over entire plots, on margins along curving paths, or as groves within other grave types.

5.9.4   Baby, infant and child graves

I am not aware of any natural burial sites that provide entire sections of these graves. Nonetheless, an individual request for such a burial must be anticipated, and if they are to be accepted, a policy needs to be formulated.

The principal consideration with all baby and child deaths is the strong emotion involved, which can extend to a large number of people. Consequently, the amount of memorabilia placed on these graves can be very high. The family and friends are rarely given the opportunity to say farewell at the time of death, as occurs with anticipated adult deaths. The need to leave tokens of love and friendship overwhelms. It is amazing how many expensive floral arrangements, football scarves, dolls and toys, helium balloons and other gifts are left on these graves. The parents are often not in control of the memorabilia because if the child was of school age, school friends may visit the site without a guardian and leave their own mementoes.

Conventionally, much of this material is plastic and garish, and as it ages, no one feels able to pick it up and dispose of it because of its emotional attachment. Many visitors to conventional cemeteries become very upset about what they term 'plastic tat' even where regulations do not prohibit it.

My approach to this at municipal cemeteries has always been to meet the needs of the bereaved, but this may be more difficult given the environmental stance at a natural burial site. It is all too easy, and I am guilty of this, to back off and allow baby and child graves to become a mass of memorabilia, even when this flouts the regulations. It appears callous and insensitive to approach parents to ask them to tidy the grave, and it is stressful for the person given that task. The involvement of the media must be anticipated, perhaps where a request for burial is refused, and secondly, when memorabilia is removed from a grave. Ultimately, it is a matter for site managers to consider how best to handle such requests and provision.

It would be easy to suggest, as in conventional cemeteries, that all baby and child graves could be contained in a designated area and that this could be screened so that the memorabilia does not impede on the rest of the site. I do not believe that sufficient requests would arise for this to be feasible in a natural burial site. I am more inclined to believe that such burials will arise where baby or child deaths occur in a family who already own a natural burial grave, or where the parents are committed to the concept and want the child placed in a grave into which they can be interred at a later stage.

Hospitals routinely make arrangements to cremate or inter stillbirths, although I am not aware of any natural burial sites being used. In recent years this policy has been extended in some areas to include fetal remains, i.e. 12 to 24 weeks' gestation. Although currently rare, the parent or parents can take custody of the body or fetus and make their own arrangements for a funeral.

5.9.5   Pet grave

Pet graves are unusual in conventional cemeteries but those that are being provided are similar to cremated remains graves with regard to location and usage, varying according to the size of the pet. The few provided by local authorities are usually restricted to small domestic pets like cats, dogs and cage birds and not horses, sheep or goats. For natural burial sites wishing to provide this service it is essential to define precisely what pets would be accepted in any planning application.

Knowing and understanding the pet market would be essential in defining what commercial opportunities exist. Where pet bodies are left at veterinary facilities for disposal, bulk pet cremation is normally arranged. This can be at a private, often family-owned crematorium or an industrial-size operation, the latter also handling dead farm stock. This bulk disposal option and the private pet funeral option need to be considered separately.

The bulk disposal option is not suited to burial and the focus of natural burial sites is on the more lucrative private pet burial, which can include carrying out the entire funeral. Private pet burials are generally sought by those people who take personal interest in the disposal, and are concerned that the identity and care of the pet is maintained. Although this might be anticipated at a family-run crematorium, the industrial-type operations have received some very bad publicity. The transparency evident at a natural burial site, especially if managed by committed pet owners, will be seen as having integrity. Some natural burial pet sites allow small inscribed tablets, and whether such a service would be successful without memorialisation remains to be proven. Pet burial is also an ideal way to increase contact with people that may choose natural burial for themselves.

Clearly, owners of larger animals such as horses and donkeys can be very attached to their pets and distressed when they have to be disposed of using impersonal industrial cremation. The handling of large animals can be difficult and the graves large so the charges will need to reflect these factors.

Pet burial combined with human burial (companion graves) appears to be an attractive proposition. As many pets can die during a person's lifetime, the pet grave should ideally be separate and adjacent to the human grave so that pet bodies are not disinterred for the burial of the owner.

5.10   GRAVE NUMBERING

Grave numbering methods vary throughout the UK, some being extremely complex, especially in the Victorian cemeteries. At Shrewsbury cemetery a three number reference was required; first, a number for each plot, then a letter for each block of 16 graves within that plot (4 x 4), then a figure of 1 to 16 on each grave. The immediate problem with this system, was that the plot number and grave number could be the same, for instance 16 – H – 16, and this duplication of numbers can lead to errors.

In the Victorian period they tended to block and number the entire area before roads, features and plot boundaries were drawn on the site plan. That meant many blocks were cut in half by a curving road shape creating half graves, which were later used for the burial of children or cremated remains. As path edges tend to creep, after decades it became uncertain whether the graves along paths were a half, three quarters, or a full grave. Frequent visits to the grave were required to check the position and size of the grave before accepting a burial order, which was time consuming. Some interment orders were accepted without such checks, which resulted in graves protruding into drives and in odd positions, as is visually apparent in many Victorian cemeteries.

If that sounds complex, later cemeteries ignored this process and issued a consecutive number for each grave as it was sold, so that every grave had a different number. Because graves on site could often be selected by families from anywhere within a plot, and because the cemetery often managed two or three different plots, one for each religion, the consecutively numbered graves were no longer side by side but were often some distance apart on different plots. Decades later I have known staff spend hours studying several old cemetery plans to try to locate a grave number, and sometimes failing to do so. The numbers, once they reached, say 10010, contained various identical figures, so errors were still possible. If this number is given to a funeral director by a distant relative of the grave owner, who then passes it on to the cemetery office, who pass it to a cemetery supervisor, it is easy to see why mistakes occur.

It appears quite straightforward upon opening a natural burial site to number the graves consecutively 1, 2, 3, and so on. Over time later burials will extend onto plots to the left, then years later to the right, which illustrates how the grave numbering can become so complex. There is no simple and perfect process. Ideally, the entire site will be divided into logical plots and each given a simple prefix such as A, B or C. If a more descriptive or marketable name is preferred on plots, such as the oak or ash section, or similar, then the prefix can change to OS1, OS2 (for oak section) or AS1, AS2 (for ash section), etc. This prefix locates the grave on a specific section, provided trees with the same initial letter are not chosen.

The important point is to ensure that each plot is physically and visually obvious using dividing tracks or paths, or some other feature such as boulders. Otherwise, it is easy to stray over an unseen line and find the correct grave number, but on the wrong plot. Each plot can then be numbered one upwards and in blocks or rows. If tracks cut across a grave leaving small land portions they could, if so wished, be used for cremated remains or child burial at some stage but these will need to be given a consecutive number from the start. This will prevent odd numbers appearing around the edge of the plot after some years have passed, when the grave is actually used.

In the UK in the last 40 years media coverage has exposed serious errors in cemetery grave numbering resulting in hundreds of graves not being individually identifiable. It is certain that smaller instances will have occurred in municipal cemeteries but have been kept out of the media. The distress caused by such errors is profound, both for the bereaved people and the staff concerned. The reason for these errors is usually due to a practice that has arisen in the last 50 years of separating the cemetery administration office from the actual cemetery site. This office issues grave numbers but does not check that the actual graves on site match the plan they are using. Meanwhile, the cemetery supervisor is entering the grave numbers on his/her plan, confident they are replicating the plan at the administration office. This might go on for years, the cemetery plan might even disappear or the cemetery supervisor, who has the entire cemetery plan fixed in his brain, retires or dies. Typically, after many years, a second burial is required in a specific grave, the office issues the number but the mason, under direction from the cemetery supervisor or site plan, finds the grave but notices the memorial is inscribed with a different name, and the mistake is realised. A massive administrative exercise then occurs to devise a definitive plan, but in the worst cases this has not been possible. Typically, a grave owner contacts the local press, and the bereaved lose all confidence in the cemetery authority.

One principal difference between a conventional cemetery and a natural burial site is that the former usually has stone memorials placed on graves. Provided these are correctly located, they can greatly reduce reliance on using the actual grave number. For instance, if you are planning to re-open an existing grave which has no memorial then you might note down the numbers of a few nearby graves, and the names of the interments in them. On the basis that a memorial can be found on at least two such graves and that they validate the numbered position of the grave sought for re-opening, then this is treated as confirmation. This process is often taken to its ultimate in churchyards where only graves marked by a memorial will be re-opened for further interments. This is often because churchyards never had a grave plan, or if there was, it was later destroyed or mislaid. All too often the churchyard grave plan is in the sexton's head, and goes with him when he dies.

Finding a grave in a natural burial site without memorials, and perhaps without marker trees, can be extremely difficult as time passes. The solution to this problem, whether the office is on site or not, is to maintain a single definitive grave plan in the durable plastic type paper manufactured for this purpose. A computer plan should not be considered as an alternative as it cannot be used on site. The grave numbers can be initially penciled in, but should not be inked onto the plan until the grave has actually been physically inspected on site. The inked-in number then indicates that the grave is ready for sale, and selection by the bereaved. If this is not done, then the danger is that a grave will be sold to the bereaved which was not intended to be used at that early stage, perhaps to allow access through to a new plot, or into a glade between trees.

An acceptable alternative approach might be to use the graves in sequence and then arrange for a regular topographical survey to be carried out by a specialist firm. This updates a paper plan and fixes all grave positions to within a few centimetres. The problem is that, apart from the cost of this, it is still difficult for the public to understand this type of plan if sections blend into each other without physical path edges, and finding a grave without staff assistance may be impossible. The need for staff to take visitors to graves increases in due proportion to the number of graves sold, so can be expected to increase year on year.

My preference is for each grave made ready for sale to have a permanent number physically placed on the grave, one that cannot easily be moved. The Victorian cemeteries understood the value of this and created markers cast in iron, made of fired clay or cut into sandstone, which are still legible over 100 years later.

At Carlisle's natural burial site, I used cheap, heavy, concrete building blocks, with an aluminum spiked number set into them using cement. Each block was set one inch below ground level at the centre of the foot end of the grave with the number set flush on the top. It meant that years later, a few minutes with a spade would, without fail, locate it and confirm the grave number. These aluminum grave numbers are often sold as purpose designed grave markers but, in themselves, are too weak and poorly riveted to just sit alone in the soil. The identification of the grave can be assured if an electronic marker peg (microchip) is placed on the grave. The chip can be read, and advanced systems will indicate the deceased's name and grave details. The cost will be between £10.00 for the basic and £20.00 for the advanced markers (2010 prices). These markers are intended as identification confirmation, and not as a means of actual grave location.

Some natural burial sites currently use oak posts, or stumps, up to 24" (61cm) high to mark graves. These are usually made of non-tanalised wood to maintain environmental credentials, and will last perhaps 30 years. What happens after that period has expired needs to be considered. The answer might be to set up triangulation stones or rocks from which at least two tape measurements can be taken to locate the centre of any grave. These points need to replicate the pillars used by the Ordnance Survey, so must be relatively big and immoveable. Rough hewn sandstone, granite or slate would suffice and fit in well enough in a wild or semi-wild environment.

Finally, people arrive intermittently seeking a grave for a number of reasons, many quite personal, perhaps even to 'talk' to the deceased for a while. Recently interred graves are often marked with flowers and easy to locate, but decades later, after trees have grown and any memorial is obscured, might be impossible to find. The usual routine for personal or postal enquiries is to mark the grave position on a map, and rely on the enquirer to find the right plot and possibly the actual grave. From experience I am aware that few people can read a map and too often they fail to find the correct plot and leave feeling very disappointed. An obvious plot sign, perhaps set on a huge granite boulder, is the answer. At all times every opportunity should be taken for the site manager to personally lead visitors to a grave as it is an ideal opportunity for customer feedback, PR and marketing.

5.11   ORIENTATION OF GRAVES

In most natural burial sites the orientation of graves will not be an issue, other than in regard to access to paths. If an area is to be consecrated it needs to be considered, especially if the graves in the local churchyard are orientated east towards Jerusalem and/or if the local minister would value this. Likewise, a section for Muslims must be aligned so that the deceased's face can look towards Mecca. Members of the local Mosque would give advice and should be present when the graves are aligned, usually using a compass.

Orientation is important if memorials are to be placed. In some conventional cemeteries where the east orientation is traditional, the graves on the eastern sides of roads have their headstones placed at the head end, which means they are then backing onto the road from where they will naturally be viewed. This looks absurd and from comments I have received, many relatives find it both annoying and upsetting.

Although the grave plans show graves in grids, nothing suggests the orientation of the coffin in the grave. Sometimes, the numbers are positioned on the grid to indicate the head of the coffin. With conventional lawn graves, it is usual to use two rows and place the burials head-to-head. The advantage is that a 2' (61cm) head border can then be formed within which two rows of headstones are erected backing onto each other. With the remaining 8' (244cm) of grave to the foot end, plus the same 8' (244cm) on the next row, this creates a 16' (488cm) wide obstruction free strip, readily mowed using larger mowers. Ideally, if the grave numbers are shown on grave plans back-to-back then it is visually obvious that head to head burial has occurred. Head-to-head burial may be an advantage in those sites where memorials are to be placed and/or frequent mowing is intended.

Grave sizes can be increased from the usual 10' x 4' (305cm x 122cm) if the land is available and the graves are costed to reflect this. If a grave is 10' (305cm x 305cm) square then it would allow the bereaved partner or family to decide how to orientate on a radius of 360 degrees, and give more space for tree planting, if needed. If further burials are intended in the grave, the precise burial position and head would need to be shown on the plan.

The regimented side-by-side grid plan of graves is typical in local authority cemeteries, often because plots are rectangular to fit into a grid of pre-constructed roads. This crams in many graves and is simple to lay-out and mow thereby holding down already very expensive costs. Yet the notable Victorian cemetery designers such as Loudon recommended curving rows that are linear to add grace and elegance. Curves and shapes are more expensive because they use more land, are more difficult to plan in the drawing office and lay-out on site, but do add character.

5.12   MEMORIALISATION

The subject of this section is grave memorials, and not grave markers. I usually associate grave markers with numbering the grave, and not as a means of memorialising it. There is no reason why a marker cannot include the deceased's name, of course, but I would suggest that this then defines it as a memorial!

The placing of a memorial impacts on the entire natural burial concept and cannot be considered in isolation. If a memorial is placed it potentially influences the appearance of the site, and affects the grave, habitat, mowing and the administration and design. When a memorial is allowed the bereaved might anticipate the incorporation of a vase, and often families will add vases depending on who will be visiting the grave. Memorials ordered by executors, perhaps a solicitor, are often without vases as there may be no family left to visit the grave. Because of the association of memorials with floral tributes see also section 1.3.5.

The aesthetics of memorialisation I leave to others. Suffice to say that I appreciate the artistic qualities of a hand-carved memorial and those created by 'Memorials by Artists' are exemplary. The machine-cut modern memorial headstone looks sterile in comparison, the gilded inscriptions look garish and have no longevity and the variation of stone colours and types often jars. One writer used the term 'greetings cards' to describe modern headstones, which seems apt.

The decision to be taken is whether to prohibit all memorials, to compromise with a communal memorial scheme, or to allow individual grave memorials. I consider each of these options in turn below.

5.12.1 Prohibition on all memorials

Environmentalists might anticipate a prohibition on all memorials at a natural burial site. There are a significant number of people in the UK with similar views, evident in many cremations taking place without any memorial placed subsequently. Even in conventional cemeteries where memorials are routine, a small number of graves are never memorialised. This may be because no survivors exist to place the memorial order, or a memorial cannot be afforded. I have met a number of people who consider memorials a waste of money and find other ways to remember the deceased.

To prohibit memorials at a natural burial site has many advantages. Management costs are reduced, the maximum number of habitats can be created with limited maintenance, and there will be fewer visitors, with less waste, less water usage and less carbon impact. Without a grave memorial, site visitors are usually content to visit the site without going to the actual grave.

It is important to remember that just because there are no memorials, it does not mean that the burials are somehow forgotten and not recorded. The reality is that each burial is recorded for posterity on plans, and in register form, either written or computerised. In addition, as so many Victorian memorials have been destroyed, especially the cheaper less substantial ones, huge numbers of conventional cemetery graves are no longer memorialised and the bodies lie beneath unmarked lawns.

In the early period of the natural burial site at Carlisle when the only memorial was a tree on the grave, it was decided to survey the site users for their views. Half of the bereaved felt that a tree was the only memorial required and half felt that they would like some form of inscribed memorial. Considering that the scheme was in its infancy, it is perhaps surprising that so many people were prepared to forgo the elaborate and very personal memorials of conventional cemeteries and to accept the anonymity of natural burial.

5.12.2 Communal memorials

At Carlisle natural burial site, the needs of those who wished to have some kind of memorial was satisfied by having a communal memorial. This epitomises the Parish War Memorial or cenotaph inscribed with the names of the deceased. It keeps the memorialisation in a contained area thereby reducing the impact of individual personal memorials throughout the site. It also creates a sense of unity between the many disparate people buried on the site, regardless of their beliefs, sexual orientation and ethnicity.

The council opted for a circular, traditional sheepfold made of recycled sandstone, which was constructed by two Cumbrian stone wall builders. Inscribed plaques were placed on the inside of the wall and in the centre of the sheepfold a local artist built a three-sided, tricorn-shaped wood seat. This enabled the bereaved to sit in some privacy and view their plaque. A memorial wall, lich gate, cairn or such feature could be considered. It is a compromise but without the operational and sustainability problems implicit with individual memorials.

The communal memorial is also ideal for sites that cannot allow access to graves for operational reasons, such as the farm type. The sheepfold or some other rural or agriculturally themed memorial would be suited to such sites. An alternative might be a small, memorial garden with seating for quiet contemplation.

5.12.3 Individual memorials

As previously stated, individual grave memorials validate grave visits and the placing of memorabilia and as a consequence, the habitat must suffer. Apart from mowing, constant walking near trees will compact the soil and restrict growth.

A further compromise might be to accept individual grave memorials but with conditions. These could stipulate an objective to create a natural habitat within a set period, and define and implement a strategy that will achieve this. The provision of a biodegradable wood memorial that will naturally degrade in, say, 30 years, could achieve this. There could be an associated right to place the memorial upon the grave for the period, perhaps included in the grave rights. A period of 25–30 years appears to be accepted by most people as extending far enough into the future. Commercial sites might prefer, at the outset, to increase confidence by allowing them to renew the right, say, after 20 years has elapsed. That might require a new memorial, or at least refurbishment of the old one. My experience suggests that after 30 years very few will renew the right.

As outlined in section 5.2, it is essential to state clearly what the standard of maintenance is for any defined period. If it is to cut the grass once per year, the memorial will not be visible for perhaps half the year. Some might suggest that to sell a memorial with associated mowing standards that make it difficult to see, or approach on foot, is inappropriate. A solution would be to mow the grass regularly throughout the 30-year period, and then reduce to conservation mowing. Alternatively, less expensive and preferred for the environment, would be to reduce the mowing in phases over the 30-year period. This ensures that unsustainable maintenance costs are not carried beyond year 30, at the very least.

Memorials are mowing obstructions and as they increase in number, mowing becomes more onerous. Mowers damage memorials, either through the blades or mower body causing chips or by constant wear by nylon line cutters. The more memorials and the closer they are, the smaller the mower needs to be with a relative increase in the mowing cost. Horizontally placed plaques are the least visible and can be mown over, whilst wood crosses, stumps and posts are very real obstructions. Each stump or post needs surrounding in mulch, or cutting with a nylon line strimmer, both of which are time-consuming. Wood crosses, stumps or posts also look very obvious after mowing and influence the appearance of the site.

Horizontal plaques in wood, made locally using wood from a sustainable forest might suffice but can be damaged, stain when wet, crack when dry and the inscription can be difficult to read. Stone plaques are not biodegradable and have a high carbon footprint. This could be acceptable if a natural burial site is near a local, small scale quarry producing, say, slate. Scottish and Cumbrian pink granites are still quarried and small-scale production of some beautiful English sandstones, limestones and Derbyshire Gritstone still exist. The supply must be local to avoid road haulage, and relatively small, say 12" x 12" (31cm x 31cm) maximum, to reduce the quarrying impact.

A number of memorial stone importers exist to serve the conventional monumental masonry trade. Little, if any, UK stone is sourced and shiploads of Indian and Chinese stone is now the norm. Accusations that the stone is cut by families including children arise periodically, but I cannot cite any evidence to prove this. The carbon impact of stone sourced from abroad is so high that it ought to be discounted in a natural burial site.

I have discounted cast bronze, which is readily available and well-suited to small plaques. Perhaps this is unfair because a 6" x 6" (15cm x 15cm) bronze plaque can be sent by post or courier, can include a massive number of letters or figures, wears extremely well, and can be recycled at the end of 30 years.

Whatever type of memorial is chosen, a process to ensure that it is placed on the correct grave is essential. It can be assumed that the memorial will be delivered some weeks after the funeral. By this time any floral tributes may have been cleared and there may be no marker whatsoever on the grave. At such times it is all too easy to place the memorial on the wrong grave, the more so if the person placing the memorial is less than familiar with the grave numbering scheme.

5.12.4 Additional inscriptions

A high percentage of enquiries will relate to additional inscriptions to be added to the memorial. As I anticipate that all non-municipal natural burial sites will be the sole supplier of any memorials, I have not described any controls regarding external memorial masons working on site, or regarding the safe erection of memorials. If this is intended, a specific management process would be essential.

Conventional memorials are usually erected with a memorial inscription to the first burial, and allow sufficient inscribing space to add one or two further inscriptions to match the anticipated number of burials in the grave. Often, because cremated remains are added, it is sometimes necessary to supplement the original memorial with a plaque in matching stone in order to create additional inscribing space.

If double-depth or even deeper plots are planned on a natural burial site then this issue needs to be considered. If, as anticipated, the plaques are small and therefore relatively low cost, a new second plaque could be added next to the first, and so on. This suggests that a process to add extra plaques and their positioning upon the grave needs to be considered from the outset. If the memorial is in the form of an incised wood plaque, cross or stump it is rarely worth attempting to add incised inscriptions directly into old wood. In such instances, it may be possible to affix new wood or metal plaques to the surface of the old memorial.

5.12.5 Separate plots

The decision to allow individual grave memorials can be varied throughout the site. Different plots might be used for different types of memorials, for instance plaques on one plot and wood crosses on another. I would not recommend mixing the different styles on one plot, for aesthetic reasons as well as the fact that mowing is then made more difficult.

The three options of no memorials, a communal memorial, and individual grave memorials could also be offered on a single site as long as each area is well demarcated. It would provide choice without impinging on those people who dislike memorials. The main challenge would be marketing the options, especially when a third party is involved such as a funeral director, as it is essential the burials go into the appropriate section. If a body is put into the no memorials section, and the family say they asked for the section with memorials, then a potential dispute arises.

5.12.6 The culture of memorialisation

Memorialisation has extended well beyond the confines of the actual grave. There are burial chapels and certainly crematoria where artistic windows, the pictures adorning the walls, the pews, service books, hassocks, bier and even the organ are memorials to a burial or cremation that has taken place. The bereaved appear to be more than willing to memorialise any item, especially those seen or used every day. In a natural burial site, this list could extend to walling, fencing, stiles, gates, lich gates, the coffin carriage or cart and perhaps even the horse or donkey! Donated memorials are more readily marketed if a small memorial plaque is subtly included, or reference made in promotional leaflets. In a charitable or social operation the desire to support the aims of the organisation, whilst also gaining a memorial that has operational value, is an even stronger motivation.

I have known bequests to be left in wills for the maintenance of crematorium grounds and of one family who paid for the expensive construction of a scree garden. I have never found that the presence of a memorial inscription on anything involved with funerals has been a problem for other bereaved families.

It is essential to sensitively promote a desire for memorialising proposed improvements, existing features or equipment, or perhaps their replacement. Donation schemes are quite common in local authority crematoria and some cemeteries but might be less acceptable at a commercial site charging market fees. The planting of trees, butterfly beds, bulb walks and water features, or anything to improve the environment are always attractive to the bereaved.

5.12.7 Unauthorised memorials and memorabilia

It is a cliché in conventional cemeteries that where unauthorised memorials or memorabilia are left on graves, it spawns an increase. In fact, most people are reasonable, and if they know the regulations, will abide by them, even when seen to be ignored by a small minority.

Dealing with this problem varies throughout the UK. Some authorities remove items without any form of warning, and are thereby featured in the media! Others try to telephone or write to the grave owner, leave a written request on the grave or approach the grave owner personally when they are at the site and ask them politely to remove the items and not bring them back. Sometimes, the response is that they did not know that the items were prohibited. As outlined in section 6.2, sending every grave purchaser a copy of the rules and regulations and preferably getting them to sign acceptance is more effective.

If the grave owner fails to act on the request then the next stage is to remove the items, which should be placed in a compound where the owner can retrieve them. The items should never be destroyed as denying the owner the opportunity for repossession is a form of theft. The problem is that some people will then simply return the item to the grave and this distressing cycle repeats itself *ad infinitum*. If the situation becomes intransigent, some managers often choose to ignore the situation. The stress is considerable and it can culminate in being portrayed in the local media as a jobsworth or petty bureaucrat. It can be expected that complaints will arise from other grave owners and ignoring the situation is unlikely to satisfy them. It is always necessary to patiently explain what has been done to resolve the issue.

The problems with memorabilia can often arise from the children and grandchildren of the deceased and not from the principal mourner. To take presents to grandpa's grave in the form of helium balloons would appear appropriate to a child and they would have no awareness of the environmental consequences or aesthetics. Likewise, teddy bears, rag dolls, and suchlike are left by siblings, and football regalia by friends of young deaths. A real problem is created for management when other grave owners take exception to the items, repeatedly stating that they chose the site because such material was prohibited, and demanding action.

At conventional cemeteries memorabilia can be seen as a virtual wave of grave mementoes sweeping along the line of recent interments. The wave diminishes both in measurable amounts and as a visual impact as the interments become less recent, and the widow or widower also die. It can be anticipated that natural burial sites will receive less memorabilia, especially those sites that prohibit individual memorials. From the outset, there must be a positive message opposing memorabilia together with rules that prohibit the material, and then routine policing of the graves. This might allow prohibited memorabilia to remain for a short period, and then it will be removed. The policy that graves will be regularly checked must be seen and understood by all site users.

Chapter 6

HOW SHOULD NATURAL BURIAL SITES BE MANAGED?

6.1 CONTACTING THE SITE, BOOKING A FUNERAL AND REGISTRATION

6.1.1 Contact by the bereaved and visitors

In 2008 I located two natural burial sites on the internet, with the intention of visiting them with friends who are interested in the concept. The information stated that neither site was staffed but a telephone contact number was given for more information. Several telephone attempts over a number of days and weeks were unsuccessful, which is a reminder that immediate reliable contact is essential in the funeral market.

The bereaved and visitors expect a personal telephone response at least during normal office hours, say 9am to 5pm Monday to Friday, and if this is extended to the weekend and evenings it would represent an enhanced service. An answerphone should be available when the office is unmanned giving contact details and when a call will be returned. Neither do closures at lunchtime suggest a customer-focused service.

A website is essential and should include information about natural burial, the type of site being offered, how it can be contacted, its location, opening hours and access using public transport. Photographs showing the appearance of the site and perhaps the grave types are always helpful. An email contact would be expected on the webpage, and again some indication as to when a response could be expected. All too often contact sites are not checked daily and replies initiated. Also, for the less well-sighted, the text should immediately be in a font size that is easy to read. Written details of location should be accompanied by a map that indicates precisely where the site is situated.

Computerised records are much faster to access than paper records when responding to enquirers about forthcoming funerals and the location of graves and burials. Telephone enquirers are often surprised that grave records from decades earlier can be accessed within seconds of the enquirer finishing speaking. Nonetheless, computerised registration and booking systems are expensive to buy, and an annual software support charge is also necessary. A paper recording system can be used, at least in the first few years. As funeral numbers increase it is relatively simple to backdate the existing records onto software. It is essential to work towards one system because it becomes time consuming and very frustrating if old paper burial records have to be manually searched whilst more recent records are computerised.

A staffed office on site makes contact much more reliable and efficient but is expensive. In the initial few years of operating a site it may not be feasible but contact via a mobile phone is essential. I am aware that many private site owners make themselves available by telephone every day and evening of the week, often personally if living on site. To ease this burden, and to ensure that funerals can be booked, a group of natural burial site owners could unite to form a central booking service during normal office hours, perhaps extended into evenings and weekends. The service should allow bookings by families carrying out a funeral independent of a funeral director.

A serious shortcoming can arise regarding private natural burial sites when people wish to locate a burial some years later. If, for instance, someone is researching a family tree then they will logically first check the churchyard for the parish where the deceased resided. If that fails then they might assume cremation and enquire at the local crematorium, and if that fails they look to the local municipal cemetery. These all logically serve a defined area and any enquirers would end up with being given directions to these sites. Most municipal burial and cremation authorities are also making enquiries much easier because they are starting to place their burial or cremation databases on the internet, often using internet companies now experienced at facilitating access to records. Currently, few people will think to enquire of natural burial sites, which are fewer in number and often serve a much wider geographical area. This will change over time but it also suggests that natural burial sites need to work together to ensure that records can be accessed, or they need to employ internet companies that currently serve the municipal sites.

6.1.2   Contact by funeral directors

Funeral directors are routinely available to the bereaved seven days a week, and have staff available for call-out at night. Many people telephone a funeral director in the middle of the night when a death occurs, and expect the body to be collected within hours. Even at this time the bereaved may suggest on what day they want the funeral, or they will meet the funeral director the following day to finalise this. The funeral director cannot proceed with the arrangements until he or she has made a provisional funeral booking with the natural burial site. This must be for a day and time when the funeral director also has the required hearse and limousines available. With this provisional appointment, they can then contact the minister or secular officiant to confirm the appointment is convenient, and that the Coroner's Order or Registrar's Certificate can be issued to allow the funeral to take place.

It goes without saying that funeral directors welcome a wide choice of booking times, and appreciate some flexibility. Unlike cremation, burial bookings are rarely allocated at set times and are booked to give the funeral director whatever time is required. Typically, one hour would be allocated to cover a service in the celebrant's hall plus a grave-side committal. It needs to be borne in mind that after the committal on a warm dry day the mourners will congregate around the grave to talk. Any member of staff who attends the funeral may need to be present for perhaps 90 minutes before everyone leaves the site. This also delays staff waiting to backfill the grave, and potentially delays these staff from moving on to any subsequent funeral.

With a burial booking, it is not unusual to have odd times requested by the funeral director, such as 10.50am or 11.25am, in order to fit in around a prior church service held elsewhere. As such times are not printed on a booking sheet, as with cremations, and have to be entered by hand, mistakes can easily occur. In addition, when enquirers ask what time the funeral is, a time such as 10.50am or 11.25am is much more difficult to remember than times on the hour, or half hour. These factors should be considered in any training given to staff.

Often funeral directors need to release the hearse from a funeral as soon as possible, as it may be required on another funeral. If the funeral process on the site is such that the coffin can be removed near the entrance, or at the celebrant's hall, and moved on site by bier or other means, it enables the hearse to quietly move off, a factor that might be appreciated by funeral directors. The availability of a hearse often dictates funeral director capacity, as limousines can be more readily hired.

Conventional cemeteries and crematoria vary little, and follow traditional opening hours. Private crematoria are often much better with a centralised 24/7 staffed telephone booking service. Companies offering computerised crematoria and cemetery registration packages can usually supply an automated 24/7 telephone booking process, at least for cremations. Using a PIN number, the funeral director can personally access the diary and book a day and time out of hours, and confirm this the next day.

Automated systems are more difficult for burials, as unlike cremations, they cannot operate on a 30 or 45-minute booking diary. The grave excavation takes time and relies on the availability of shoring equipment, and if graves are close to each other, or other funerals are taking place, excavation is often delayed. In addition, the bereaved will select a grave if given the option, so even the grave number might not be available for some time. If excavation capacity is sufficient, perhaps because in-house staff is used rather than contractors, a fixed number of burials could be handled each day. This might be assumed at one per morning and one per afternoon. This would ensure that each burial had sufficient time and that two funerals could not coincide. In these circumstances an automated booking process might be feasible. An average of two burials a day, ten per week, must be considered high turnover as few conventional cemeteries complete more than 200–300 burials each year, excluding the burial of cremated remains.

Burials are normally anticipated Monday to Friday, and if Saturday is offered it represents an enhanced service. Christian burials on a Sunday can be a problem for ministers because they are routinely conducting church services. Nonetheless, we live in a society where most Christians do not set Sunday apart, and where atheists, humanist and other non-Christian religions abound, and restricting funerals on Sunday, as well as a Saturday, is outdated. Premium fees being charged for weekend services, a common ploy at local authority and private sites, should be challenged. Funerals should be equally costed over seven days to offer more choice. Weekend funerals avoid people having to take time off work, and suit those struggling to keep small businesses operating, and those caring for young children between Monday and Friday. Seven day operation also increases burial capacity and avoids Friday being typically overbooked.

6.1.3   Making a provisional funeral booking

As well as funeral bookings for new graves, within a short period there will also be burials in re-opened old graves. Further bookings will arise in both new and old graves, if cremated remains burials are accepted. The bookings are a complex juggling act to ensure that the grave can be prepared in time, that mower and excavator noise do not impinge on services, that funeral parties do not coincide on site and that vehicles are managed. This is together with ensuring that staff is available to meet funerals, and backfill the graves.

The funeral booking procedure is the same for all municipal and private cemeteries as well as natural burial sites. The details required include:

- Funeral date and time (this is when the funeral arrives at the gate).

- Name and address of the deceased.

- Grave number (entered on the grave deed if an existing grave, otherwise this will be the new grave number).

- If new graves are dug for more than one, the number of burials anticipated for the grave, to ascertain the depth for excavation.

- Funeral director's name and contact details.

These minimal details, usually taken by telephone and noted on a booking sheet, allow the site staff to identify the grave and prepare for excavation. The following details can be added to the above or included on the written Interment Notice, sometimes called a Burial Order, which will be submitted by the funeral director within an agreed timescale:

- Coffin size, including handles.

- Funeral type (whether straight to grave (committal) or in any chapel or celebrant's hall at the site).

- Religion of deceased (to enable staff to anticipate the style and length of service).

- Age of deceased (if young a very large funeral can be anticipated).

- Sex of the deceased (especially if not obvious from the name).

- Name and address of the purchaser of any grave right.

- Special requests, e.g. vehicle free funeral, etc.

Interment notice

The site manager should have a free printed form made ready and distributed to funeral directors to formally order the burial, which also serves as the binding contract for the work and costs involved. This notice must include all the information outlined above, and is often required at least 24 hours prior to the funeral. Payment of any fees might also be requested from the funeral director at this stage. Often the notice is delivered together with the Coroner's Order for Burial or a Registrar's Certificate, but either could be accepted when the funeral arrives at the site. If the Order or Certificate is accepted as late as when the funeral arrives, but is mislaid then the funeral must be delayed until a written declaration in a prescribed form is obtained confirming that the necessary order or certificate has been issued.

Ideally the Interment Notice should contain a brief description of the grave type selected and any restrictive conditions related to this choice. This might relate to mowing frequencies, whether a tree is included and other such detail. Any aspect that needs clarification, especially anything that could potentially upset the bereaved at a later stage should be highlighted. Restrictions regarding the type of coffin or placing of memorials, or the prohibition of embalming are obvious examples of this and are set out in section 6.2. If the person applying for the grave right is asked to read and then sign this contract, the potential for later dispute is minimised.

The Interment Notice should also include a section related to any grave being re-opened for a second or further burial, or the burial of cremated remains. Where the body or remains being interred is not the owner of the grave right, then the signature of the owner approving the burial must be obtained.

After the provisional booking is made the grave registers and/or grave plans are checked to locate the grave and to confirm any ownership details. The grave location is physically checked, especially if an old grave, to ensure that there are no impediments to excavation, e.g. trees. A new grave will be allocated and pencilled out on the grave plan. An order to excavate the grave will be issued and should include the coffin size including handles. At times of high death rates, new graves (called stock graves) can be partially excavated in advance, say to 4' (122cm) deep, and then deepened and trimmed to the coffin size once a booking is accepted. The preparation of graves and dealing with the funeral is outlined in Chapter 8.

Even with efficient booking and grave checking processes it is worth noting that in my 45 years' work at least two funerals arrived which the funeral director had entirely forgotten to book!

Registration

It is worth noting that in the past, cemeteries were always managed by the Superintendent and Registrar. Although the modern title 'manager' has become commonplace there is no reason why the site manager or owner cannot be given the title 'registrar' or 'manager and registrar' of the natural burial site. For the public, it suggests that a person is specifically in charge of the records.

The responsible person will, as soon as is reasonably practical, make an entry in the statutory register of burials. In England, private sites need to comply with the rather obscure Registration of Burials Act 1864, but in practice mimic local authorities. They comply with the Local Authorities Cemeteries Order 1977 (LACO) as amended. The register can be in book form or computerised. If in book form, the entry must be in durable black ink (not biro) in a strongly bound book made of durable paper, on numbered pages, with headed columns to read:

- Sequential number of burial.

- Date of burial.

- Full name, address and age of deceased.

- Grave number.

- Other particulars, such as reference number to Registrar's Certificate/Coroner's Order/details if body exhumed.

- Signature of person making entry (could be site manager or Registrar).

Where the burial is of a stillbirth, the entry 'stillborn child of' and the full name and address of at least one parent is entered, with the age left blank. In practice, it deeply upsets parents who have given the child a name not to have this recorded, so the entry could read 'Rosie Ann, stillborn child of ...'.

The private burial of fetal remains (pre-24 weeks of pregnancy) is now more commonplace, rather than leaving the burial or cremation arrangements to the hospital authorities. Fetal remains are outside the usual registration law but they can be accepted for burial, and registered similar to a stillbirth, the entry preceded by the words 'fetal remains of ...'. Again, if the parents gave the fetus a name then this can be recorded. As there will not be a Coroner's Order or Registrar's Certificate, evidence of the fetal loss from a midwife or doctor at the hospital involved should be obtained. Parents are often very emotional about the entry for fetal remains and stillbirths and if possible the name to be recorded should be discussed and agreed.

The burial of cremated remains must be recorded as such. It is useful to record the crematorium name and cremation number in the 'other particulars' column, which might be useful to anybody researching the death at some future date.

The burial, including cremated remains, is also entered in the alphabetical index to the register. The index is in surname order and the grave number is included so that the entry in the register of graves can be located. The register of graves is maintained, in grave number order, showing the name and address of the purchaser of any right of burial, the period that this covers, the cost and grave depth, and details of the burials in the grave. This ensures that any future enquirer, typically only aware of the name of the burial, can locate the grave and full ownership and other details. The registers can be purchased from Shaw & Sons.[1]

The purchase or granting of a right of burial should be confirmed by issuing a document, often referred to as the grave deed or grant. Burial grant stationery can be purchased from Shaw & Sons.[1] The deed is usually posted to the purchaser of the right or sometimes given to the funeral director making the burial arrangement. If so, it should be borne in mind that the funeral director might retain these until such time as the funeral account is paid. The ICCM organises regular training on granting, exercising and transferring exclusive rights of burial.

When a new burial is complete, the initial deletion of the grave on the grave plan in pencil will be inked over to ensure it is never selected again in the future.

Within 96 hours of the burial, the detachable portion of the Coroner's Order or Registrar's Certificate must be sent by the site manager

---

1   For more information visit www.shaws.co.uk, or call 01322 621100.

to the Registrar of Births, Deaths and Marriages of the sub-district involved indicating the date and place of burial. It is important to note that the place of burial is not actually recorded by the Registrar and subsequently locating the place of burial through the Registration Service is not possible.

The natural burial site office remains the only place where the burial is recorded and will be the focus for any further enquiries related to the grave or burial. The law requires that searches of the register of burials should be possible at all reasonable times. This comment probably anticipates normal office hours, but at sites without permanent staffing or a designated office, the ability to make an appointment to carry out a search would suffice.

The destruction of the burial records by fire is a real risk. If the process is computerised then a copy of the records can easily be taken off site every night. If not, at the very least a purpose-designed fireproof cabinet ought to be bought, sometimes available as a reconditioned unit. This must be placed on a ground floor to avoid collapse from a higher level. In really hot fires the records may still be charred and unreadable. If all hard copies of the interment forms are stored in a separate building it at least enables the register of burials and of graves to be rewritten. Maintaining a second copy of the grave plan is not that onerous, and this ought to be kept off-site at all times.

6.2 RULES AND REGULATIONS

I am not an advocate of prescription and I could have substituted the heading 'Rules and Regulations' with the words 'Information for the Bereaved'. A number of sites prefer to use 'Terms and Conditions'. I prefer to soften prescription because it also accords with the spirit of the Charter for the Bereaved. The rules and regulations ensure the site is managed to meet its promotional aims and it might be assumed that the more environmental the aims, the stronger the prescription.

It is easier to defend logical regulations like prohibiting alien plants but far more difficult when aesthetics are involved. Consequently, plastic should not be prohibited because it is considered visually unacceptable but because it contravenes environmental objectives, perhaps because it cannot be recycled. Some local authorities issue massive lists of rules and regulations that will never be read, and include ridiculous regulations such as to prohibit the placing of seashells on graves.

As to what rules and regulations are needed I can do little better than quote the details given in the Ministry of Justice publication called

Natural Burial Grounds – Guidance for Operators published on their website in 2009 and to which I contributed:

"Access rights to the grave

- *The period of grave (rights) ownership and details on whether the right can be transferred/extended in the future;*

- *The operator's legal interest in the land and what long-term arrangements are in place for the future of the burial ground;*

- *What provision is made to ensure people with disabilities have access to services.*

Bereavement services

- *Information for bereaved people on how to deal, understand and cope with their loss of a loved one. Such information can be obtained from organisations such as Cruse Bereavement Care at www.crusebereavementcare.org.uk*

Burial procedure

- *Care of the deceased person before burial and whether they can be embalmed;*

- *Types of coffins to be used e.g. biodegradable materials such as wood, cardboard, shrouds, wicker, bamboo and similar;*

- *How family and friends can be involved in the funeral.*

Complaints procedure and handling

- *Operators should plan both to deal with complaints and to learn from them. Complaints are most likely to arise from:*

- *Disagreement with the burial authority's policy, e.g. the level of fees or site maintenance regime; or*

- *Where things go wrong, e.g. booking the wrong day for the funeral or allegations of rude or insensitive behaviour by staff.*

Operators should ensure that they provide users with readily available information about how to complain and that complaints procedures are not unduly bureaucratic. For authorities (and private sites!) who are signatories to the Charter for the Bereaved, reference can be made to the charter organiser. Local authority cemeteries are subject to their own authority's complaints procedures.

Environmental policy

Information on:

- *The environmental benefits anticipated for the scheme over a period of no less than 100 years;*

- *The current and future size of the site;*

- *Where trees, shrubs or other plants are sourced and whether these are 'native';*

- *Use of herbicides, chemicals, fertilisers, baits and any other substance that might impact on the environment;*

- *Land management, e.g. frequencies of mowing, replacement of dead trees, when tree planting will take place, ultimate tree cover, pest controls, water features, protection of historic and archaeological features (e.g. veteran trees);*

- *Waste and litter disposal from the site and whether green waste is composted;*

- *Support and/or advice of local wildlife trusts, or other agencies involved in conservation and the environment.*

Exhumation

- *Operators should make clear whether or not they are prepared to allow remains, once buried, to be exhumed from their ground.*

Management

- *Information on the burial ground management, directors, trustees, managing body or similar, with relevant qualifications given and membership of the Association of Natural Burial Grounds, the Federation of Burial and Cremation Authorities, the Institute of Cemetery and Crematorium Management or equivalent organisation.*

Memorials

- *What can be placed on the grave by mourners, e.g. real or artificial flowers, plants from a prescribed list, personal items such as toys or mementoes;*

- *Whether any form of individual grave memorial or marker is allowed and, if so, details on the position, size, inscription and materials permitted, and ongoing maintenance arrangement.*

Pricing policy

- *Itemised price lists for the various services provided;*

- *Methods of payment accepted;*

- *Any administrative charges, e.g. for a change of mind.*

Records

- *What details are kept on file, why and for what period of time, and where such records are to be found;*

- *What burial plans and records are held, the arrangements for public access to them, and any fees payable.*

Site maintenance

- *How the burial ground will be maintained and if this will impact on memorials set up, access to graves, and how the landscape character may change, e.g. through selective thinning of trees, which may impact on a tree planted especially individual memorial trees;*

- *operators should make it clear that the site is managed for wildlife and visitors and grave owners should expect presentation and experience to be different to conventional cemeteries."*

To the above list I might add:

- Control over vehicle speeds and access.

- The site seasonal opening and closing hours.

- Whether unaccompanied children are allowed on site.

- Whether dogs are allowed, and if so, under what conditions.

- A total prohibition on any glass item placed on graves.

- Whether the owner of the grave right can maintain the grave, such as regularly cutting the grass.

As local authorities operate under the Local Authorities' Cemeteries Order 1977 (LACO) as amended, they are given access to legal powers to prosecute in certain circumstances related to criminal damage to buildings, graves, trees and plants. In practice, these powers are rarely, if ever, used. Private sites cannot use LACO and as they rely on normal police response regarding theft, damage and graffiti, it would appear pointless to create any regulations to cover these issues.

Local authorities may also possess various useful byelaws, and that might include the control of dogs and dog fæces. Private sites ought to consider this aspect as dogs are often a point of dispute. This is especially the case where large numbers of urban dog walkers might use the site. If thought necessary, rules on drinking alcohol, holding picnics or playing games might be considered.

Two issues remain, the first on how much of this detail can be conveyed in leaflets, and the second on developing a process that ensures the rules and regulations are fully understood by every grave purchaser.

6.2.1 Information in leaflets

All or some of the above rules and regulations could be set out in a formal list, but that is following the naïve approach of many local authorities. By far the majority of the rules ought to be written into the leaflet(s) which describe the site, its purpose and its range of services. Simple statements such as the following:

> *"Greenland natural burial site is for those who want to create the perfect habitat for a barn owl. Burial is in native wildflower graves, each of which can be marked by a wood cross and accessed along mown paths through the meadow. As part of this natural approach we only accept coffins made of earth-friendly materials, do not accept embalmed bodies and prohibit the use of any horticultural or other substances that might damage the environment."*

At least seven points in the Ministry of Justice publication have been addressed in one paragraph. The more objective regulations such as vehicle access and the control of dogs might be listed on the back of the document. Because people fail to see or specifically internalise lists of blank text, computer graphics can be used. Against a picture of a dog and a car the appropriate text can be appended on an A4 sheet. A picture draws the eye and focuses attention but it is difficult to prove whether it is more effective. The advantage of keeping objective rules and regulations on a separate, single sheet is that they can be retained on a computer, and amended and printed as needed. If they are integrated into an expensive colour printed leaflet, as hand alterations look unprofessional, changes are only possible at a reprint.

As an example of the need to add a rule, I recall a complaint by cemetery visitors that they had not been warned that when adjacent graves were excavated, the spoil prevented them visiting their grave

151

for a few days. Using computer graphics, a picture of a grave was created, and text appended to warn that the right to do this was reserved. This was added to the list of existing rules and regulations, and passed to every new grave purchaser, which appeared to stop the complaints. The flexibility to readily add and remove rules and regulations is useful.

6.2.2   Ensuring the information is received

It is evidence of efficient management if a process is in place that ensures the rules and regulations are conveyed to grave purchasers, even though this does not ensure that they have been read and understood.

Most local authorities send out this information as part of a package enclosing the grave deeds. The creation and sending of the package is then a routine which, in theory, should never fail. In local authorities the grave deeds are routinely dispatched in the weeks following the burial in the grave. The risk is that the funeral director may not have fully explained the site rules to the grave purchaser, so they will receive this information some weeks after the funeral. A natural burial site that provides an integrated funeral directing service will not experience this potential communication failure.

A new approach at some local authorities is for the potential grave purchaser to apply for each specific type of grave on a prepared form, which could be an integral part of a site leaflet. The rules and regulations, in full or part, are detailed on the form, and a signature can be seen as a binding declaration that they understand and agree to abide by the rules. As this would need to be signed prior to the funeral, the funeral directors would need to maintain a stock of the forms. This sounds rather bureaucratic but it is the most reliable way to avoid potential communication disputes.

It must be understood that the person signing the form is often the widow or widower of the deceased or a parent of a dead child. They will often be distressed and confused by the precipitate nature of the death, which is why such events are often referred to as a crisis purchase. Much of the time this person is so distressed that the conditions that might apply are neither recognised nor understood. Because of this the assistance of a son or daughter, or a friend or neighbour who could act as an advocate, is often helpful. In knowing the bereaved they can often interpret the information to ensure that they will understand the commitment that is being agreed to. As the advocates may also be future grave visitors, they will obtain their own perspective as to whether the site rules are acceptable or not. It is essential that those people, who will find the natural burial sites ethos unacceptable, arrange a funeral elsewhere. People cannot grieve properly if the grave is attended by unacceptable conditions.

The site rules and regulations often support a particular habitat. This effectively becomes a contractual agreement between the site and those people who purchased a grave and thereby endorsed such values. Consultation ought to occur before any changes are made that might significantly alter such an agreement. Where grave right owners, or other visitors, transgress, then action needs to be taken. The first stage is a more subtle prescription, perhaps pricking the conscience by reminding them that the site's objectives cannot succeed, for example if grass is mown short. The last resort is to suggest that their actions would not have been approved by the deceased. Ultimately, where inappropriate memorabilia is placed or the grave is otherwise mown or distinguished in some other way that contravenes the regulations, reference back to a signed agreement is often a potent influence on behaviour.

6.3   PARTICIPATION BY THE BEREAVED

Funeral services in the 1960s when I began work were sometimes referred to as 'Churchillian'. This was because they were seen as conservative, concentrated on religious sentiment rather than the deceased, and truly British in avoiding emotions. It was typical not to mention the name of the deceased during the ceremony.

Natural burial has been a significant force in changing funerals, not least in allowing and supporting the bereaved and other grieving people to participate. I recall the death of a father who died too young. His children, in accordance with his wishes, arranged a natural burial and ordered a white cardboard coffin with the intention of artistically decorating it. Subsequently their funeral director contacted me because he felt that I would be as concerned as him about the decoration.

I personally met the funeral at the burial chapel but the children lead the funeral service themselves. They spoke of their dilemma a few days earlier, a coffin bereft of decoration and the challenge of what to put on it. After much discussion, a younger child had suggested writing on the words that their dad regularly used, the everyday familiar words that immediately made him seem with them again. The coffin lay on trestles in front of us all and along the sides and ends it read 'Shut that bloody door'.

Although natural burial is not the only type of funeral with such flexibility, one of its advantages is that being relatively new it has not become slick. A routine burial and especially cremation can be reliably expected to take place within a set period of perhaps 30 minutes. The crematoria sets the agenda and the minister and funeral director have to teach the bereaved their part and together ensure that the conveyor belt is not interrupted.

Most people seem content with this process and consequently, the cremation rate has increased over decades. The question that arises is whether, given the opportunity, the bereaved would prefer to be more involved in funerals and services? To achieve this they would need an open process, which encourages and supports their participation, without severe time restrictions or any suggestion that there is such a thing as a typical funeral. A natural burial site has this opportunity, and they ought to foster a more relaxed and supportive approach.

Many psychologists advise that participation in the funeral is therapeutic because the death is internalised and its reality accepted. Supporting people to do this is very satisfying but it is important not to imply that a failure to participate is in any way unusual or unacceptable. Many people will feel challenged or stressed when given an open licence. Others may feel that as the deceased had a good long life, the short perfunctory service is appropriate, and a small number will have no wish for any form of service at all.

6.3.1 Participation in the funeral service

It should be remembered that when family members speak at a funeral it is not uncommon for them to become very tearful, even to break down. The fact that this may happen ought to be discussed as an acceptable part of the experience. Psychologists suggest that children should be encouraged to attend funerals and participate if they so wish as this will prevent the development of funeral phobias. The fear of seeing bodies, of talking about the dead, even of participating in services or entering a cemetery, are learned behaviour and less likely if not observed in adults.

This is not a book dedicated to creating a funeral service or decorating a coffin. *The Dead Good Funeral Guide* by Sue Gill and John Fox is eminently more suited to this purpose, especially for those seeking more involvement, to introduce art into funerals or to make their own coffin.

Site owners will need to be aware of what could happen at services so that the design of their celebrant's hall will be suitable and meet any requirements. Participation by the bereaved might include:

● Decorating the room with photos of the deceased, or their hobbies or interests; with flowers; or with streamers, balloons, etc.

● Placing the coffin in a variety of positions within the room.

● Moving the chairs into various positions, such as around the coffin.

● Focusing lighting on the coffin, or placing candles around it.

● A desire for more performance elements using speakers, singers, playing music and instruments, etc.

● A desire that speakers in wheelchairs or people with disability can fully participate, e.g. radio microphone, absence of high podium, steps, etc.

6.3.2 Involvement in the whole funeral

If a wider participation is sought, a supportive funeral director is essential. This may not be an issue if the natural burial site operates an integrated funeral directing service. Alternatively, the family will need to arrange an independent funeral, i.e. without a funeral director, see section 10.3.

The principal areas of participation include:

● Supplying a coffin – many funeral directors include a coffin as part of the funeral package and do not accept independent procurement or a homemade coffin. The coffin would need to be strong enough to support the weight of the body, and not collapse whilst being carried. It can be seen as little more than a sturdy box and I know of one person whose coffin is currently the oak linen chest in her bedroom.

● Decorating the coffin – modern chipboard coffins, the type supplied by most funeral directors, are not suited to artwork unlike plain pine, deal, or white cardboard. Solvent-free paints such as those manufactured by Auro should be used. Coffins are being painted in football team colours, pictures of favourite cars, or leaves and flowers. The less artistic are using standard stencils bought at art shops, collage or dried flowers or covering the coffin with a homemade pall.

• Digging the grave – I know of no municipal cemeteries that will allow the family to excavate graves, usually on the basis that health and safety requirements demand trained gravediggers. If permitted, it would be prudent to have a disclaimer signed, and only accept people experienced in manual work, as it is skilled, heavy work as described in section 8.1. If accepted, then it might be expected that the usual excavation fee is cancelled, or reduced sufficient to cover the essential supervision and provision of equipment and safety wear. A token part of the excavation work might satisfy the family, and not necessarily the entire excavation.

• Backfilling the grave – many conventional cemeteries allow this, as it is considered a cultural need for those of West Indian or African ethnicity and some religions. As a cultural issue some confusion exists as to whether health and safety legislation applies, but the backfilling work should be supervised as if it does. The backfilling work is described in section 8.1. It is also essential to confirm whether the family require a token backfilling, or wish to complete the entire operation taking perhaps 20–30 minutes. Tools and gloves would be expected, and some washing facility might be appreciated as mourners will be dressed to attend the funeral, and not to carry out dirty manual work.

• Bearing the coffin, which is described in section 8.6.

6.4   HORSE AND HEARSE

The use of the horse-drawn carriage for funerals has increased dramatically in recent decades, not least for cremations. This has not been an environmental initiative but one based on a return to the Victorian and Edwardian funeral, the emphasis focused on black ostrich plumes rather than reducing the carbon footprint. Nonetheless, a carriage-style hearse drawn by four Belgian black horses is dramatic and elegant. I am unable to add the word 'environmental' because the large truck used to convey the horse and carriage to the site might have travelled some distance. Although the use of a horse or horses pulling a Victorian carriage or a decorated cart has a bucolic charm, all too often it is no more than a status symbol fostered by modern consumerism.

I defer to natural burial site owners as to how they respond to this fascination for horses, which might extend to mules and donkeys. If the animal is stabled nearby and its use with a carriage genuinely displaces a carbon-fuelled vehicle, it is environmentally sound. Where the horse and carriage are transported to the site in motor vehicles simply to move the coffin, it is not environmental.

I have been to natural burial sites where the restricted gate entrance and absence of a turning circle makes them unsuitable for a carriage. A traditional, horse-drawn hearse looks dramatic entering an impressive gate and proceeding up a tree-lined drive, which is why most Victorian cemeteries were designed to emphasise the drama of the approach, both to the chapels, and then to the grave side. This is an important promotional factor and one that must be considered before the site design is finalised.

Chapter 7

DEAD SET AGAINST THE PLANNING APPLICATION?

7.1 ANTICIPATING OBJECTIONS

When considering this section on planning applications for natural burial sites it was difficult to ignore the cheap jokes in newspaper headlines such as 'stiff opposition to cemetery' and 'plan for corpse copse now buried'. Planning applications for cemeteries seem to generate such humour.

The development of land and buildings is regulated by the planning system, which is managed by the local authority, referred to as the planning authority. Changing the use of a piece of land usually requires planning permission, and any new building or changing the use of, or alteration to an existing, especially listed building, is similarly in need of permission. If this is assumed to be difficult in normal circumstances, consider that planning guidelines in the past stated that cemeteries should be considered bad neighbours.

Although the information in this section is primarily directed at those who wish to open or support a natural burial site, it is just as useful for those who oppose or may wish to modify an application.

If stiff (oops!) opposition is anticipated when a natural burial planning application is submitted it might be assumed that the reasons why the site ought to be approved are evident, at least to the site owner, and the argument to support these well-formulated. Many applicants prefer to employ a firm of planning consultants to manage the planning application for them. A successful application is going to require an effective strategy based on an analysis of local need, allied to some passion for the proposed scheme. In effect, the planning application ought to be presented as the first stage in marketing the natural burial service developed for that specific community.

The marketing policy must be considered at this stage. Although I identify the marketing objectives below, I would anticipate perhaps a measure of each of the listed components to form the final project. The balance between the different components might be the final

159

arbiter leading to success, or failure. The content of this book suggests that the reasons would include:

7.1.1 Consumer benefits

1. More choice for the bereaved.

2. Local option for the bereaved.

3. Potential low-cost funeral.

4. Potential for a green funeral.

5. Potential for a meaningful funeral.

7.1.2 Environmental benefits

6. Create new habitats

7. Potential to increase community green space.

8. Potential for low-carbon funeral.

9. Potentially reduces cremation disbenefits.

10. Potentially educates about the environment.

7.1.3 Community benefits

11. Creates a new local business.

12. Improves local resilience regarding pandemic.

13. Replaces need to extend local churchyard or cemetery.

14. Reduces deficits of the local cemetery if it had been used.

15. Potentially supports other local businesses.

Few planning applications, other than for nuclear power stations, upset people as much as a proposal for a new cemetery. In the planning applications I have researched, the language used by objectors shows the passion and fear that can be generated. Quotes I have seen include: 'ultimately some 21,000 corpses', 'an almost industrial scale' (of the number of burials), 'short of poisoning the water table', 'by virtue of the noise and odours associated with cemeteries', 'they might be surrounded by a cemetery, an environment few of us would choose for ourselves', and 'the regular depressing sight of mourners'.

It is rather sad that death is so harshly observed by people who will eventually themselves need the facilities of a burial ground or crematorium.

7.2 THE PLANNING APPLICATION

The application will be submitted to the local planning authority and will outline the area of land involved, any change of use and details of access, parking areas, tracks, landscaping, buildings and other works.

The phasing over time of the burials, areas where no burials will occur, areas of open grassland or conservation meadow and any changes or re-grading of land surfaces, must be detailed. Also, any new or revised vehicle and pedestrian access and the areas and numbers of parking spaces will be necessary. The accommodations made for the disabled and less mobile will be important.

Precise details will be required for new planting or screening, the tree species and whether native or not. Any trees that exist on the site, especially those covered by a Tree Preservation Order (TPO), must be considered. It may be necessary, perhaps advisable, to catalogue all trees. As the trees dictate the character of the site, any new planting must be compatible and expert advice may be advisable.

The locations from which the site can be viewed, especially residential properties, is an important consideration. Objections from the owners of abutting properties can be anticipated and ways to mitigate this impact must be considered. Security and site locking are often important to property owners and local people.

The planning process favours sustainable development so it is important to emphasis this, highlighting any new habitats and reduced impact compared to conventional burial or cremation. If the site can reduce oil dependency or generate its own energy needs, then it will enhance its sustainability.

The number of daily, annual and overall interments must be detailed, defined as full body burials and/or cremated remains, and the days and hours of funeral activities as well as site opening times given. Care must be taken not to suggest unrealistic burial figures, which could support local objections that the proposal is commercial and out of scale for the area.

The application will be advertised as acceptable to, or a departure from, the Local Plan created for the area by the planning authority.

For instance, natural burial might represent development in the countryside of a form which is not covered by any policy, and might be seen as the loss of prime agricultural land which the Local Plan seeks to prevent from occurring.

The application will be screened by planning officers prior to registration in order to determine whether an Environmental Impact Assessment (EIA) is required to be submitted, typically necessary for significant schemes.

7.2.1 Revising the application

It is essential to be prepared to revise the application before it is formally submitted to the planning committee. Planning officers may advise modifications as a means of supporting approval, or it might become apparent that local opposition is already developing and early changes might counteract objections. Examples might include changing the appearance of buildings, reducing working hours or adding, or removing, a footpath link. Being ready to compromise might be essential to success.

The planning process can be viewed in two parts, first, the consultations, and, secondly, the policy and planning considerations.

7.2.2 Consultations

The planning authority will advertise the application, write to those who are near the site or erect local notices, and set a time in which responses must be made. Anybody has the right to take part in planning consultations, whether to object, support or request modifications. The purpose of consultation is to highlight aspects that might otherwise pass unnoticed and to clarify the proposals.

It makes sense to ensure that the application does not take those most affected, such as immediate neighbours, by surprise. An early outreach policy should be considered in order to get as many neighbours, local people and organisations as possible to support the application, or at least not object.

It is helpful to identify those most likely to take an interest in the application. As new sites are invariably in the countryside, the focus for most objections will be the parish council. They often act as mouthpieces for significant, vocal, local residents. Indeed, such people may be the local parish councillors themselves! Their objections often begin with statements such as, 'You should note that this meeting was exceptionally well attended, clearly indicating the depth of feeling felt by residents against the proposal'.

All too often emotion is the driver, and as the fact that they just do not want a new cemetery is not a valid objection, emphasis will be placed on issues such as groundwater, loss of arable land, traffic predictions, appropriateness of a cemetery of the size proposed and consequences to immediate neighbours. In fact, most of these issues will be subject to separate expert analysis, and it is to these that the planning authority will ultimately defer.

The position of councillors can be compromised. For instance, parish councillors and those councillors acting for the planning authority are often part of a local authority that manages a conventional cemetery, perhaps even one with a natural burial service. They may even be on the committee managing such a cemetery. I have experienced such councillors commenting that a new natural burial site would create unwanted competition to an existing council cemetery, and they might have acted, perhaps even voted, against it. A declaration of interest might have been appropriate.

Parish council objections may well reinforce the negative findings of, say, the Environment Agency regarding drinking water. Often, if they feel the Environment Agency are too weak they will highlight the potential pollution by exaggerating the data.

The loss of farmland is a frequent objection, often as if an exceptional wildlife resource is being destroyed. It may be necessary to point out that prime agricultural land is heavily artificially fertilised and herbicides are used to control weeds in the monocrops grown. Consequently, farmland has the potential to be far more polluting than a natural burial site, and is often habitat poor.

The loss of farmland for food production is potentially a valid objection. The Agricultural Land Classification scheme (ALC) defines five grades. The finest is Grade 1 – intensive arable, the poorest is Grade 5 – rough grazing. If this is expected to be a strong objection then perhaps a farmland natural burial site should be proposed, or more emphasis placed on returning the land to some farming enterprise at some future stage.

Concern is often expressed about the size of the burial operation and whether this is too large for what might be a quiet rural area. If the number of estimated burials is well beyond what can be attracted locally then such a proposal will require some defence. Again, it is the content of the Local Plan which matters, and if that seeks to protect farmland, rural quiet, and avoid development that attracts traffic to rural roads, the application is more likely to be refused.

The need for green travel plans, and sustainable transport, is a growing requirement. Remote sites that can only be visited by car are more difficult to defend, especially where they replicate conventional cemeteries. The provision of mown graves upon which memorials can be placed implies a need for the bereaved to routinely visit subsequently, using their own vehicle.

The data about the site traffic, and subsequent visitation by bereaved visitors to graves, may well be exaggerated by objectors. Also, they may suggest this traffic will contribute to local road accidents and accident blackspots, and that funeral cortèges will bring local villages and towns to a standstill. The traffic position ought to be analysed very carefully before the application is submitted. The rule is the more public transport that is available, the better. If access roads are narrow, there may be a requirement to build passing bays to avoid vehicles having to reverse.

The site impact on neighbours will be highlighted, and traffic, noise and even odours might be cited, as well as a lack of screening. In fact, my experience proves that the neighbours of cemeteries I managed invariably felt that the area was enhanced by the trees, the silence and the wildlife. It is essential to anticipate such comments and mitigate them by highlighting the fact that cemeteries are far quieter, odour free, and more secure than farms, where vehicle and stock theft is routine.

Care must be taken to define precisely what type of natural burial is provided within the application, and not use casual terms such as green burial without defining what that means. In addition, words like 'parkland' and 'woodland' are not always clear to planners as well as objectors, so definitions are essential.

The planning authority will be aware that parish council written objections can be copied and submitted by individual parish councillors and other objectors. Duplicated letters or wording used by objectors are usually spotted and may well be taken less seriously. Neither are petitions taken as seriously as unsolicited letters.

Submissions might be anticipated from the County Preservation Society and County Wildlife Trust, so they ought to be contacted well before the planning stage. An application that protects local vernacular buildings or species, creates habitats and protects priority Biodiversity Action Plan species is far more likely to gain support.

Consultation with the Environment Agency is potentially the most difficult. Typically, the Groundwater and Contaminated Land team at the Environment Agency are consulted at an early stage. Meetings ensue with the applicant and any consultants they might employ, and detailed reports and monitoring data are used to make an assessment. They must consider that the burial site poses no significant risk to controlled waters but may well apply some conditions such as no burials shall take place within 10 metres of any ditch or watercourse, in saturated ground or within 50 metres of any well or borehole.

The Highway Authority must not object and it may be necessary to meet conditions, perhaps on road access or visibility or preventing water from running on to the highway.

The County Landscape Officer or County Council Countryside and Environment Service might comment if they identify conflict between the site proposals and the local character. If so, they might request more or less native planting, or a more detailed explanation of what is meant by words like 'parkland'. They may be concerned about artificial lighting, or the creation or protection of hedging or stone walling. Natural England might seek an Ecological Appraisal for the site on how biodiversity might be increased.

The County Council Archaeological Service will consult if there is known archaeology adjacent to, or on the site. They might require a desktop appraisal and/or site excavation to establish the extent, nature and survival of any archeology. Their principal concern will relate to ground that will be disturbed by burials. They may state that there are no grounds to consider refusal, providing that conditions requiring an archaeological programme of work to be undertaken prior to the commencement of any development on site are accepted. This work must be funded by the applicant and can be both open-ended and expensive. In one authority that I managed in 2003, over £12,000 was spent, and far from being conclusive, it resulted in demand for a second phase of site excavation.

The County Council Rights of Way Team, and possibly the parish council, might consult on footpaths that run through and close to the site.

Residents Associations are normally restricted to urban areas, but might be expected to submit comments where they exist. They are often closely associated with local councillors so may be prompted to act on behalf of other objectors.

Individual comments from neighbours, most often objections, must be anticipated. These might run into hundreds but if a huge number arise from one address, they lose much of their impact. The planning authority will report these objections under their individual topics, such as traffic, nuisance, loss of farm land, impact on view, etc. All too often the comments can be puerile and absurd in exaggerating impacts related to odour, dust, traffic and health. However, if they highlight significant factors such as old covenants or historical land facts, then they might influence the decision. Nonetheless, the applicant needs to anticipate these objections and do their utmost to avoid conflict and to be seen as an advantageous neighbour.

It is important to be prepared to refute objections with sound facts. A broad understanding of the topics in this book is essential. For instance, objectors often cite the presence of a local crematorium as a reason to refuse natural burial, and the case against cremation might need to be expressed.

7.2.3   Policy and planning considerations

A wide range of local authority and national policies need to be taken into account. These are constantly changing but need to be identified and considered prior to the submission of a planning application.

This part of the process will be completed as a report by planning officers to the planning committee. It will highlight existing local and regional plans and how they influence the application. Such plans might include commercial activities within the countryside and may even anticipate the opening of 'green burial' sites, although this term is rarely defined. The plans may well state that green burial should be accommodated on 'under-used land', again not defined, rather than on agricultural land. Clearly, the use of poorer quality land is more likely to be approved. Even so, a departure from this policy may be acceptable if the application involves tree planting in, say, an area devoid of trees. Increasing policy guidance can be anticipated on the need for green travel plans, and planning officers will highlight this issue.

The planning officers will interpret the planning considerations directly related to how the site is to be developed and managed. It is here that any weaknesses in the application will be highlighted, especially the definition of what 'green' actually means. One natural burial planning application stated that metal caskets and zinc coffins would not be permitted, to support their green ethos. In fact, use of these is rare and yet the site's unquestioned acceptance of chipboard/ MDF coffins was ignored, perhaps an example of disinformation? Also, embalming was to be discouraged but how this was to be achieved was not explained.

The planning officers will state the case for natural burial, as set out in the application, so this needs careful preparation. Overall, the need must be justified with realistic projections for the future. This will be balanced against existing provision for natural burial, and perhaps the absence of conventional local burial. If adjacent natural burial sites are smaller in scale or completely different in design and operation, this might be highlighted. The planning officers can be expected to summarise the natural burial scene nationally so that the planning committee can understand the movement.

For the planning application to succeed, the view of the planning officers should be that the applicant has demonstrated that the natural burial site is essential in terms of meeting a need within the district. The officers can be expected to highlight topical issues, which are likely to include the following.

Traffic

The applicant's figures regarding the number of vehicles at funerals related to the operating hours and impact with peak traffic periods will be reported. Reduced operating hours, say to 3pm, might be demanded to avoid traffic congestion at peak times. Parking will be detailed, as well as access and any necessary works demanded by the Highway Authority. Access by public transport will be an important consideration. The officers might conclude that the absence of buildings, especially chapels, perhaps toilets, might attract fewer people and vehicles to funerals.

Contamination of groundwater

The planning officers will report on, and defer to the Environment Agency report. The EA do not report on health risks, and if these are alleged through consultations, an alternative community health expert might be cited. The applicant may need to highlight the fact that many rural people live next to churchyards without health implications.

Residential amenity

The officers will summarise the impact on residential properties regarding noise, disturbance or a loss of privacy. They may indicate conditions they have demanded to mitigate this, such as moving a car park, or screening.

Landscape impact

The planning officers will summarise the landscape issues, and may well indicate conditions they have applied. This might be to refuse non-native tree planting, protect hedges, and perhaps better define what parkland or other such site descriptions actually mean. The officers may also suggest to the planning committee that they have the option to make conditions if they are not satisfied about specific issues.

Planning officers are skilled and usually very fair in their assessments. Often they summarise by stating that the proposals represent an opportunity to enhance the appearance of the site or area, perhaps over a number of years. Planning officers are rarely horticulturalists or landscape architects, so they rely on advice on these, as well as other topics.

Wildlife and biodiversity

The planning officers will defer to Natural England and others on these issues. External specialist ecological appraisal provided by the applicant may be valuable. Often, this advice will highlight the existing poor diversity of most farmland sites and prove that most natural burial sites, perhaps with specific management, will increase diversity. The potential to create and improve wildlife corridors should be included in the application. Where the applicant works with, or otherwise supports, the County Wildlife Trust, it is likely to find favour.

Facilities on site

The intensiveness of the site use is a concern to planning officers, so the absence of a chapel, etc. might ease such concerns. One officer summary even supported the absence of site toilets by stating that 'many graveyards do not have toilet facilities', which clearly meant churchyards! The fact that a number of men will urinate behind trees, whilst the women will just get very uncomfortable, was not mentioned. As concern for disabled access is typically high, it is inconsistent to ignore the value of toilets.

To reduce artificial path surfaces, grass paths are often specified by applicants. These might be seen as an accessibility problem by planning officers, especially if distance and undulation are involved. To overcome this some applicants provide an electric golf buggy to transfer the infirm to the grave side.

Loss of agricultural land

This topic will be detailed and related to the existing Local Plan.

7.2.4 Summary

The planning officers will finally state whether they can support the application, and may list their concerns, what elements are uncertain, and the positive aspects overall. They may then recommend to the planning committee that the application be approved, perhaps with a series of conditions related to the issues discussed above. If the application is rejected an appeals process is available. Information on this and a wealth of planning advice is available on the Government's planning portal, see www.planningportal.gov.uk

Chapter 8

HOW ARE NATURAL BURIALS CARRIED OUT?

8.1   GRAVEDIGGING

Charlie Tomkins of Shrewsbury could neither read nor write, yet he was an artist whose medium just happened to be soil. He was a short man, taut, an athlete who trained by excavating one grave each working day over a long life. If he was short of a grave to excavate, he would dig over a patch of ground in the plant nursery, where I first met him when I was 15 years old. Each sod was cut, hardly lifted, which would be to waste energy, yet deftly turned so that it formed part of a chequerboard of unbelievable neatness. He was the last of a type, and I never saw such a skilled worker of soil again. By the end of his working life he was already being replaced by a tractor-mounted, backhoe digger on new graves. Now, very few new graves are hand dug.

The early gravediggers wore wood clogs, with an iron plate fitted to the instep to protect against contact with tools, which quickly cuts through the sole of a standard Wellington or boot.

Digging graves is an acquired skill and I am aware of at least one new natural burial site manager who found digging their first grave extremely stressful. To avoid the coffin becoming wedged a huge grave was dug and when lowered in, the coffin looked rather lost in the expansive void! What is evident from this and other comments is that all too often gravedigging is not given the respect it deserves. It should not be performed without training, and even where contracted gravediggers are used, they should possess some evidence of formal training. Specific training courses are provided by the ICCM.

Although the training is available I am aware that there is no readily available description of the process in print. With the knowledge that gravedigging is occasionally being carried out by the bereaved for garden burials and perhaps at some natural burial sites, a description is required. In addition, with so many inexperienced natural burial site owners entering the market, they will gain some insight into the process before they employ a gravedigger, or contractor. Many gravediggers at private sites, churchyards and parish cemeteries are not formally trained and often use too little shoring and timbering in and upon the grave.

The first consideration is whether gravedigging is to be done by hand, or with a mechanical excavator. Hand excavation is environmentally sound but such hard work that few people are skilled or willing to be trained. If burial numbers are expected to increase, and manual excavation not feasible long term, mechanical excavation is essential from the start. As the activity of gravedigging is fundamental to the success of the site, I propose to consider the entire process, from staff issues to the final reinstatement of the grave.

8.1.1   Staffing

In the past, the gravedigger had the highest employee status and was expected to dig a single grave each day. Often he (as women did not undertake this work in the past) supervised the use of the grave for the funeral, and its backfilling after the committal service, so that it was an integrated task from start to finish. This ensured that responsibility for the safe excavation, and the correct selection of the grave for the funeral, rested with a single person.

Although the excavation of a grave can be achieved using a single staff member, safe work practice now demands two staff. This ensures that when one person has entered the grave, the second is always available to give immediate assistance in the event of a soil collapse or other incident. In the past, the second employee was called the 'topman' to separate this role from the gravedigger.

8.1.2   Manual handling

All gravedigging and associated tasks involve heavy lifting and manual work. In the past, the gravedigger would perform these tasks everyday and develop the physical strength necessary. For new staff unused to such work, and where gravedigging is only carried out spasmodically, it is important to approach the work with care, and allow time for the body to adapt to the demands.

All staff involved should undertake manual handling training prior to the work. It is also useful to appreciate that slow, steady work is more suited to the human body. Short periods of excessive labour with intermittent periods of rest, is liable to lead to body strain. When using tools such as shovels and spades, the smaller tool is often the most efficient. Larger tools can encourage the lifting of too much wet, heavy soil, which will put an excessive strain on the back muscles. In wet soil, especially clay, stainless steel tools tend to throw off the clinging soil more efficiently and are easier to use.

8.1.3   Health and safety

This work, as with all site operations, must be risk assessed. All gravedigging staff must wear safety helmets, because stones regularly fall from spoil heaps back into the grave. Safety boots with steel toe-caps, gloves, visor or other form of eye protection and overalls are all essential. Ear protection will be necessary if working with a mechanical excavator. For work in wet graves, safety Wellingtons might be preferred. All gravediggers and grounds staff should be routinely immunised against tetanus.

I am not aware of any deaths due to grave excavation in recent decades and accidents are infrequent, but may have gone unreported. In the past, I recall an employee working alone in the grave being trapped by the legs when a side wall collapsed. His shovel was buried and, unable to extricate himself, he had to wait some hours before a cemetery visitor heard his cries.

8.1.4   The gravediggers' maxim

- Save labour by excavating the grave as small as possible.

- Work at a steady, consistent rate.

- Share the work with a second person and never work alone.

- Share the lifting of all weights.

- Think safe at all times.

- Work in a neat and tidy manner avoiding damage to surfaces especially turf.

- Do not leave equipment and tools lying around.

8.1.5   Initial preparation

It is important to ensure that all the equipment and materials are taken to the grave side before the job starts. If items are forgotten, their later collection requires that one person leave the site with the other staff member then working alone, an action that must always be avoided. A checklist of all the equipment needed for each job can be drawn up, if considered necessary.

Where gravedigging is routinely occurring on a single plot, it is sensible to store the heavy timbers and other equipment on or near the site. This requires that a secure storage building or compound is available, as visually, it looks poor to leave the equipment in view. Where tools, grave shoring, timbers, etc. are moved by dumper or truck, it is important that they are securely placed and cannot fall off en route.

8.1.6   Marking out the grave

It is essential that one person checks each grave on the office grave plan and confirms that the actual grave excavated on site is identical to this using both the number and physical orientation.

It makes for an efficient excavation process if the site office issues a temporary grave marker for all excavated graves. A spiked wood plaque or a spiked plastic plaque of the kind often used to display plant names in horticultural nurseries is ideal. The grave number and name of the deceased can be written on using marker pens, or a card attached. The marker is then taken by the person allocating and checking the actual grave and inserted into the ground at the head end. The marker can stay on the grave after excavation, through the grave dressing and funeral, perhaps to the point at which any memorial is placed, and then returned back to the office for re-use. This process is not suitable if there is any danger of children moving such markers as a prank.

With the presence of an allocation marker, the gravedigger has visible evidence that the grave is the correct one and will confirm this against the grave excavation order he or she has been given. Two planks will be placed along each side to the correct width, and the turf cut along the edge of the planks. The turf should be cut into identical neat pieces; ideally using a purpose designed turfing iron.

The actual position of the excavated grave merits some consideration. It is not unusual to visit a cemetery plot currently in use and see rows of graves where each grave is obviously out of line with its neighbour. An error of one quarter of an inch per grave means that 100 graves later, a row might be over two feet out of line. Then, as the graves are visually picked out by trees, plaques and even flowers in vases, the error becomes more obvious. Relocating the precise grave decades later is more difficult if it is some feet out of line.

Ideally, the grave markers (not the excavation marker!) in stone, cast metal, etc. or just a wood peg should be placed, as agreed, either at the top or bottom centre of each grave. The entire grave row should be lined out so that error is avoided against the grave plans. The marker must be secure and at turf level so mowers or other ground operations cannot hit or move it.

As the grave itself is much larger than the actual excavation, it is useful to define precisely the point from which all excavation begins. If a tree or memorial plaque is to be placed on stable ground at the head end, it makes sense to begin the excavation 2' (61cm) from the head end grave marker. Assuming a 7' (214cm) long excavation in a 10' (305cm) long grave, this will leave a 1' (31cm) width at the foot end. This will create a 4' (122cm) border between head to head grave rows on which plaques or trees might be placed.

8.1.7 The shape of the grave

In the past, graves were excavated coffin-shaped, with a taper at each end. This kept the removal of soil to a minimum, and allowed wider and therefore safer 'midfeathers', the term for the soil wall between graves. The widest part of the grave is dug at the shoulders, which is the widest part of the coffin. Often, cemeteries following this practice had wood boards cut and fitted onto angled metal brackets to create a template, two of these being used to cut the coffin shape in the turf. Subsequently, they were used for the bearers to stand on when the coffin was lowered. Such shaping is much more difficult with mechanical grave excavation and is now rare.

Where a grave is excavated using a mechanical excavator it is usual to excavate with straight sides to the grave. Even with straight sides, the foot end is still tapered to the narrower width of the coffin, and with a wider midfeather, makes for a safer grave. The grave for a casket must be rectangular in shape.

8.1.8 Coffin and casket sizes

Graves are excavated 4" (10cm) wider and longer than the coffin or casket, which allows a 2" (5cm) gap all round. This is the safety margin to ensure the coffin does not bind against the grave sides or shoring. Care must be taken that the submitted coffin size includes any handles,

175

as occasionally these can extend beyond the coffin. It is essential to ensure that the funeral director, when giving coffin sizes, does not also add a safety margin and submit an oversize measurement. If a 2" (5cm) tolerance to either side seems too little when inexperienced, this can be extended by a further 1" (2.5cm) on either side, and reduced as experience increases. It is important to consider that every 1" (2.5cm) extra width on a 6' deep x 7' long (183cm x 214cm) grave is equal to 3.5 cubic feet of soil, and greatly increases labour costs. Of equal importance is that a wider grave requires more backfilling, and as this settles, more reinstatements.

When excavating the grave for coffins, the width of the tapered end is usually estimated based on experience. The inexperienced will need to telephone a funeral director and obtain the relative measurements between the shoulder widths and foot widths of standard coffins. As biodegradable coffins can be very variable, specific foot and head end measurements might be necessary at all times.

8.1.9   Dealing with spoil

Before the excavation begins, the placement of spoil needs to be considered. The deeper the grave, the more difficult it becomes to neatly retain the soil. The spoil may be removed entirely from the grave site, but this is energy expensive and raises the carbon footprint. It also necessitates the excessive use of dumpers or other vehicles and muddy tracks are then inevitable, and all too often, soil is spilled on road and path surfaces. It is not recommended, and it would be environmentally detrimental to natural burial.

The spoil from shallow graves is often loosely placed on a couple of 8' x 4' (244cm x 122cm) ply boards butted together. Such a level surface makes it much easier to shovel the soil back into the grave compared to placing the soil on the bare ground. Adding three sides to these boards, to form a spoil box, is even better as it holds the soil higher, and closer to the grave edge, all aspects that reduce the effort of backfilling whether manually or mechanically. Spoil boxes also look neater, are safer in spreading the weight, and make it easier to cover the spoil in wet or freezing weather. The spoil box can be designed to sit on blocks or legs if it is necessary to hold it above herbage that needs protection.

As commercially manufactured spoil boxes have been available but of poor quality, some cemetery authorities have spoil boxes made locally by a carpenter or fabrication firm. The whole must be built up in easily carried sections and form a level base, with 2'–3' (61–92cm) high corner posts into which panels are slotted. This is placed on the side of the excavation, as close as possible whilst leaving room for the coffin lowering and bearers. If the base of the spoil box is raised by a few inches, it makes it easier to shovel the soil over the edge and back into the grave. Mobile spoil boxes have been used at times, but were never popular.

The spoil should be placed on solid ground wherever possible, and not over used graves with the potential to collapse. If only used graves exist around the excavation, access to one or more of these will be denied to any visitor who arrives after the spoil heap has been created. Consequently, graves obviously visited regularly should be avoided, or ideally, the grave owner notified that the excavation is to occur. Such excavations should be delayed as late as possible so that access is quickly recovered, and every care taken to avoid damage to the surface of the covered graves.

8.1.10 Excavation

It is important to understand how soil responds to excavation. Once dug, a grave cannot be disguised because the solid walls and the backfilled soil do not bind together for hundreds of years. If the backfilled soil is removed during this period, the soil falls away from the walls until the grave is exposed with its original dimensions.

The excavation of a new grave begins by neatly stacking the turf where it will not get damaged. The top soil is now removed to a spade's depth, called the first spit, and, keeping the soil profile in mind, this valuable topsoil must not be carelessly mixed with subsoil. Traditionally, the first dumper load is trucked away, either for the reinstatement of graves, or retained or used elsewhere on site. This load is in lieu of the space taken in the grave by the coffin, and the fact that the same volume of soil cannot be backfilled after it has been disturbed. All dumpers or vehicles used to move soil should be driven parallel to the grave sides, so there is no danger of clutch failure or driver error causing the vehicle to surge forwards and into the grave.

The grave is then progressively deepened. If by hand, a sharp spade is used to cut down the side walls, a fork is often used to loosen the soil but must not dig into and weaken the side walls, and a shovel is used to throw the soil out. A pick is used to break up hard ground, but if this is consistently necessary, it suggests the grave is too hard for hand excavation. When using a pick, eye protection should be used, especially on flinty or stony soils. Hand excavation has a low vibration factor, and with no mechanical excavator sitting on the surface, the soil is much less likely to fracture and collapse. As hand excavation proceeds, a depth of 3' (92cm) should be considered the maximum unshored depth whilst a lone gravedigger is working in the grave. The gravedigger can throw the soil into the spoil box with ease for the first few feet, but this gets progressively more difficult as the depth increases. A second person is necessary to move the soil back into the spoil box at the later stage. Ideally, the soil profile will be maintained in the spoil box so that the deepest excavated soil is at the front, and is the first backfilled to its original depth. Gravediggers must always access the grave using a ladder, and not climbing down the walls or shoring.

When mechanically excavating, the machine is always positioned on solid ground at the foot or head end of the grave. Care needs to be taken to avoid excessively striking the walls or ends of the grave with an excavator bucket, as once weakened, they pose a permanent hazard. A smaller bucket causes less vibration than a larger one, and is much preferred. The soil is progressively removed and placed in the spoil box. A second employee watches the excavation proceed and gives guidance when necessary.

Whether hand or machine excavated, care must be taken to ensure the grave walls are smooth and vertical, and a plumb line should be used if doubt exists. Tree roots or stones sticking out will snag coffins and must be removed. The base of the graves must be smooth and level so the coffin is not tilted when it is released by the bearers. If a large boulder or obstruction appears, and excessive vibration is involved in removing it or it is too heavy, the grave should be abandoned. An occasional tree root can be removed using a hand saw.

8.1.11 Re-opening graves

The re-opening of a grave follows the same pattern as a new grave. The removal of the soil is much easier and falls away to the shape of the first excavation. If this is wider than the grave size needed on this occasion then it is shored to the original size. If it needs to be wider then virgin soil will have to be shaved off one or both walls. Re-opened graves are usually surrounded by other used graves, so access, the placement of spoil and the potential for offensive water in the grave, needs to be taken into account. Often, re-opened graves are dug by hand because access to the grave by the excavator is over visited graves, which may cause offence.

Re-opened graves already contain a body, which might have been interred a week, or perhaps decades previously. The 6" (15cm) depth of soil left over each coffin was intended as a hygiene barrier to protect the gravedigger from fouled soil. Where the gravedigger removes soil right up to the previous coffin, especially one interred recently, then the soil can contain blood and body fluids seeping from the coffin. These have a particular odour, and personal hygiene should be paramount at such times.

Although it is advisable to adhere to the six-inch barrier, in some parts of the country it is local custom and practice to expose the previous coffin, or at least its cover, called a coffin board. This is traditionally prepared by the funeral director for placement by the gravedigger over an interred coffin. The board protects the coffin from stone damage during the backfilling. When the grave is re-opened, the gravedigger is expected to expose the board. The board also protected the coffin against damage caused by the gravedigger. He or she also had a hard surface to slide a shovel along which, unlike the coffin top, was free of screw heads, nameplates or other impediments.

8.1.12 Mechanical excavators

Machines can be hired or directly purchased. Hired machines may not be fitted with an efficient excavation bucket for cutting graves. Many excavators are noisy so the decibel rating must be considered with regard to the operator, grave visitors and funerals present on the site. Rubber track laying mini-excavators are usually quiet, cause little damage and are more stable than wheeled machines.

Large, highways mechanical excavators are far too powerful for routine gravedigging. They destroy turf, lay mud along roads, and their weight and vibration undoubtedly contribute to grave collapse. Their one redeeming factor is that they might be constructed such that the boom and bucket can be slid to the left or right. This enables the boom to be lined up at 90 degrees to the grave sides, and thereby cut the grave more efficiently, and often without any hand trimming. Excavators without this facility have to move their tracks or wheels in order to place the boom at 90 degrees, which can be time consuming and more difficult if the ground surface is damaged by tracks or hydraulic rams.

Excavator buckets that minimise tearing and facilitate square cut corners should be selected. In compacted soil conditions, cutting teeth may be essential. Mini-excavators can be operated over ply sheets in order to minimise turf damage. It is necessary to ensure that mini-excavators have sufficient power and the ability to get to the required depth. For new machines, a site demonstration should always be arranged.

8.1.13 Grave shoring

Many differing types of shoring exist and it is not my intention to consider these individually. Where just a small number of graves are to be excavated, timber shoring is the traditional and acceptable method. The simplest timber shoring technique is to use standard scaffold planks 10' x 9" x 1.5" (305cm x 23cm x 4cm) cut the length of the excavation. Timber suppliers can often metal band the plank ends to prevent them cracking. Two planks are placed opposite each other on the grave walls, and 3" (7cm) square wood crosspieces, the width of the excavation, are hammered between them, in the past using a wood mallet. A choice of crosspieces or props and wood wedges are often stocked to allow a variety of grave widths to be covered without sawing wood. The crosspieces have to be wedged across the plank ends to the specified width of the coffin, plus four inches. If the grave sides show signs of swelling due to water, or if the grave is to remain unused for some days, a third crosspiece might be wedged across the middle of the excavation, and removed prior to the funeral arriving.

The wood crosspieces or props can be replaced by re-usable metal braces. In the past these were called acro-props, and were shaped like two butterfly wings either end of a threaded shaft. A metal bar was used to turn the shaft and expand the butterfly ends against the timbers. Trench struts or braces, rather like an expanding car suspension strut, are currently manufactured and might be considered.

In unstable soils, sets of timbers butted together can be placed one above the other down the full depth of the grave, which is called 'closed timbering'. The deepest timbers are extremely difficult to remove when the coffin is in place, so the last 18" (46cm) of depth is rarely shored. If shoring is essential to the full depth, the lowest shoring can be removed just before the funeral arrives. Closed shoring is specialised, as are other techniques to hold back unstable soil or sand. Skilled gravediggers should always be used in such conditions and gravedigging abandoned unless absolutely essential.

The minimum safety standard is to place at least one set of side timbers six inches below the surface. This protects the gravedigger whilst excavating and ensures that the grave edges will hold up during the funeral. The gravedigger must not enter an unshored grave once it exceeds 3' (92cm) deep. The placing of a strong metal ladder down each end of the grave will prevent the two planks crushing together and injuring or trapping the gravedigger if a collapse occurred at this stage, so is good practice. In good soil conditions, gravediggers will sometimes cut grooves along the grave sides and inset the timber planks so they are flush with the grave sides, which keeps the grave as narrow as possible and reduces excavation.

Shoring units manufactured in aluminium with hydraulic rams are the safest, and easiest to use, but are also expensive. The traditional side timbers are replaced by aluminum panels, perhaps 12" (31cm) deep and the length of the grave, these being secured across the ends by hydraulic rams. As a box unit, they can be lowered into an excavated grave, and the rams pressurised, from the surface. This avoids the need for a gravedigger to enter the grave before it is shored. One unit can be placed on top of another to the full depth of the grave. At the time of backfilling, the ram pressurising fluid is released from the surface and the units removed without anybody accessing the grave. This technique is extremely safe and neat, but the expensive units need to be stored securely to prevent theft. They can be heavy to lift, especially the deeper panels. The companies purveying these units will demonstrate their use, and often provide advanced training, which is a skilled task.

With at least one set of aluminum or timber shoring placed close to the surface, the excavator bucket needs to work inside the shoring to deepen the grave. This needs precision especially where expensive and easily damaged aluminum shoring is in use. Old excavators with loose joints might be more difficult to use in such conditions. A smaller bucket might be preferred. A second operative usually enters the grave to do any necessary grave trimming with hand tools.

8.1.14 Soil types

An important consideration in grave excavation is soil type. A continuum would see standard loams in the centre, with these considered as the safest medium. As one moves right on this continuum towards more open soils like sand, gravels and shale, the risk of collapse increases but the graves are usually dry. These are often easy to excavate, but may need closed shoring to prevent the loose material sliding into the grave. As one moves left on the continuum towards dense soils like clay, the soil becomes heavy, often wet, and in some conditions, very inclined to collapse. This is most likely when clay is sodden with water, and especially when it overrides running sand or a spring line. These issues will be evident the first time such a grave is excavated. At a certain depth, water may seep from the sides of the excavated grave, which can be almost imperceptible. Where the water flow is more obvious, silt and small blobs of clay will fall away and these can be heard from above the grave dropping into the bottom. Any excavation below this point will fill with this water, and it is surprising just how much can accumulate overnight. Once the water fills to the point where it enters, it will flow away following the course it had before the grave excavation intruded into its meandering silent world.

The signs of collapse must be watched for at all times. If the grave edge begins to fret, if tension cracks appear, or any ground begins to slump, or shoring bows or creaks, then care must be taken and adequate shoring used. Gravediggers usually get to know their soil profile with experience, and act accordingly. If water or collapse is anticipated, the grave can be excavated and shored, say, to 4' (122cm) depth and then covered over. The following day, just prior to the funeral, the final depth can be excavated. The limited time before the funeral arrives might ensure that only a small amount of water accumulates, and this can be obscured by leaves or grass clippings.

The words 'grave collapse' can too easily be correlated with the potential for injury to the gravedigger. In reality, in my 45 years of work I never experienced a single instance of an injury due to collapse. Rain is the principal cause of grave collapse and, like death, mostly seems to happen overnight. This is because rainwater runs over the edge of the grave, washes soil from behind the shoring, which unsupported, moves and allows the sides to run into the bottom of the grave. On perhaps two occasions I have been called to an excavated grave the morning after heavy rain, to view a virtual crater of wet clay, perhaps ten feet across. On both occasions, the backfilled soil lying over coffins in adjacent graves had washed away and exposed the coffins. No funeral was cancelled but to prepare the grave involved many staff working in filthy conditions in order to board over the collapse and excavate the slurry.

In really cold weather the frozen graves tend to hold up well and are less likely to collapse, but soil frozen in the spoil box is a real problem.

At such times, old mats, carpet or even leaves can be used to cover the spoil and keep the frost out. In the past coke braziers were burned over graves to thaw the ground sufficient for working.

8.1.15 Surface timbering

Overnight, and during all periods when the grave is not attended, it should be safely covered. A ply sheet is ideal as it is heavy and, unlike planks, difficult for children to move. If children access the site, or where safety is paramount, commercially manufactured vandalproof shutters can be purchased to fit aluminium shoring units, and these lock down. Trip hazards are an important consideration so the surface should be left as even as possible, and no shoring, timbers or equipment should be left lying about.

Excavated graves should be checked at least daily, preferably both morning and evening, to ensure they are covered, that the shoring is secure, that no collapse has occurred and to ascertain the water situation.

8.1.16 Gravedigger shelter

A shelter is necessary for hand excavation, in part for the comfort of the gravedigger, but principally because wet timbers, ladders and tools become more hazardous to use. Various manufactured tent structures were made for gravediggers in the past, mostly rather poor metal frames, built with a low ridge, which with heavy canvas, could be dark inside. Shelters are still commercially available although a tent or gazebo could be used, provided the sides can be removed in the lee of the wind. Any shelter must be securely tied down to ensure it does not dislodge during strong winds.

8.1.17 Backfilling the grave

Before backfilling, the webbing used to lower the coffin must be removed. Often, this gets trapped, especially where it was placed through coffin handles, or around snagging wicker or such materials. It is often necessary for somebody to descend onto the coffin to release these.

Backfilling might appear a rudimentary task, just a matter of shovelling or using an excavator to drop soil into the grave. In reality, it is far more complex, if carried out properly. From my experience, and comments made by other professionals, the backfilling of graves worsened dramatically when contractors were introduced into gravedigging. The dips and holes in used grave beds are a visual example of this all over the UK. They tended to backfill quickly, and the time necessary to tread the soil was often not accounted for when the job was priced. Hence, the first time heavy rainfall occurs, graves can drop 18" (46cm) or more overnight as the water consolidates the soil. If not noticed and remedied by staff, it deeply upsets the bereaved as it suggests that the coffin has collapsed. Wreaths can also be washed into such a recess and become wet and soiled.

It is essential to consolidate the soil as backfilling proceeds in order to remove as much air as possible. The human body clad in a pair of heavy, metal toe-capped boots, is ideally designed for this purpose. The problem is that getting in and out of the grave to tread the soil is tiring and time consuming, so often avoided. Nonetheless, work omitted here creates far more deferred work through reinstatement.

The initial backfilling must be extremely careful, so that the soil does not immediately damage a fragile coffin. Neither is the sound of backfilled stones bouncing off the coffin an example of good customer care. The soil down the sides of the coffin must be consolidated with a boot. If a fragile coffin has been used, which cannot be stood upon, this is more difficult until the coffin is amply covered in soil. Then, as backfilling proceeds, every 12" (30cm) or so of soil should be well trodden especially down the edges and corners so that as much air as possible is expelled. The shoring will be removed as the soil is backfilled, and not removed en masse before the backfilling starts.

It should be noted that clay exists in the ground under some pressure. Once excavated, it swells and simply cannot be replaced in the grave at the same density. As it is often removed in large clods by an excavator, these can be extremely difficult to tread down to exclude air. Sand and loose soils are much easier to work and infill well. I have avoided any reference to compacting the soil. This is because wet soil cannot compact, and pressure simply displaces it to one side or the other. Dry soils will not bind, so neither can they be compacted. Damp soils can be compacted, but if excessively so it will prevent water percolating and cause pooling. Mechanically powered whacker plates compact well, but should be discounted because they look and sound appalling to the bereaved.

It is usual to finish by leaving a small grave mound, say 6"–9" (15cm–23cm) high. This has the additional benefit of channelling precipitation to the sides so that it drains down the solid midfeathers, rather than into the grave over the coffin. Over some months, sooner if it rains, this should settle roughly level with the surrounding soil. With the topsoil placed last, the pre-existing habitat and typical surface vegetation of the plot should recover. If the soil in the grave sinks below ground level the topsoil should be removed, subsoil placed underneath, and the topsoil replaced.

The final act is to place any floral tributes neatly over the grave mound. These should be inspected daily, especially after strong winds and replaced as necessary. These should remain for an agreed period, say 10–14 days, before being composted or recycled, and the remaining waste sent to landfill. This period ought to be reliably notified to grave owners, as the removal of wreaths, and the potential destruction of wreath cards, or other mementos, can be a contentious issue.

8.1.18 Water in graves

As new natural burial sites are unlikely to gain planning approval if water is expected to be a problem, the historical problem of water in graves should at least reduce. Nonetheless, during inclement spells water will accumulate. Many existing cemeteries are situated on wet ground, and mechanical pumps are routinely used to pump water out. Apart from pump noise and the cost of labour and equipment, disposing of the water is restricted to the length of the outlet pipe; so silty, sometimes offensive, water is spewed over the surface in the vicinity. As pumping often accompanies inclement weather, the entire area around an excavated grave can become very muddy and unpleasant.

In wet ground, it is not unusual to find an excavated grave completely full of water the following morning, perhaps 3'–4' (92–122cm) deep. This is usually pumped out immediately prior to the funeral arriving, and sometimes the pumps are operated until the funeral arrives at the gate. As soon as pumping stops a 2"–4" (5–10cm) layer of leaves or grass clippings is spread over the grave base. As some of this organic material will float, it obscures any water entering or in the grave until after the mourners leave.

If water is anticipated in graves, perhaps due to heavy rain, a small sump is often dug at the foot end. This collects any lying water and a long-handled scoop, or a bucket can be dipped into the sump and the water, or most of it, removed with ease. Where the water table is high or in extremely wet periods, the soil removed from re-opened graves can have an unpleasant odour. If this is likely to be noticeable during the service, disinfectants can be used to mask the odour, but are environmentally harmful.

8.1.19 Grave reinstatement

Backfilled graves sink periodically as the air is displaced by consolidating soil, often dramatically so after heavy rainfall, especially if this follows a long dry period. The topping up of such graves with fresh soil is referred to as grave reinstatement. The number of grave reinstatements varies according to soil type and the quality of backfilling. Few conventional cemeteries manage without perhaps six reinstatements, but they have to create a level lawn suitable for intensive mowing. In a natural burial setting, fewer reinstatements will be necessary, but if not done, the surface will become very uneven and difficult to walk over. If a surface recess is created it will pool water and channel this down onto the coffin. On heavy soils, it may take a couple of years for the surface to consolidate. The final sinkage will occur, perhaps decades later, when the cavity around the coffin collapses.

To reduce labour costs, the topping up of graves is best done routinely by the gravediggers preparing to excavate other graves. They can remove the first spit of topsoil from a new grave, and transfer it to reinstate graves used in the past weeks or months. This keeps all topsoil at the surface and avoids the double handling of soil. If the turf is retained to cover the excavated grave mound, this is laid aside on the reinstated grave, the soil topped up, and the turf replaced. Experience will quickly be gained as to when the final reinstatement can be made, and the turf allowed to knit and grow. Getting cut turf to grow during the summer is almost impossible, unless rain is constant, but readily achieved in the other seasons.

If gravediggers are not employed to reinstate graves on a routine programme, then an alternative inspection process is essential. Otherwise, grave visitors will attend graves and if they find them sunken, will complain.

8.1.20 Mud!

An important consideration is to keep mud off the shoes of those attending funerals. In a natural burial site the problem is potentially much worse because hard-surfaced paths are rarely laid for gaining access to graves. Mud is a problem for funeral directors, especially when limousines are fouled up and have to be cleaned before a second funeral can be managed. Mud is no less a problem for private car owners. The problem is worse on clay and silt sites but considerate work practices and sensitive management can overcome most problems.

I outline in the next section the need to dress graves and in part this is to reduce the impact of mud. Maintaining a permanent turf surface undoubtedly reduces mud, which is feasible if hand excavating, but less possible with mechanical excavation. The larger the excavator the more difficult it is to protect any turf, and the worse the mud. Many conventional cemeteries consider it a given on current burial plots to ignore surface damage, on the basis that at some future stage the entire area will be renovated and re-turfed or seeded. Financially this might prove cheaper in the long term, but all bare soil implies neglect, is less safe for pedestrians, and the potential for mud to spoil funerals and grave visits is real. With natural burial, the turf is an important habitat in itself, full of worms, insects, larva and organic material, so it should be protected and reused. Any new turf brought in will introduce alien soil and seeds and potentially pests and diseases, so it should be avoided where possible. Turf is also very expensive. The use of native grass seed reduces these problems, but the growing seed cannot be walked upon for some weeks, so restricts grave access.

Using the same access for gravedigging works as that used for funerals is a common mistake. It is essential to create a works access to the graves from the back of the plot or anywhere that avoids the route taken by funerals on their approach to graves. Constant works access across turf, even if just walking and using hand barrows, causes mud in wet weather. As soon as mechanical excavators are introduced, even the lighter rubber tracked models, a degree of mud is guaranteed. It may be possible to alternate access to some degree so that grassed areas can be rested at times to recover from trampling. If access is limited and so must be shared, or if mud is a local issue then it is better to surface the area with ground bark or similar mediums from the very start.

8.2   DRESSING THE GRAVE

The dressing of a grave is not defined, but usually refers to the placing of artificial grass mats over the spoil heap, and perhaps the grave edges. This probably started with the Victorians, perhaps to obscure what they saw as the cruder elements of a burial, particularly bare soil and stones. The dressing may have been expedient if it also covered over the bones of previous burials. Some may see the covering of the soil as an example of the denial of death, or perhaps just another task for which a fee could be charged. Grave dressing is considered here as the preparation prior to the arrival of the funeral.

The earlier grass mats were made of sisal or hessian and dyed green. The green dye used to run after rainfall, colour the timbers green and the hands of those handling the mats. In recent years, plastics have been used, which are longer lasting, retain their colour, and in shedding water are lighter and easier to dry. However, their environmental credentials can be assumed as poor. It is easier to slip on the modern mats so care must be taken. All mats need periodic washing and hosing down after use in muddy conditions.

The principal is to use a selection of grass mats, large ones to cover the spoil heap, and smaller ones to hang over the edge and perhaps hang two feet into the grave. Sometimes the mats are used to cover the surface timbers, whereas others will place them under the timbers. Wet, muddy, timber walk boards can be a hazard so the grass mats may be a safer option at such times.

Natural burial sites appear to vary in their dressing of graves. In some, grass mats are used in a similar way to conventional cemeteries. Others, perhaps based on an objection to using plastic-based materials, do not use grass mats. Some use cut foliage to obscure the spoil heap. The use of natural foliage has a spiritual element but should only be started if a constant supply is available, the transport of the material does not add to the carbon footprint, and the material can be composted afterwards. A considerable amount of foliage will be needed once burial numbers begin to increase.

Part of the dressing process included placing leaves or grass cuttings in the bottom of the grave 2"–4" (5–10cm) deep. Apart from obscuring water in the grave, this covered the soil and stones and ensured a soft landing for the coffin when it was lowered. Where inexperienced family bearers are used, the coffin can hit the bottom a little hard at times, so it is a useful practice. Dead leaves (leaf mould) may also introduce decomposing bacteria to the coffin, and hasten the process. The grave dressing is completed early on the day of the funeral so is also a final check that the grave and shoring is secure.

Part of the dressing process is to ensure that the coffin bearers, and anyone standing close to the grave edge, are safe during the grave-side service. If the surface timbering remains in place, such as ply boards, and these extend right up to both sides of the grave edge, then this will suffice. Otherwise, a plank can be placed along each side of the grave edge, as a walking board. This ensures that nobody can stand on a soil edge, which can be anticipated to collapse, especially if bearing the weight of a heavy person.

In the past an extra fee could be paid to the cemetery authority to individually decorate a grave prior to the interment. The gardening staff would do this by wiring laurel leaves, flowers, etc. onto the grass mats that extended into the grave so that the coffin was lowered through a grave aperture adorned with flowers or greenery. Families with environmental or horticultural interest might welcome advice and support in order to do this for themselves.

The final part of the dressing is to lay two timber putlogs, each 3" (8cm) square and at least 48" (122cm) long, across the grave, each about 22" (56cm) from the head and foot end of the grave. The coffin is placed onto these by the bearers, where it rests until lowered on webbing. The webbing is laid across the grave alongside these putlogs, on the head end and foot end. Each webbing must be long enough to lower the coffin to the foot of the grave, allowing sufficient to remain in the hands of the bearers. A length of 22' (672cm) is usual for a six foot grave. The webbing is usually passed through any handles to prevent it slipping off the ends of the coffin, especially with family bearers. The ends can be folded neatly on the grave edge, or stretched out over the ground. An additional third webbing will be needed in the centre of the grave if six bearers are expected.

The webbing can be made of nylon-type material, which is strong, but if silky and smooth, it can burn the hands if the coffin is released too fast. Webbing made of natural material like flax is easier to hold, does not cause friction burns but is more likely to tear with age. The webbing should be clean and dry, inspected regularly, and discarded as soon as signs of wearing appear. The webbing snapping whilst a coffin is being lowered is not unusual, but might be due to sharp edges on a coffin.

Coffin lowering methods vary in the UK and in some areas hooks are fitted into the ends of solid coffins and a single lowering rope attached to each end. This enables just two bearers to lower the coffin, which may not be safe and certainly lacks finesse. Expensive US stainless steel lowering frames are available, which lower the coffin very smoothly. Some would see these as pretentious and not very green. Some sites use ropes instead of webbing while others appear to leave the provision of lowering webbing or ropes, entirely to the funeral director.

Often a container of soil or sand is included in the dressing. This avoids mourners seeking soil at the committal stage in the service, and in wet weather, and with clay soils, avoids muddied fingers.

A dressed deep open grave is a potential hazard and if visitors are expected in the vicinity, or if children have access to the grave, it ought to be covered, or supervised, until the interment occurs.

Finally, it is essential to remember that when the funeral cortège arrives, a dressed grave will be the one that everyone assumes is the correct grave for the funeral. It has been known for burials in incorrect graves to occur simply because two or three graves had been excavated but the wrong one was dressed.

8.3   HOW FUNERALS VARY

When a natural burial site opens the site manager will be expected to understand how funerals vary and to give advice. For a person without funeral experience, the first 20 or 30 burials are a steep learning curve, and potentially stressful. Each site manager gradually realises that they have become the centre of a death network and the archivist of the local dead. Most people seem to find this social perspective invigorating and not something to fear.

Similarly, any person experiencing their first death and funeral will understand this lack of familiarity. Too many people assume that funerals are all the same, but this is not the case. Although it might appear clichéd, each funeral party is an entirely unique gathering of people that will never reassemble. Neither is a re-run possible if things go wrong or wishes are not fulfilled. It requires a team effort, with the site manager, the person taking the service, and any funeral director involved, working together. They have to co-operate and support each other in the delivery of a service which is adaptable to the varying needs of the bereaved.

Since the early 1990s natural burial has influenced funerals and changed attitudes. Although, in theory at least, a conventional cremation or burial service could be varied, this was rare. The change has brought about greater family involvement, new service formats and the introduction of green and artistic coffins and burial shrouds. Rosemary can replace soil for the committal, Guinness can be poured on coffins and farmer's motor pick-ups can be used to carry the coffin to the grave.

The behaviour at funerals is conditioned by experience. Typically, the aged person's funeral will attract the fewest mourners all aware of the traditional norms of behaviour. They will be quiet and restrained, dark apparel will be worn, everybody will be well mannered and very self-conscious, the wreath cards will be repetitious and based around 'rest in peace'. Conversely, the young man who died in a road accident will attract a very different gathering. There will be large groups of weeping young women, sometimes extravagant wailing, perhaps even the threat that somebody is going to jump into the grave. The mournful cry 'I will never leave him' might echo around the site. The wreath cards will say 'Love you Smackers', and 'I hope you can drive in heaven'. The aged in attendance will be shocked at this unrestrained behaviour but their actions simply reflect a celebrity and media-influenced society. It is not uncommon for people to be overwhelmed by the occasion and faint or even have a heart attack. Providing a glass of water, a chair or calling emergency services must be anticipated.

Often, the range of vehicles at funerals reflects lifestyle and 4 x 4s and a mass of wreaths are rare at current green funerals, but standard fare at a conventional burial in a grave topped by a large Italian marble angel. In the past, funerals of publicans and auctioneers attracted a huge congregation, but less so now. The bowling club and cricket club members will attend in their club jackets, like a great wedge of pink or red. Some, like the Buffs and pagans will perform their specific rituals. Occasionally, something especially tragic will happen such as a double funeral of mother and child. Perhaps a mourner will arrive chained to a prison warder or the police may attend to watch drug dealers at the funeral of a drug victim. All of life is reflected in a funeral.

8.4   WHO TAKES THE SERVICE?

The majority of services are taken by 'ministers', the term I use to cover all religions. There has also been a dramatic increase in secular officiants, sometimes called celebrants, and mostly Humanists, in the past few decades. As a matter of care, as well as an important promotional issue, the site should support ministers and officiants wherever possible. In crematoria they are used to a vestry for their personal use to enable them to compose and robe themselves, as well as their own toilet. The site manager should always greet them, to ensure that they have all they require to carry out the service

Ministers and officiants are generally very skilled and caring, and take their funeral role very seriously. I recall a minister's annoyance when funeral directors had already discussed the format of the religious service and selected the hymns before he had seen the family. The minister ought to meet the family as part of their pastoral care and, as with secular officiants, perhaps to ensure that the names of individuals are mentioned in the eulogy. I recall one family deeply upset that they had forgotten to ask the minister to mention the grandchildren's names. Issues arise even as late as the funeral arriving at the natural burial site, so must be anticipated. Women deacons now frequently take services and have rid the Church of England of much of its male starchiness.

I recall in the 1990s a family who did not want to use a minister or officiant, but did not feel confident about managing the ceremony themselves. They asked me to act as a master of ceremony at the service. Using the text they created, I managed the service, committed the body and introduced family and friends to participate as agreed. If supporting the bereaved like this is possible, it is socially beneficial and reflects well upon the site.

There is a convention, now perhaps less common, that the funeral director, after confirming the deceased was Church of England, would notify the deceased's parish minister about the death. The family may oppose this, perhaps because they do not use the church or dislike the minister. Often, they prefer a hospital or hospice chaplain met during the deceased's final illness, with whom they have developed a relationship. Whatever their religion or belief, if the family do not know a minister or secular officiant then they rely on the advice and contacts of the funeral director. This can lead to the funeral director repeatedly using a retired minister, sometimes referred to as a 'tame minister'. They have few church commitments, are readily contacted and flexible in fitting into the funeral director's programme, unlike parish ministers. It is all too easy to make cursory attempts at contacting the parish minister, and then fall back on booking the retired minister. Where this happens, the parish minister is unable to perform his or her pastoral role.

Retired ministers often have a wide experience of funerals. Being more relaxed on dogma they often create a bespoke rather than routine service through mentioning the deceased's and other names, and creating a small eulogy. Neither have retired ministers any reason to encourage the bereaved to attend the local church, so any embarrassment as a lapsed churchgoer is also avoided.

I have sensed increasing tension with clergy if it is suggested that the bereaved are buying a religious service, as if it were a consumer purchase. Ministers are trained to provide pastoral care, and not to deliver what might be considered a religious funeral performance. This is relevant in that some ministers and churches do not charge a fee for regular churchgoers.

The issue of what makes a good funeral service is interesting, and as a good service is remembered, it might be seen as an effective promotional tool. This can be considered as part of a funeral continuum with those committed to religion to the extreme left, the committed secularists to the extreme right and between the two – the indeterminate majority! Both the religious and secular groups are often defined communities, familiar with a minister or officiant. With this familiarity, these services have a certain unity and are often relaxed, warm and emotional. I do not recall that I ever had a complaint from such groups that a service was in any way, cold and informal.

The complaints, or rather grumbles of discontent, tend to arise from the indeterminate majority. They are neither active churchgoer, nor have the confidence to be secular. They usually take the pseudo-Christian line and ask for a Church of England minister. As the minister has no relationship with the family then the service may seem superficial and cold. As the funeral director also needs to promote a good image, they might suggest only retired ministers who deliver what they define as a good service.

When the service ends, the minister or secular officiant usually expects to shake hands with the congregation. Likewise, the partner or spouse of the deceased, or close family, might want to greet everybody leaving the chapel or grave side, so this needs to be kept in mind. This can take a long time, especially with a large congregation, so the timing and the most ideal place to do this, should be given consideration.

The natural burial site should be aware of their local ministers and officiants, and those who would turn out immediately if a funeral arrives without a minister, or the minister is taken ill. Otherwise, the site manager ought to have a copy of a funeral committal service ready and be prepared to deliver it, if requested.

8.5   THE FUNERAL SERVICE

In conventional cemeteries and crematoria the funeral service is handled as two distinct parts, the full service and the committal service. Although originally entirely religious elements, in more recent decades they have continued in usage because the non religious have adopted the same two-part approach.

In the past, established religions in the UK all tended to hold a full service in church followed by a committal ceremony at the grave side. The cemetery expecting just a committal service would know that their on-site chapel, if one existed, was not being used and the cortège would go 'straight to grave'. This ceremony might take only five minutes, perhaps less if the minister read the religious text in church and left very little to be said at the grave side. When people enquired of me about attending the committal I always considered it advisable to warn them that it might only last a few minutes. Otherwise, complaints would arise about the short length of the service, especially if they had travelled some distance to attend.

The full service will take perhaps 20–30 minutes, although this can be extended where large congregations attend, or where a number of people wish to give a eulogy. This full service can be held at the grave side immediately before the committal, so that both parts are unified, but without seating and protection from inclement weather, this could be uncomfortable. If still preferred, the unified service could be pared down to between five and ten minutes.

Similarly, both parts can be unified within the celebrant's hall or chapel, so that no grave side service actually takes place. If this is arranged, it is still possible for just one or two family members to witness the lowering of the coffin into the grave. This avoidance of the grave side is rare, although I suspect that few people are aware that it is an option. With an increasingly aged society, and a need to reduce car travel, dispensing with the grave-side service should be promoted as a virtue. With cremation, the equivalent action would be to watch the coffin placed in the cremator, but this is extremely rare. The walk to the grave and standing in inclement weather is onerous for the aged and infirm, as well as for obese people who may also have health and mobility problems. The comfort and health of the living should always be a consideration.

Most committals follow a similar process, which must be understood because the site manager is responsible whilst the funeral is on their site. The cortège travels to the grave side whether directly in vehicles or on foot from a car park or from any chapel or celebrant's hall on site. Staff need to ensure that the funeral director knows where the grave is located, and on complex sites may need to meet the cortège at the entrance and guide them to the grave. The route and grave site will have been checked to ensure no litter, dog fæces or mud exists and the surface is safe for pedestrian access. The staff member, if not with the cortège, will meet it near the grave, at a spot known and acceptable to the funeral director.

Often the funeral director and sometimes the minister or secular officiant might want to view the grave before the service commences, just to get the lay of the land. If a mourner is in a wheelchair, or if some less able-bodied people are attending, the means of help and the best grave-side position for them will be considered. Traditionally, the cortège will be led by the minister or secular officiant, with the bearers and coffin following, and then the funeral director along with the family and mourners. The coffin is traditionally carried feet first, although a minister's coffin is carried head first. The minister or secular officiant will stand at the head of the grave, the coffin placed onto the putlogs with the feet away from the minister or secular officiant, the webbings pulled around the coffin and held by the bearers so that it is ready for lowering. The family usually stands along the spoil-free side of the grave and, on the instruction of the funeral director, or sometimes the minister or secular officiant, the bearers lower the coffin. The presence of the bearers, especially six, intrudes to some degree and the partner or family may not see the grave. Usually, after the coffin is lowered, the bearers stand aside and the funeral director is able to draw the partner or family closer to the edge of the grave so that they can look into the grave and see the coffin.

The minister or secular officiant may have been reading text during the lowering of the coffin and they may dictate other aspects of the process. Typically, they develop their own routine and staff become familiar with these over time. During a catholic service the priest will usually have the coffin retained on the putlogs and will give a blessing and sprinkle holy water over the coffin, after which it is lowered.

The moment arises when the body is committed to the earth and as the minister or secular officiant reads the text, a staff member or funeral director will sprinkle soil on the coffin when the prayer or secular alternative is read. Sometimes the minister or secular officiant will prefer to do this themselves. The religious committal service will finish with the Grace and often the family will be invited to take a handful of soil from the tray to scatter on the coffin. Catholics might be given the opportunity to sprinkle holy water on the coffin, and sometimes funeral directors supply flowers for the partner and perhaps the family to strew on the coffin as a ritual farewell.

The site manager will stand discreetly near the grave throughout the ceremony, and is often expected to remove the two putlogs as the coffin weight is taken by the bearers. As representative for the site he or she is ultimately in control and must ensure everyone is safe whilst on site. They must be prepared for a grave collapse, a coffin getting trapped part way down the grave, a mourner falling and the control and parking of cars. Where a funeral director is involved, they are responsible for the actual ceremony and for controlling the mourners. There is a fine line between these dual responsibilities, a point worthy of consideration in any site staff training and in consultations with funeral directors.

The partner or family, perhaps through their funeral director, must give due consideration to the religious dignity of any ceremony, as well as the personal feelings of any minister or secular officiant. If hard rock, music with sexual references or violence, or poetry or text with doubtful content is required, it might need to occur after they have left the grave side. The site manager should be aware of such requests or arrangements.

The site manager has a responsibility to inter the correct body in any grave used, as set out in the guiding principles in the Charter for the Bereaved. As direct viewing of the body or body identity tags is not possible, they have a responsibility to confirm that the name written on the coffin nameplate accords with the name on the submitted interment form. The name should be identical, and if familiar names are used, this should be checked with the attending funeral director.

If the coffin nameplate is to be checked, how and when is often the most disputed issue with funeral directors. Many oppose such checks, especially where they are obvious, as it implies they might be careless. Access to the coffin nameplate is not possible in the hearse, and if the coffin is immediately shouldered by bearers, it is too high to be read. Even if access is possible, the coffin is often covered in wreaths, so the nameplate cannot be read without it appearing obvious to the mourners. The most opportune time is when the coffin is placed on the putlogs over the grave, and when any wreaths are removed. The last opportunity is when the coffin sits in the bottom of the grave, by which time the service might have been held over the wrong coffin!

Once a coffin is lowered in the grave, it is legally interred, even though the soil is not backfilled. Removal at this stage, perhaps because the nameplate is incorrect, is possible only if an exhumation licence is obtained. If this occurs, the grave must be temporarily covered and the Ministry of Justice contacted over exhumation.

Over my working life I experienced three entirely incorrect coffin plates, all cremations. On two occasions the funeral director immediately accepted the error, cancelled the funeral and later re-arranged it with the correct body. The third funeral director told me the body was correct, and that just the coffin lids had been mixed up. A new lid was supplied and only later did I discover that this was a lie, by which time the body had been cremated.

The point at which a natural burial site takes responsibility for the body is not defined. In a crematorium it is generally accepted that once the coffin is placed on the chapel catafalque, it is under the care of the cremation authority, and no longer the funeral director. With burial, it is only when the coffin is placed in the grave, and the bearers retire, that the funeral director ceases to be responsible for the body. This suggests that by leaving the actual coffin identity check to that stage is an acceptable decision by the site manager even though, potentially, it might have allowed the service to occur over the wrong body.

It is the site manager's responsibility not to allow a service to take place before its advertised time. Occasionally, funerals arrive early, perhaps because the funeral director is trying to gain time because of other funeral commitments. Despite assurances that everyone is present mourners can and do arrive at the appointed time and consequently can miss the service, much to their distress. These aspects reflect upon the site and rarely upon the funeral director.

Funerals are also often late, and if other funerals are expected can stress the entire day. The reasons can be based on the widow who needed to go back to the toilet or her insistence that the cortège passes her late husband's pub. Natural burial sites should accept this with good grace, and if the site anticipates late arrival, it comes as no surprise. Persistent late arrival by a specific funeral director must be addressed.

Finally, it is unacceptable for the gravediggers to rush to the grave and begin backfilling before the mourners have left the site. This is assuming the bereaved have not asked to participate in the backfilling, or watch it proceed.

8.5.1   Funeral service for cremated remains

Although much of the foregoing information can apply to cremated remains, the process is often very different. First, the family often arrives at the site in possession of the cremated remains, with no funeral director and often, no minister or secular officiant involved. This might be for reasons of cost or because the family desire an informal interment. All too often such services are allowed to proceed too quickly, partly because no one takes control of the process. I suspect the bereaved leave many sites feeling that a little more could have been said and done for the deceased.

The majority of families have no idea how to proceed so it is essential to give guidance and lead the process. Site staff should be ready to greet the family on arrival and then explain the procedure that is usually followed. The flexibility within this process must be highlighted and must allow for the participation of the family or partner wherever possible. For instance, they ought to be given the opportunity to personally carry the remains to the grave, and perhaps lower them into the grave. The site, whether private or local authority, should have a short service available, including a specific committal for cremated remains, and to be prepared to deliver this for the family. This could be religious or civil and might include some suitable poems. A few spoken words slow down the process and encourage communication with the family or partner. Ideally, these details can be discussed with the family or partner when the cremated remains burial is arranged but this can be difficult over the telephone.

Kneeling down to lower a casket into a small grave is difficult, especially for the aged. The casket can be lowered on a re-usable harness made of webbing and Velcro, which can be removed after the ceremony. Alternatively, two strips of tape made of natural materials can be cut and attached with pins. Nothing looks worse than carrying a casket of remains in a casual manner and it is more dignified to use a wood or woven willow tray. Velvet-covered pads are manufactured for this purpose but may look slightly garish for a natural burial site. Even if not used for the carrying, such trays can be positioned by the grave side, upon which can sit the casket during the first part of the service.

The ceremony might begin with placing the casket on the tray carried by the deceased's partner, who then walks with the staff member to the grave. The tray and casket can be placed beside the grave. A poem can be read and the casket then lowered into the grave on tape by the partner while a short committal is read along the lines of: "We commit the cremated remains of (name) to this grave, to be forever at peace in this beautiful location looking over the South Downs". A tray of dry sand could be available for those attending to scatter on the casket, or could be substituted by flower petals, or rosemary for remembrance. Another poem could be read to emphasise the final parting from the deceased and the completion of the service. The staff member should then retreat and allow the family some personal time around the grave to say their last farewells. If a suitable room exists, a cup of tea could be provided for the mourners before they leave the site.

8.6   BEARING THE COFFIN

I have not seen any guidelines for bearing coffins, so it is worth a little consideration. Although the word 'bearer' is professionally used, the person in the street often uses 'pallbearer', which the *Collins English Dictionary* defines as 'a person who carries or escorts the coffin at a funeral'. This relates to when a pall, often a black cloth, was used to cover the coffin, the edges of which were held by those walking alongside, separate to the bearers of the coffin. Over my working life, funeral directors have moved away from using full-time bearing staff, often younger men, to using retired men paid per occasion. Some of these aged retirees have looked decidedly wobbly when carrying a heavy coffin. Coffins can be surprisingly heavy, at 20–25kgs (44–55 lbs) and with the added body weight of, say, 76 kgs (12st), the total weight, not including any wreaths on the coffin, is around 101 kgs (15.8st). I would suggest that this is the limit for the typical four bearers, and for increased body weight, six bearers are necessary.

The most difficult part of the bearing can be the first lift of the coffin and the final lower, especially down onto the putlogs over a grave. This is because the bearer's knees and backs are at their most vulnerable at this stage. It is at this point that a further two people can assist lifting or lowering, one placed at the foot and one at the head end, to relieve much of the weight from the four or six bearers. This will be essential when a heavy body is involved. Rehearsing the process, or at least explaining what must happen, is essential if the bearing is to be competent. Family bearers need to be told to carry the coffin feet first and how to align it at the grave side.

The way the coffin is carried varies, perhaps as a regional tradition and sometimes at the preference of the funeral director. The simplest method is to carry the coffin at waist height but the most formal method, seen by many as the most impressive, is shouldering, typically preferred by the armed forces. Both methods can look ungainly when performed by amateurs, especially compared to shouldering in the armed services, which is well rehearsed beforehand.

The bearers should be paired up side to side based on height, especially if the coffin is to be shouldered, the tallest pair at the head, shortest at the foot. Otherwise, the tall bearer takes excessive weight, which can be really painful on the shoulder, and the shorter carries little weight. Shouldering is fine over short distances such as into a chapel, but ought to be reconsidered for longer distances, such as to a distant grave. For longer distances, and perhaps where untrained family bearers are used, a bier is a much safer and more comfortable option.

Most coffins do not have proper carrying handles, and where handles are fitted, they are often just decorative. The standard chipboard/ MDF coffin has slots cut in the base just under the side panels, so must be carried from below. Most biodegradable coffins, often in varying shapes, are most safely carried this way. Unfortunately, positioning the hands side on whilst walking forward is a difficult movement, as it twists the back. The experience of carrying a Victorian style coffin or casket with full side carrying bars contrasts with how difficult it is to carry modern coffins.

In the Scottish lowlands, perhaps elsewhere, carrying sticks are used. Each of a pair of hardwood sticks is placed under the coffin, each end held by one of four bearers. This spreads the coffin weight, allows the bearer to hold the stick across their body enabling them to stand erect and thereby protect their backs. Overall, these are safer, have a touch of finesse and should be used more widely.

Bearing is safest on level surfaces, and it is preferable to walk further if it avoids slopes. Paths must also be mown through long grass so the bearers can concentrate on the coffin, and not worry too much about placing their feet. Resting places for the coffin, perhaps a large flat stone or a design feature of a lich gate can be incorporated in long routes so the bearers can rest. Alternatively, a pair of coffin trestles can easily be carried alongside the bearer party, and placed under the coffin when a rest is needed.

Many would consider that bearing the coffin is the final act of homage to the deceased and thereby therapeutic. If the carrying is too heavy, the provision of a standard manufactured bier makes this achievable. Biers can be purpose designed for the site, perhaps with large carriage wheels and some rustic or artistic work on the structure. The bereaved may still consider it bearing if they are holding or stabilising a small cart or carriage, perhaps drawn by horse or donkey.

Even if not bearers, the bereaved can still lower the coffin into the grave. Patience is essential by whoever is supervising, in part to ensure the webbings are equally placed, and that everybody is ready to lower together. Uneven lowering can be expected such that the coffin scrapes the sides, perhaps get wedged once or twice, and then occasionally is released too early and thuds on the grave bottom, but major problems are rare.

At my late sister's funeral in 1995, her nieces wanted to bear her coffin. This reminded me that in over 45 years I had never seen a woman bear a coffin, so it was a good time to break another taboo. They had no problem with the bearing, though we shared a relatively light coffin between six bearers, and they appreciated the responsibility and involvement.

Chapter 9

HOW TO MARKET NATURAL BURIAL

9.1   MARKETING

9.1.1   Introduction

Marketing is not synonymous with natural burial, and some of the private sites I have visited in the last few years have clearly ignored this subject. This is dispiriting because it suggests sites open on a whim of an idea, with no clearly identified aims other than to sell a few graves. Unfortunately, local authorities are also complacent and still imbued with the culture that customers will find them without any marketing. This is probably because marketing is seen as the prerogative of the private sector seeking profits and less about developing socially valuable services.

Marketing any form of disposal option is difficult because the majority of people do not consider their death. The funeral then becomes a crisis purchase, with little awareness of options or discussion within the family before the funeral is precipitately arranged. The social message is that to be seen as caring, we need to consider our death because it ensures the issues are discussed with our spouse, partner and family; it ensures that in knowing what was wanted by the deceased, the survivors find it therapeutic to carry through those wishes. The subsidiary message is that with this approach, both the deceased and survivors will have the ability to be in control of the funeral, and in control of the anticipated costs.

The counter message is that those who refuse to consider their own demise, or their funeral, present their partner and family with difficult decisions. These have to be made whilst under assault from a well-honed marketing machine developed by commercial funeral directing. The potential for manipulation is increased and often results in higher and perhaps unnecessary funeral expense.

These messages tie in with other messages such as making the funeral more meaningful by integrating it with lifestyle choices. Natural burial cannot operate in a vacuum and these messages are ideal when talking to individuals and groups; they are transparent and can be delivered entirely without any commercial intent. These are not messages conveyed by mainstream funeral directors, who prefer funerals to remain a crisis purchase. Few local authorities deliver these messages, and most just highlight practicable aspects of cremation and burial. They ignore the potential for change, the need for consumer rights and the challenge of sustainability.

9.1.2 The definition of 'marketing'

The Chartered Institute of Marketing has defined 'marketing' as:

> *"The management process responsible for identifying, anticipating and satisfying customer requirements profitably."*

This definition suggests that the process is determined by profit and that other objectives exist which might be relevant. More recently, in October 2007, the American Marketing Association adopted the following definition:

> *"Marketing is the activity, set of institutions, and processes for creating, communicating, delivering and exchanging offerings that have value for customers, clients, partners, and society at large."*

This definition, with the words 'have value for customers', suggests that profits are not the principal concern. It is far more embracing and moves beyond the usual profit-based provider and customer relationship in the earlier definition. The new definition identifies 'clients', whom we might define as the people the site manager advises and educates on funeral options, who might subsequently buy a grave and become 'customers'. It mentions partners, those groups or organisations who might support a private company, or a not-for-profit group, to provide natural burial. Finally, in focusing on 'value for society at large' it similarly embraces the local authority ethos of serving communities. This definition is ideally suited to natural burial, a far more complex sale or 'offering' than say, the purchase of a car.

In writing this section I propose to avoid wherever possible the use of jargon, a common problem with all marketing. Unfortunately, words like 'offerings', e.g. products and services, and 'set of institutions', e.g. relationships, networking, etc., still have a touch of jargon about them. Putting this aside, the definition requires that the natural burial offering is defined, created and delivered, which is achieved through a marketing plan.

9.1.3   The components of the natural burial marketing plan

It is essential to define precisely what is being offered at every natural burial site in order to create a recognisable brand. This needs an understanding of basic marketing which requires a return to the 1960s, when the four Ps were introduced, often called the 'marketing mix', and these are used to create a marketing plan:

1. Product

2. Place

3. Price

4. Promotion

The four Ps were intended for selling low value consumer products and not for selling services. As natural burial is product-led, with the service element subservient, it is appropriate to use the four Ps as the basis of a simple marketing plan, and they will now be considered individually.

9.2   THE PRODUCT

Natural burial is a complex mix of a product (i.e. the grave), of a service (i.e. the funeral ceremony) and the site reputation. In marketing terms this can be called a 'bundle of benefits' and it consists of tangible and intangible elements, which are covered below.

9.2.1   Tangible elements

The tangible, that which can be touched, is principally the natural burial grave which, with appropriate management, creates one or more habitats. The marketing of graves was first introduced by the Victorians, and turned into a fine art. This historical perspective is worth considering, as it might suggest a way forward for sites with commercial aims, and what to avoid for sites with more social and environmental objectives.

No Victorian purchased grave was marketed as cheap, so grave choices would be described as good, better, best, a marketing approach still used by the American cemeteries today. The good (a euphemism for the cheapest) was often a standard grave on the inside of plots, to which there was no direct path, or the path was simply a narrow space between memorials. To better this, the next price would be a standard grave adjacent to a surfaced path, which was easier to access. The best, or most expensive, would be graves on the main drives, especially near the chapels.

The graves were marketed in perpetuity, as the Victorians clearly allowed commercial returns to obscure any thoughts of sustainability. It is possible they might have considered that after 100 years the majority of grave deeds issued to grave owners will be mislaid, and the possibility of anybody pursuing rights as remote. As the interest in graves after that period is extremely rare, the perpetuity grave offer can be seen as a marketing ploy.

Some natural burial sites already price graves according to location, and it might be anticipated that enhanced grave locations will be introduced as a marketing feature. The Victorians preferred to recreate Egyptian or classical themes. Sites seeking an environmental image might create lakes and market graves in themed zones. The marketing of green, greener and greenest graves reflecting the number of habitats created might be anticipated. Clearly attractive sites, perhaps landscaped to include lakes, will be more expensive and must command higher fees. This approach demands greater maintenance, marketing skills, promotion and salesmanship, so is not without inherent cost.

Some people prefer a choice so even if just one type of grave is offered, having a selection of these graves in different areas is advantageous. These might vary between shaded or sunny locations, away from trees and perhaps nearer the toilets or car park. Customers appreciate being able to view a selection of graves and to have some say in the location. Giving the grave areas distinctive names, perhaps relevant to specific trees or other habitat, is a selling aid and helps everybody to focus on the right plot in all communications.

Widening choice requires the opening of a larger area and has operational cost implications, so a balance is essential. A further benefit of increasing grave choice is that it spreads the funeral activity over a wider area. This prevents too many funerals occurring on one small plot, which in itself can restrict the time allowed for each funeral, and also avoids a mass of visually intrusive wreaths and floral tributes. These aspects suggest an overtly commercial operation whereas dispersed funerals suggests a more relaxed ambience and greater privacy.

The grave as a product has two values, one as a personal place to visit, the hallowed spot, so to speak, and the second, in how the grave contributes to the other graves in creating a habitat. The promotional messages must highlight these values, and leaflets must clearly explain what they mean. The leaflets are potentially the first items from the site to impact on people. As tangible items they are used by people to inform wider family and friends of the concept. Fine artwork and colour add quality, but can imply a commercial ethos. Recycled paper should always be used and where a site is focused on the environment, cheaper leaflets without colour might be cited as a virtue. The text is a significant influence, and considered later under promotion.

The final tangible elements are those of the infrastructure, the quality of entrance gates, boundaries, buildings, toilets and site signage. They do not have to be built of expensive materials, but ought to be well maintained. Site signage, in guiding and informing people visiting the site, is tangible evidence of the interest, ability and objectives of the site owner. The opportunity to use salvaged or recycled materials should be taken wherever possible. This adds to the promotional opportunities and reinforces the sense that the site owner is both innovative and caring about the environment.

9.2.2 Intangible elements

The intangible benefits are intellectual and psychological. The psychological relates to reducing any cognitive dissonance experienced by the bereaved in adopting a concept like natural burial, which is innovative and radical. For instance, promoting the environmental benefits and how these manifest themselves to create benefits for society at large will give users confidence. This 'feelgood' factor will be reinforced as the site increases in size, more habitats are created, and especially where local media highlights supportive statements from, say, the County Wildlife Trust. A non-profit, environmental organisation managing a natural burial site would inevitably possess greater promotional advantage on environmental and social issues than a commercial site.

The intangible benefits are reflected in the experiences of consumers, and potential consumers, in two specific areas. The first is people's perception and confidence in what they see at the site, and similarly in what they see and hear through leaflets, advertising, and talks given by the site owner or manager.

Support for the product is also an intangible factor. For instance, people have confidence when burial is provided by local authorities, as there is a proven track record over a long period. Private natural burial sites do not have this advantage, so need to increase confidence in the product by informing users about their long-term planning, financial strategy, and if the site is sold, how continuity is assured.

9.2.3   Unifying the tangible and intangible

If the tangible and intangible are unified, the product of natural burial has potential variations that can be 'positioned' for an identified 'segment'. In simple terms, this involves identifying various segments of society as potential customer groups. For a natural burial site, the green consumer is the most obvious segment, but we could include a Church of England adherent, or a Muslim. The product would then be positioned, that is mixed or tailored, specifically for that segment. Consequently, green consumers would value a mix of a biodegradable coffin and burial in a grave that creates habitat. These aspects might be marginally attractive to an adherent of the Church of England, but the offering of a consecrated grave might be the overriding decision factor. The fact that a mounded grave could be offered at a natural burial site, which might not be allowed at any of the conventional cemeteries in the area, may make such an offering attractive to Muslims. The skill is in identifying the various segments and positioning the widest range of products.

As well as identifying segments of society, there are also three potential niche products that a natural burial site can offer. These are the cremated remains grave; baby and child graves; and pet or companion's grave, as outlined in section 5.7.

9.3   THE PLACE

The well-known cliché is that there are three important factors regarding any new business: location, location and location. Two categories of location are typical with natural burial. The first is those sites appended to existing local authority cemetery facilities, often urban, and the second is private sites, usually rural. The marketing differences between the two are considered below.

9.3.1   Local authority sites

The adding of a natural burial site to an existing conventional cemetery, which often includes a crematorium site, conforms to another marketing principle, that it is better to locate similar businesses in the same area. For instance, several fish and chip shops or estate agents are better clustered where people see and know they are all located. The area then becomes synonymous with their particular product.

The conventional cemetery will have been a purveyor of graves for perhaps 100–150 years, and a huge proportion of local people will have either interred a family member there, or will have attended a funeral on the site. The location, perhaps even the area name, becomes synonymous with death and funerals. The place becomes the first thought the moment a specific funeral need arises.

A further advantage is that such old sites often contain the infrastructure to service funerals. Chapels exist, often old and picturesque Gothic buildings, along with toilets, shelters, offices and often very attractive, varied grounds. At Carlisle cemetery for instance, a sense of place exists which supports the feeling that the site is the right and proper place for local burial. Even the local wit that refers to the site as the dead centre of town has been influenced by promotion, whether intended or not.

The marketing disadvantages of these sites are often the reverse side of the same coin. An aged cemetery, its memorials, perhaps its buildings, can all have a neglected appearance. Too often this is because budgets are poor, and too much emphasis, and finance, is apportioned to the cremation service. Also, some people attracted to natural burial will be so opposed to conventional burial and cremation that they would not want any association with it.

Another issue is that more often than not, local authority managers can only use land for a natural burial site that the local authority already owns so can be seriously compromised in having to promote what is often a poor location. The site might be boxed in by houses and factories. Apart from a poor outlook, there can be vandalism and constant background noise from roads, all of which detracts from the serenity and contemplation needed in a natural burial site. At such a location it is better to have the site outside the conventional cemetery perimeter, if reserved burial land exists, or at least located or screened so that the grave visitor can look out of the cemetery, and not over, old burial plots and memorials. Also, the local authority natural burial option might not be promoted as positively by management compared to a site offering only natural burial. It might be seen as just another option, along with conventional burial and cremation.

9.3.2   Private rural sites

The majority of private natural burial sites are situated on attractive rural locations, often with extensive views. In fact, this may have been the prime motivator for creating the service. Evidently, many of these sites attract compliments from the bereaved and this feedback suggests that it is a primary reason why people use them. That many also mow the grass frequently and do not promote any social and environmental objectives suggests that green funerals were never their principal focus. An attractive rural location does not a natural burial site make!

A significant disadvantage of some sites is their remoteness, whether real or perceived. I visited a site in the south of England by rail in 2009 where none of the taxi drivers in the local town, a mere five miles away, had any idea where it was. The site name was similar to other farm names in the vicinity, so I was initially taken to the wrong place, where I was informed that many people on their way to a funeral were repeatedly misdirected. The need to be known, and easily found, is fundamental to success.

This relative remoteness is often reinforced when the site has no infrastructure. Although I acknowledge that some sites are promoted on their remoteness and lack of infrastructure, the potential market must be small. It is possible that the absence of toilets or a celebrant hall is not foremost in the minds of those choosing burial at such sites. The romance of a beautiful location seduces many people when viewed on a balmy day, and they cannot visualise the funeral held in inclement weather or the need for a toilet. Perhaps these shortfalls are noticed by the bereaved subsequent to the burial and a cause of cognitive dissonance, a point that only further research can elicit.

These potential weaknesses of remote private sites need to be recognised by local authorities who provide well-serviced sites. Their promotional strategy should highlight the importance of facilities in supporting what might otherwise be a visually unattractive location.

9.4   THE PRICE

In considering the price of the product, two factors are important: first, that the pricing structure is easy to understand, and second, that it is transparent. Transparency suggests that the fees list must be immediately available on request or online. Before the actual product or service is individually priced it is worth considering:

- That the smaller the fees list the easier the overall administration.

- That the fees list can be minimised by making them inclusive where possible.

- That each fee should be structured and justified by the work content.

- That an extensive list of options and supplementary fees implies the site has a higher level of commercial intent.

- That the more options and fees on the list, the greater the assumed need for salesmanship skills.

At a natural burial site the fees list might include the following:

Fees that are VAT exempt	Fees with VAT at standard rate
Grave rights for each grave type.	The supply and planting of a tree or other plant.
Interment fees to cover babies, children and adults (including cremated remains).	Dressing the grave with flowers and/or foliage.
Use of celebrant's hall, provision of music or organist.	Provision and fixing memorials, plaques, seats, book of remembrance, etc.
Funeral out of hours (late evening, Saturday or Sunday).	Inscriptions on memorials.
Use of horse-drawn bier on site, etc.	Ongoing individual grave care.
	Ongoing memorial care.

9.4.1 The fees table

Pricing at most conventional local authority and parish cemeteries is simply the 'going rate', with little recognition of real costs. The going rate too often reflects mediocre local authority cemeteries, often heavily subsidised, none of which have experienced real competition. Nonetheless, some comparison by private natural burial sites is essential as part of the pricing exercise.

Local authorities usually revise their table of fees annually on 1st April. The increase is often based on last year's fees, plus the rate of inflation, and on the fees of adjacent authorities so that some regional parity is maintained. This historical process might have gone on for decades, during which the fees were never properly priced.

It might be anticipated that private sites will be more commercially astute at setting the price but, in reality, the market is more complex. Unlike easily comparable items, natural burial is a complex combination of services and products. Some sites consider high prices an incentive, that it suggests a unique quality product, others promote low-cost funerals as a social aim, whilst others focus on the environment and simply accept the going rate. Logically, as the fees get more expensive there is a corresponding reduction in accessibility, as fewer people can afford to pay.

All sites should set their fees using absorption costing, whereby all overheads and costs are recognised and a profit element added. Sale of the standard grave right is the principal income source with each grave sale absorbing a specific percentage of the total costs. This suggests that once the forecast level of grave sales is reached, which also assumes a specific number of associated burials, all fixed and variable costs are then covered. Each grave sale and burial beyond that figure represents increasing profit less variable costs, e.g. excavation costs. This is extraordinarily difficult but essential in order to set a sound base for financial management and periodic analysis of the business.

It is evident from my visits to private natural burial sites that absorption costing, if it is adopted, is made more complex by other businesses operating on the site such as farming, forestry and pet cremation. This means that the day-to-day costing of staff and the owner's time input is often just guessed. Farm staff might be drafted in to mow grass and not charged at cost or perhaps a token figure is placed in the natural burial account. This is similar to local authorities utilising staff across various departments and estimating departmental share of large externalised grounds maintenance contracts. Many sites are also located on land owned by the site owner's family for decades, so even the market value of the land might be estimated. Too many guestimates mean that the end of year accounts mean little.

Those entrepreneurs who opened the first sites in the 1990s played a dangerous game. The lure was that for each rural acre they owned, worth perhaps £5,000, they could sell 600 graves, and perhaps 1,200 burials, about £150,000 at that time. It really was too good to be true! The principal concern is the long-term maintenance of graves, a liability usually included in the sale of the grave right. This is impossible for me to estimate as site objectives vary so much. For instance, a site where the graves will revert to a nature reserve and where no maintenance will occur beyond, say, ten years has very low liabilities. These low liabilities also apply to a site where trees are grown on graves in order to create a permanent woodland reserve or shelterbelt, or even where the timber might be harvested in 100 years. Mowing the grass dramatically increases liabilities and financial risk, and this is the scenario I can illustrate in the following financial model.

9.4.2   Financial model

The model assumes a new natural burial site with sufficient land to provide graves for 75 years, at which point the law may allow the graves to be re-used, and the business includes this as part of its strategic approach. The principal income source is the sale of new grave rights supplemented by some profit drawn from interment fees, and perhaps from the separate sale of memorial plaques. The fee for new grave rights must absorb the costs set out below:

Fixed costs (that do not vary with output)

- Rent and business rates.

- Salaries and pensions.

- Depreciation (land is not depreciable, but accountancy advice should be sought on landscaping and planting costs, etc.).

Variable costs (costs that vary with output)

- Office and administration costs including computerised registration for each grave and burial x 75 years.

- Site costs such as chapel heating, repairs and maintenance, water usage, waste, health and safety checks, grave markers or microchips, etc.

- Grave maintenance costs including machines, fuel, etc. (in-house or contracted out) per year x 75 years (some consider this a fixed cost!).

- Gravedigging costs including equipment and fuel (in-house or contracted out).

213

- Cost of plaques, fixing and any agreed maintenance.

At the start of year 76, the graves sold in year 1 can be resold for a further burial(s) assuming that grave reuse, called 'lift and deepen', is approved. As far less graves will be sold in year one than are sold in year 76, income will fall unless some new graves are still available to fill this shortfall. The above financial model will have to be revised at that time because the exhumation costs will be a new expense, but as the site construction costs were absorbed by the first sale of grave rights, they will not apply to the reused grave rights. We might assume that this saving will be mitigated by increased expenditure for the repair and maintenance and/or refurbishment costs of the original infrastructure of roads, etc., which will then be 75 years old.

The second consideration is that the new graves sold in year 75 will still have to be contractually maintained for a further 75 years, so the site must continue maintenance of at least those graves, and the infrastructure, for 150 years overall.

That portion of the fee for grave rights covering the 75-year maintenance period is the most contentious; should it be treated as income for the current year, or should it be reserved in a sinking fund? Setting up a sinking fund can be compared to passing a sum of money over to any Trust set up to continue the management and maintenance of a site after the burials have occurred. It can be assumed that most natural burial sites, as is the case with conventional cemeteries, fail to create a sinking fund. The sinking fund is the sum calculated for the variable grave maintenance as set out in the bulleted list above, being retained in a bank account. This sum should represent the year one grave maintenance cost inflated for each of the following 74 years. In theory, by charging the annual maintenance cost for each grave against the fund, the charge in year 75 should render the individual grave fund to zero.

When the sum equal to the annual cost of maintaining each grave is withdrawn from this sinking fund, it is treated as income for the year upon which it is drawn. This sum should then fund all historical grave maintenance expenditure, and remove this cost from expenditure estimates for that year. As the accumulating cost of maintaining old graves is so significant in natural burial sites and cemeteries after a few decades of trading, the potential to trade at a profit for that year is significantly enhanced.

Most conventional cemeteries treat all income as annual income, and fund the maintenance from this. This is easily managed in the first few years, but the income in year 75 then has to fund all maintenance for graves sold in the preceding 74 years, which becomes onerous. This ever-increasing liability reduces profits and would be an important financial consideration for any purchasers should the site be sold. A sinking fund also ensures that in the event of the natural burial site having to cease trading at any stage, a budget exists to continue grave maintenance for the contracted period, which will reduce the impact on the bereaved as consumers.

The fact that local authorities fail to consider sinking funds should be discounted. They have a mandate to raise whatever finance they need from council taxpayers, and this tends to create an insularity from good business practice.

The perennial problem with sinking funds is just how much to place into them. The evidence suggests that all such funds proved to be insufficient after two or three decades. This is evidently the case in the USA where legislation demands that councils operate more like private businesses, and a sinking fund is mandatory in case the council ceases to exist. The shortfall occurs due to a desire to take too much income immediately, and the difficulty in calculating inflation over such long periods.

I annually assessed the actual cost of grave maintenance in the cemeteries I managed. In 2006, the cost per grave was between £4.50 and £5.00 each year to cover all costs. This meant that the 60,000 graves that the local authority maintained, mown 16 times each year, cost close to £300,000. As an established site with a large number of graves, the cost per grave is much lower than at a new site. I recall that in the late 1990s relatively new conventional cemetery sites were estimating these costs at £15.00 per grave per year. This is because the ratio of graves per employee is low, and the ratio of unused to used graves is high. The cost is much lower where mowing is once or twice a year, but it is nonetheless still significant over time.

The next consideration is what level of annual inflation to use over the 75-year period. Local authority accountants were minded to set this at 4% per annum, but it is evident that periodic inflation peaks can play havoc with this assumption. These calculations are fundamental in creating a sustainable business and I illustrate below how even small variations can dramatically increase costs over the full 75 years.

Grave maintenance cost in	Inflation rate p.a.	
	4%	5%
year 1	£4.50	£5.00
year 10	£6.41	£7.74
year 20	£9.48	£12.61
year 30	£14.02	£20.52
year 40	£20.76	£33.41
year 50	£30.72	£54.41
year 60	£45.44	£88.66
year 70	£67.23	£144.40
year 75	£81.79	£184.29
Total cost of maintenance over 75 years	**£2,015.89**	**£3,770.97**

The first column of inflation rate calculations assumes a year one cost of £4.50 inflated annually by 4%, and by year 75 the annual maintenance cost per grave has risen to £81.79. The second column of inflation rate calculations assumes a year one cost of £5.00 but inflated annually by 5%. As can be seen, the annual cost of grave maintenance by year 75 is £184.29, well over double the cost based on £4.50 and 4% annual inflation. This shows how even relatively small changes have dramatic effects over long periods. Specialist financial advice would be essential on the lump sum necessary in a sinking fund so that it could distribute these sums each and every year for 75 years.

In reality, financial projections over such long periods must remain guestimates. Some conventional cemetery managers have been quite innovative in seeking ways to address this problem. The most logical suggestion is to offer, say, grave rights for 75 years and exclude grave maintenance charges from the right. These would be highlighted separately to cover, say, a 25-year period, at which point all grave maintenance ceases even though the grave right itself continues for a further 50 years. The right to extend grave maintenance in, say, 10-year increments could be offered. This protects the site against the incalculable inflation over longer periods. The problem is that at 25 years a significant proportion of grave right owners will have died, or if living, will choose not to extend the maintenance contract. In contrast, some will pay, and others will have already extended the contract as part of carrying out a second burial in the grave at, say, 15 years into the 25-year period. This will result in a mosaic of graves, some paid and some not. As the paid contracts must be honoured, and it would look totally unkempt if some graves were missed, the tendency would be to maintain the entire area.

The grave maintenance contracts can be for shorter periods, as even up to the 1960s grave maintenance contracts lasting one year were usual. It was administratively expensive to raise these invoices, and the mass of postal reminders. Added to this was the unwieldy process of having to inform staff which graves required maintenance and which did not. This approach is not to be recommended.

In local authorities, the annual cost of maintaining a grave should be reported to elected members, and if this is to be subsidised, the subsidy identified.

It is worth noting that Victorian private cemetery authorities sold grave rights in perpetuity with an implied contract to maintain these but were aware that after 30 or 40 years, most grave owners and their heirs had died. Consequently, they could then reduce maintenance standards or even abandon whole plots with few repercussions. It may not be ethical but it effectively reduced a serious financial liability for those cemeteries.

9.4.3   The sale of graves

Many people state that they own a grave, and managers refer to the sale of graves, all of which is misleading. In reality, it is grave rights which are either purchased or sold, in the past called the exclusive right of burial in a grave. The land title remains with the owner whether a local authority, company or private individual and they remain responsible for any taxes due, health and safety and other site liabilities.

Grave rights did not exist prior to the Victorians, as I outlined earlier in this chapter under section 9.2, 'The Product'. Parishioners could not purchase grave rights in churchyards, although wealthy families could obtain a faculty for large tombs. Victorian private cemeteries followed the churchyard pattern in charging an interment fee for every body interred. To increase income and effectively create cemetery class distinction, they introduced an exclusive right of burial in specific graves. The word 'exclusive' meant that the owner of the right approved all burials in the grave, and upon their own death, could be interred without any other authority. This effectively elevated all exclusive graves above those without rights, the unpurchased grave, or what people have come to call the pauper grave. In reality, the so called pauper graves were often also ranked in price according to conditions whereby the grave might be elevated to exclusive status by paying a fee within a set number of years.

9.4.4   The right to place a memorial

It was the prohibition on erecting permanent memorials that really defined the unpurchased or pauper grave. For those who could afford to buy the right of burial, they were sometimes charged a further fee for the right to place a memorial. This was also proportionately higher for the more expensive rights of burial, for instance, pathside graves and vaults. Modern conventional cemeteries have continued a similar process, although the right to place a memorial is often included in the right of burial in order to simplify the fees table and the administration.

9.4.5   Secure advance payments

Where grave rights are sold in advance (called pre-need), which some private natural burial sites might consider, the monies ought to be secure against the potential closure of the business, an issue which does not arise at local authority sites. In the Ministry of Justice publication called '*Natural Burial Grounds – Guidance for Operators*' published on their website in 2009, it states:

> ### "Financial legislation
>
> *If operators require advance payments for funerals, they must conform to the requirements of the Financial Services and Markets Act 2000 (Regulated Activities) Order 2001. Operators may wish to establish a trust fund to administer advance payments.*
>
> *Operators should have a defined plan for allowances for future financial commitments. The simplest format is to create a sinking fund into which is directed a proportion of plot sales income.*
>
> *Circumstances will vary but, as a guideline, the Association of Natural Burial Grounds have negotiated an agreement with the Valuation Office Agency (Practice Note 2: 2005: Revaluation 2005: Natural burial grounds) which suggests 20 per cent of plot sales income being treated in this way, dropping to 15 per cent when the site has been open for eleven years. Operators may wish to set up a trust fund and arrange for the burial site to be taken over when full by, for example, a wildlife charity. It should be noted that the pre-need sale*

of burial plots is not covered by the Financial Services and Markets Act 2000 (Regulated Activities) Order 2001 (Chapter XIV – Funeral Plan Contracts). Operators may wish to protect a proportion of such funds by a trust fund."

For more information, see www.opsi.gov.uk/si/si2001/20010544.

It is sensible to conform to this request to secure pre-need plot sale income so that if the site is sold it enables the new owners to call up this income when the grave right is exercised for the first burial. The figure of '20% of plot sales' (grave rights) income is rather meaningless, as the actual fee could vary considerably between sites, especially if the grave maintenance component is treated separately to that of the right.

The terms 'burial plots' and 'plot sales' used by the Ministry of Justice is misleading. The term 'burial plot' usually relates to an entire area of graves, and not to an individual grave. The term 'grave right' is much preferred.

It appears that the Data Protection Act applies to information held related to pre need sales. This data should not be released; neither should it be available to view where anybody chooses to search the registers regarding burials that have occurred.

9.4.6   Percentage share of total funeral costs

In the 1980s I spent some time considering the proportion of total funeral costs falling to local authority cemeteries compared to the proportion retained by the funeral director. Aware of the long term, unpredictable and ever-increasing costs at cemeteries, I wanted to contrast these with the funeral director's financial liabilities, which extend over perhaps one week for the funeral, and carry no long-term liabilities or costs.

I had noted that in Victorian times the cemetery proportion had been far higher. This was probably because private cemeteries were new and they were aware that they needed to finance, without subsidy, the long-term costs for administration, dealing with the bereaved and maintaining graves for at least 100 years, a scenario that now applies to private natural burial sites.

These liabilities were severely under-estimated because graves were actually sold in perpetuity, and with no grave re-use option, the mass of graves grew ever larger. With so many large memorials, grass cutting was expensive. To limit their liability, they rightly held the grave owner responsible for memorial maintenance and safety costs. This sufficed whilst the grave owner was alive, but following their death, their heirs often refused such liabilities. Most companies went into receivership.

Cemetery provision progressively moved away from private to local authorities and steadily increasing subsidy from council taxpayers. In this distorted market of the 1950s to 1980s, funeral directors progressively increased their share of total funeral costs whilst the proportion retained by cemeteries declined. This is not to suggest that funeral directors consciously managed this change or even noticed it occur. The blame for this lay with local authorities who were then, as now, naïve regarding market prices and astute cemetery accounting practice.

In the past decade, especially in London, cemetery fees have increased well above inflation and redressed this imbalance. In London in 2006, total burial funeral costs estimated at £3,800 were apportioned at £2,300 for the cemetery (grave rights and excavation) and £1,500 for the funeral director. With the cemetery retaining 61% and the funeral director 39%, this was a dramatic increase in the cemetery proportion compared to my findings in the 1980s. This problem has not just been a British one. For instance, in 2009 the ICCM publication, *The Journal*, printed an article on how South African cemeteries struggled to maintain even half decent standards for the bereaved. They estimated that the cemetery share of average total funeral costs was just 3%!

For anyone proposing to open a natural burial site, it is not difficult to obtain average funeral director charges in their area, and adding this figure to the fees charged at each of the local cemeteries and crematoria. This will indicate the local total share of funeral costs, together with the going rate for burial and cremation. After comparison with the proposed fees for the natural burial site, it will suggest whether the local going rate is sufficient to both cover costs and provide a reasonable profit. If not, fees must be increased and marketing policy prepared to justify why the fees are above the going rate.

9.4.7   Supplementary fees

Although the need for transparency suggests a menu of prices, if fees are more inclusive then fewer invoices and receipts need to be issued. In addition, the need to ask for supplementary fees can be embarrassing and insensitive. For instance, where a family has an appointment to inter cremated remains they might arrive at the site carrying the casket and are often very emotional. This is not the time to have to analyse their requirements and calculate the fees involved. The sensitive approach is to have a single inclusive interment fee regardless of how the interment is handled, e.g. whether or not a grave-side service is needed. An invoice can be dispatched prior to the appointment, perhaps with information about the site, or can be sent after the appointment.

9.5   PROMOTION

The topic of promotion is the single most important issue related to the success of a natural burial site. The raison d'être, the reasons for providing the site, should have been considered from the very beginning of the development and are an essential part of the planning process, which was highlighted in Chapter 7. These must now be used to finalise the promotional messages necessary to develop a long-term strategy. The reasons were:

Consumer benefits:	
1.	More choice for the bereaved.
2.	Local option for the bereaved.
3.	Potential low-cost funeral.
4.	Potential for a green funeral.
5.	Potential for a meaningful funeral.
Environmental benefits:	
6.	Creates new habitats.
7.	Potential to increase community green space.
8.	Potential for low-carbon funeral.
9.	Potentially reduces cremation disbenefits.
10.	Potentially educates about the environment.
Community benefits:	
11.	Creates a new local business.
12.	Improves local resilience regarding pandemic.
13.	Replaces need to extend local churchyard or cemetery.
14.	Reduces deficits of the local cemetery if it had been used.
15.	Potentially supports other local businesses

Of the 15 potential benefits shown in this list, the items numbered 1, 2, 6, 11, 12, 13 and 14, might be anticipated as automatically achieved at any new natural burial site, regardless of its type. The remaining eight points are only achieved if specific environmental or other objectives are set, for instance, reduced mowing. It is also essential that all the relevant messages unify to create the product intended, such as a green or sustainable funeral option.

9.5.1   The promotional message

The promotional messages cannot be fully compiled by a site owner before the marketing background to natural burial is considered, as well as an analysis of local competition. The sections below on natural burial as a brand, greenwashing, sourcing funeral advice, funeral advisory service, competitor analysis and the dreaded pauper grave are intended to explain some of this background.

It is surprising that 16 years after I wrote the first natural burial promotional leaflet, the same text can still be found verbatim on websites. It is preferable for each site to create an individual message in order to avoid being seen as just another natural burial location. The messages must promote the strengths of the site, contrasting these to the weaknesses of the opposition, which is the essence of the marketing plan. The messages might include:

1. More choice for the bereaved

A natural burial site adds a new dimension to local choice. At its most basic, it is just another alternative to conventional burial and cremation. At a more advanced level it reflects the wider benefits specific to the site, and its skill in using the location and management to enhance this new choice. For instance, it is evident from comments on the internet that many compliments are directed at natural burial sites using words such as 'beautiful', 'beautiful views', 'serene' and 'peaceful'. These relate purely to the right location and each of these words can form an essential message. If all alternative sites are unattractive or spoiled in some way, perhaps by an industrial estate, the genuinely beautiful natural burial site is unique. Clear advantages like this, which are rare, are called unique selling propositions, or USPs, by marketers. The word 'unique' ought not to be taken lightly, and any claim to a USP must be well founded.

Within the word 'choice' there are many individual market segments and natural burial can position itself to send appropriate messages.

For instance, those people who dislike memorials might appreciate a message that the site opposes individual grave memorials, in effect, that it is offering anonymity. As conventional cemeteries are designed around grave attendance as a virtue, a major cause of personal guilt when a grave is not attended regularly, people are given a different perspective. This segment might also include those people wanting to be subsumed into nature, or perhaps single people who have no family to care for their grave. In reality, the anonymity segment might be far bigger than anticipated, but this assertion does not have the benefit of consumer research to support it. Latent demand might also exist for anonymity, but might not be evident if the necessary messages are not expressed. For instance, established values militate against talking down the value of personal grave memorials, so very few people do this. Conversely, if a message based on the sheer futility and waste of money spent on memorials is expressed, perhaps reinforced by the reduced travel then necessary to care for the memorial, potential customers are given the confidence to take that option. Often, it is the incidental benefits of a choice like natural burial, which is its greatest, and often, hidden strength. For example, if the decision not to buy an expensive memorial is validated by the virtuous creation of a habitat, an accusation of parsimony is sidestepped.

It is a mistake to assume this anonymity to be unique. For instance, a number of people do not place a memorial on a grave in conventional cemeteries, so achieve the same state. Anonymity, on its own, does not qualify as a USP at a natural burial site. Although the natural burial site might be an additional choice for the bereaved, the grave as a product might be precisely the same as that offered in local conventional cemeteries, especially if the natural burial site utilise intensive mowing.

Marketers would suggest that 'differentiating' the product might make it more attractive to consumers. For instance, if local cemeteries do not formally consecrate graves, a section of formally consecrated graves in natural burial would be differentiated, and would also qualify as a USP for Church of England adherents. Similarly, Muslim communities often prefer mounded graves, which are not acceptable to many conventional cemeteries. As these could ideally fit the natural burial perspective, a section of graves reserved for Muslim use would be differentiated, and a USP if no others exist in the area.

Awareness of other facilities is the key to marketing successfully. For instance, a weakness in local cemeteries or churchyards might be the fact that they are built on steep slopes. The offer of level graves with easy access would be a differentiation attractive to the aged and less mobile consumer. Other access factors such as the absence of car parking, absence of water supplies, a long walk to the graves or perhaps an absence of bus services, are weaknesses that can be exploited.

Choice is given a new dimension if it is supported by integrated services. For instance, an integrated funeral service might offer a funeral managed only by women, including collecting the body, its laying out, and burial. This may appeal to all women but may especially be preferred by those who were single, Asian and in religious orders, and would also be a USP. The fact that single people are set to increase by 31% between 2009–2029, and that the greater number of these are professional women, is a consideration. Assuming that all dead people are married and have children to visit the grave sends the wrong message to single people and many others!

The combined burial of pets with humans is a further differentiation, and almost certainly, will be a USP. The promotional attraction here is that low cost, sensitive pet burial is an ideal way to make contact with people, who are then exposed to other messages related to their own demise.

2. Local option for the bereaved

This is a relatively simple message, but worth frequently repeating. Its value increases in direct contrast to the absence of alternative options, as well as the distance to these alternative facilities, particularly as road travel becomes more expensive and anti-environment. The potential for road congestion, poor access and parking difficulties at alternative sites must also be highlighted. A further powerful influence, often obscured without close inquiry, is that competing cemeteries might charge double, or triple, burial fees to those people not resident in the area or parish. Such facts, of course, should have been noted before the natural burial site went beyond the planning stage.

It is also essential to define the word 'local'. At the City of Carlisle Woodland Burial Site the majority of the early users were people who had moved into the area in recent years. These were perhaps local only during their retirement, so without family ties to local churchyards or cemeteries. The native Cumbrian users increased slowly, perhaps because many still had family connections with local churchyards, and would naturally be interred there. Others owned graves in the conventional cemetery where space for burial existed. It might take a generation for locals to take an interest in natural burial but once a family member is interred, others will follow!

People have a tendency to ignore the implications of their death whilst hale and hearty, so the apparent convenience of local natural burial might not have an immediate appeal. Nonetheless, this message combined with the potential to enhance the local environment through green space and wildlife habitats within a bundle of benefits can influence their decision.

There can be promotional advantages in forming a Friends Group for the site, as this would create local support. The feedback from interested friends will also help to shape the kinds of grave or other services they desire.

It is essential to develop a presence in the local area. A stand including a display of biodegradable coffins at local fêtes, agricultural shows, etc., can be considered. Biodegradable coffins are artistic, often very attractive, and an interesting topic for discussion. Having experienced this I have been surprised at the level of interest even though other exhibitors have been offended by the subject and once the stand had to be moved!

3. Potential low-cost funeral

The topic of low-cost funerals is too often correlated to words like 'basic', 'undignified' and even 'pauper'. Funeral directors very rarely advertise their prices because they consider it distasteful. Even where a low-cost option is available, it is not promoted and often comes with onerous conditions. The most obvious is that the funeral will occur on a day and time to suit their business, a condition that in itself psychologically reinforces the fact that this is a reduced level of service.

Any suggestion that natural burial is low cost needs to be supported by facts. Simply comparing the cost of purchasing a grave right with competitors is not in itself ensuring a low-cost funeral, just ensuring a low-cost component of a funeral. A site that requires people to use mainstream funeral directors, whose charges vary greatly and are difficult to control, cannot claim their funerals are low cost. Where an agreement with a local funeral director for a fixed price total funeral is possible, or where an integrated funeral directing service is provided, such an offer is feasible, and would constitute a USP. This would be a rare example of social marketing and clearly of benefit to those with financial constraints. This is a complex promotional issue, as the moment such a service is identified with poverty, people may reject it. At the very least, competing funeral directors are likely to talk it down as the pauper option, an issue considered below under the heading 'The Dreaded Pauper Grave'.

Promotion on holding down funeral costs through natural burial can be more subtle. For instance, the memorial placed on a conventional grave can be very expensive, so a promotional message about the prohibition of memorials, or limiting it to a small, inexpensive plaque, might well be perceived by potential customers as a way to reduce the cost of the funeral. The ability to use a cardboard coffin, which can be inexpensive but often has a large mark up by funeral directors, is another subtle message that reinforces the fact that natural burial can be low cost. Reinforcing the value of using these sustainable products is very important, as the potential customer is very likely to experience cognitive dissonance if this option suggests that the bereaved is not being given a good send-off.

It would be misleading to promote this social marketing stance whilst also appearing overtly commercial. This might be implied by an extensive price list, especially one that offers many upgrades and add-ons, and perhaps the selling of graves at varying prices according to their position, the view, the level of noise, etc.

The principal of low cost is to reduce the profit margin on individual sales, but compensate for this by an increase in turnover, what marketers might call penetration pricing. Increasing turnover to such a degree is difficult in the funeral market. Many commercial natural burial sites take the opposite approach by putting a premium on their service. With higher than market prices, they are apparently profitable with the resultant low turnover.

It might be anticipated that natural burial sites operated by local authorities possess a mandate to promote low-cost funerals, as social marketing ought to be their raison d'être, but such strategies are still rare. Fear of the sensitivity of the funeral market allied to local authorities lacking innovation and marketing budgets is partly the cause. The principal reason is the emasculation of local authorities by past and present government. They consistently laud the private sector, often in response to organised lobby groups at Westminster, and demean local authorities. Meanwhile, funeral costs consistently increase.

A local authority managing a natural burial site with low maintenance liabilities has the opportunity to reduce the cost of grave rights. They can then prepare a specification for a dignified low-cost funeral which can be tendered out to a private funeral director. The fully transparent complete funeral price can then be advertised as both a USP and a valuable social benefit for its residents.

The greatest potential for the low-cost funeral message probably lies with Trusts and not-for-profit organisations, which are currently rare natural burial providers. A social enterprise, or community interest company, a recent new legal model, could open and manage a natural burial site as a local facility, offering low-cost green funerals. The natural burial site would need to supply the full funeral, so would have to manage an integrated funeral directing service, or contract this out to a private funeral director. The value of natural burial is that it can raise considerable income, none of which, in this case, goes to owners or shareholders, and this can add value by pump priming other social initiatives that might then attract government or other form of grant aid. One pound of income might equal one pound of grant aid! In addition, as a social enterprise is essentially local, the income raised has what is called a multiplier effect on the local economy. In other words, the money just keeps on going around and around within the community.

This approach would neatly fit within the Transition Towns initiative, which is expanding in the UK, with Totnes in Devon leading the way. This is about pulling together all the energy, health, environment and food issues in the local environment so that local resilience is increased whilst also reducing dependency on fossil fuel. Green burial ideally fits this perspective, and the social benefit of reduced funeral costs would enhance this. Natural burial is just an adaptive approach to life, a simple matter of behavioural change.

I am surprised that the much-lauded pensioner power has not been more active over funeral costs. Pensioner groups could approach a natural burial site, or vice versa, to negotiate a grave price, similarly a funeral director for a funeral price, on the basis that they could guarantee a specific number of funerals.

4. Potential for a green funeral

A focus on green or environmental issues can suggest excessive concern for insects and birds rather than humanity. It is vital that green messages emphasise how environmental improvements benefit people, both physically and psychologically.

This segment appears the most obvious positioning focus for a natural burial site. It suggests a desire to complement and benefit a person's lifestyle and behaviour. At present, the green consumer segment is small but growing. It also raises the issue as to whether the more green the concept, the less commercially successful it is likely to be. Certainly, in America there was a perception in the funeral trade in 2007 that there was no money in natural burial. Consequently, it might be considered that this segment will find their way to the site by word of mouth, and that promotional budgets ought to be directed at less obvious segments, where greater opportunity might exist to increase the customer base.

A further issue is not actually green burial, but whether some people would choose burial at all. If the perception that worms investing themselves in bodies is a significant reason for people to choose cremation, then this incorrect assumption is a negative influence. The fact that poets and painters have described and painted worms in the human skull over centuries suggests this might be quite difficult to dispel. Even the term 'green burial' has more than a hint of the worm about it, and although greens might love worms, many people do not.

The green lifestyle is increasing day by day. Recently, the RHS conducted a survey of their members and found that more than 80% garden organically or are thinking of doing so (April 2009 issue of *The Garden*). People recycle, reuse and repair, so recycling the body through natural burial is extending the virtuous lifestyle. Conversely, those feeling guilt about their wasteful lifestyle may see natural burial as a virtuous end!

The delivery of this message necessitates a broad knowledge of all the issues, such as embalming, biodegradable coffins, etc. In section 9.7 a burial site can assess their ability to provide a green funeral, and a high score will qualify as a USP.

It is a fact that the clichéd modern funeral consumer will entirely deny death by embracing embalming, the satin-lined casket, the horse-drawn hearse, an abundance of air-freighted flowers together with the release of 1,000 helium balloons or white doves. After a cremation, they will have a memorial service during which the ashes will be fired into the sky in rockets! It should be recognised that huge commercial budgets are promoting this type of funeral. In contrast, the green funeral is supported by little more than passion and, in opposing consumerism and celebrity culture, is competing in a very hostile world.

5. Potential for a meaningful funeral

The requirements for a meaningful funeral will vary but will relate to the beliefs and philosophy of the deceased and their family. It can often be difficult for people to discuss these issues, partly because of the emotion and partly because they are unaware of all the issues involved. One way of focusing on the funeral is for people to complete an advance funeral directive. These can be obtained from the NDC and some Charter for the Bereaved members. If a site creates a directive specific to its own service it could be considered a USP in itself.

Death is still a taboo and creating messages acceptable and appealing to individuals and organisations is a challenge. The natural burial sites focused on the environment gain an advantage in having a topical leading subject. Their abiding message can be the many benefits that are created by choosing natural burial, a message which is life affirming and creative, and for many people, meaningful. The danger is that the environment topic can appear too scientific and may not be meaningful to those with a spiritual interest in nature. They may want to be interred under a tree without altruistic intent.

Reinforcing these creative messages by highlighting the negatives of established alternatives may be necessary. For instance, it might be a cliché that cremation is a conveyor belt process, but it is a fact that some people are offended by the process. Also, many people have told me that as a child they hated being dragged to the cemetery every Sunday to care for a grandparent's grave, which had become a shrine. Norms like this, and any associated guilt created by not visiting a grave, need to be recognised. A message that nature can care for the grave and release people from this onerous task, might be meaningful in such cases.

An innovative approach might be to create a video of an actual burial at the site. This could illustrate how the graves create the habitat and merge into views of the changing seasons at the site. The video could be integrated into the funeral service and shown whilst the coffin is taken from the celebrant's hall and to the grave for burial without the mourners leaving the room. This approach might be meaningful to the aged and infirm, and by keeping everybody comfortable indoors, would replicate the advantages of cremation services. This video could also be shown at funeral services held remotely, where the coffin could be collected and taken to the site without the attendance of mourners. This could create a low-carbon funeral and could be a component of a low-cost 'body disposal service' as described in section 10.2.

In order to provide meaningful funerals it is essential to take every opportunity to talk with enquirers and visitors and to listen to what they are saying. Any unsolicited information about the site and the service can be valuable, such as how they located the site and their means of access. As the site owner or manager needs to attend in order to supervise the funeral, they can often engage in conversation with those attending, and feelings about the site will be readily volunteered.

Often, the relationship between the site manager and the bereaved can be akin to a friendship. Such a relationship often occurs when the service is of a personal nature and a pleasant relationship might well be sought by, and a form of therapy for, some bereaved people. This friendly relationship can prevent users mentioning negative aspects of the service, so care must be taken. It is relatively easy for site managers to get surrounded by a coterie of supporters and admirers, and this might exclude useful dissenting feedback. Site managers can also develop fixed and inflexible views about what makes a natural burial or green funeral. If this irrefutable rightness is conveyed to the bereaved or any other person then they might lack the confidence to honestly respond, especially if they feel they want to contradict what has been said or done. This is similar to the green funeral director who told me he did not like cardboard coffins! It is what the customer feels and likes that matters.

The customer feedback is part of a circle, it starts with the need to convey a message, listen to the response, analyse it and if necessary, re-draft the message. I am mindful that where the person arranging the funeral has a good experience, they never forget it. Likewise, if a mourner attending a natural burial funeral finds it meaningful, they will be a future customer.

The promotional message on a meaningful funeral, as with many of the other messages, can be assumed as directed at the potential deceased person. In reality, demographics are far more important than is assumed. For instance, most aged mothers and fathers often act in response to the advice from children, whom we might assume to be in the age range of 40 to 60 years. If the children adopt the concept, although they may not die for 30–40 years, they will support its adoption by their parents. Even the grandchildren can be assumed to be at college, where the environment and sustainability is increasingly relevant. Any visits to educational establishments is an opportunity to convey messages using words like 'sustainability', 'green' and 'carbon footprint' to illustrate that natural burial can be a solution and not a problem.

Sites that offer companion graves, where a pet can be buried alongside the grave in which the owner will be interred, can really touch on the word 'meaningful'. The association between the pet and owner is seen to be valued by the site; pets are given elevated status as companions; the messages are all positive and affirming, as well as being creative. Such a service is undoubtedly unique, and is a very definite USP.

6. Creates new habitats

There is always a danger in excessive marketing; it can appear too commercial and lack conviction. It might be considered that birdwatchers, beekeepers and gardeners, people who get their hands dirty are cynical about marketing spiel. The simple fact that natural burial creates a habitat will appeal to them without undue embellishment.

If natural burial cannot change the world, it can make a very real difference to the local environment. If a proposed new site is set in a green desert, typical of modern farms, it has the opportunity to become a beacon of wildlife excellence. Even if the area is not currently poor for wildlife, it still expands existing habitats. Marketers sometimes refer to this as synergy, the fact that the sum of two merged parts might work better than in their individual state. For instance, a site that links two otherwise separate habitats will create valuable wildlife corridors, which can be highlighted in promotional literature.

Natural burial can only succeed if local people are engaged, and habitat enhancement is an ideal engagement tool. It is essential to monitor the entire site, especially from new, and note all the improvements, no matter how small, and relate this information to users and potential users. If woodland edge is created by new trees, and previously unseen orange tip butterflies appear, then this is a real benefit to local ecology. Likewise, if voles appear in permanent grassland, or crickets, then the site must highlight these new species as directly due to the concept. A slide show of these creatures and habitats is visually attractive, and can be interesting whilst also subtly conveying the benefits of natural burial. The bereaved need to know that their decision to support natural burial has directly improved the local environment. In a world full of environmental catastrophe, a small reversal is exceptional news and the local media will pick up on this.

It is essential to see natural burial as a hub of a much larger wheel. The site objectives need to be conveyed to neighbouring landowners and householders and to encourage them to extend habitats along wildlife corridors. Even thin habitat strips such a hedges, unmown verges, wider field edges and private gardens can have real impact in allowing wildlife from the site to move out and forage or feed over a wider area. This is essential where, for instance, owls might need a larger habitat than the site can provide. This promotional approach requires passion and knowledge, which will increase as each new species appears.

It is impossible to market an unplanned service. A strategy is essential to define the habitats or other wildlife benefits sought, and how and when this is going to happen. An environmental management plan can include habitat creation, and topics like this dovetail into carbon reduction and other related issues. Consumers seeking green funerals can be expected to take an interest in all these topics. Many will be knowledgeable, will ask challenging questions and will prefer answers based on science. Even where they choose the service, if the promised habitats are not created over time, they may become dissatisfied with the site and its management.

7. Potential to increase community green space

This is initially a message to the local residents, parish council, church, etc. in order to seek support at the planning stage, if the proposal is for a new site. At all times the message must relate to the direct and realisable benefits for local people and the local environment. The message is stronger if access to the natural burial site is given for leisure use, and added value accrues if the access results in extending local footpaths, improving local views, or any similar benefits. The message might be directed at dog walkers or the local school seeking a safe environmental study site. A Trust or local authority that directly builds into the plans public access to the site, perhaps after burials are complete, would consider this a principal promotional message.

Promotional activity would need to start early with a new site. The most important targets would be local councillors, who have considerable influence in most communities. If they can be won over, it suggests that the objective is appreciated and, at the very least, objections might be removed or reduced.

Once in operation, the site leaflets would need to constantly reinforce this objective. Photographs of the green space, the footpath, stiles, etc., perhaps illustrating the gradual improvements, would be tangible evidence that the promises are realistic, and being met.

8. Potential for low-carbon funeral

It is now a cliché that all companies are reducing their carbon footprint. The concern about global warming is directed at burning fossil fuels and releasing carbon, but the carbon footprint is often extremely difficult to assess. Every item of equipment used has an individual carbon footprint and the footprint over time must be calculated. For instance, a natural burial site that routinely cuts grass, even for a restricted period like thirty years, may have no less a footprint than a crematorium.

Although the related increasing global temperature weakens or destroys habitat, this is rarely understood at the local level. For instance, people see green fields, and think the countryside is healthy. Too many gloom and doom stories can make people disengage, so it is necessary to take a positive promotional stance. Adverse criticism must be avoided by the site reducing its own carbon footprint related to any buildings, insulation, storage of water, use of mulches, etc. The issue of waste must be considered and spoil not sent to landfill, nor a mass of wreaths landfilled when they could be recycled. The carbon benefit of reduced mowing and locking carbon up through tree planting are valuable promotional messages, especially when contrasted to conventional cemetery practice. All these issues must be highlighted in a comprehensive environmental management plan, available to all users either in hard copy or on the internet. A genuine commitment to these issues must impact on consumer behaviour, which is why so few cemetery or crematoria actually do anything.

A prohibition on individual memorials or restriction to small plaques also reduces the carbon footprint. If this approach is used, it is essential to undermine the assumed permanence of conventional memorials as well as the fact that the location and burial details are registered for all time, so a memorial is not necessary. The carbon impact of cutting and shipping heavy memorial stone from distant countries, and the amoral production methods speak for themselves. If grave re-use is introduced in the UK, it can be expected to reinforce the temporary nature of memorials.

Natural burial sites that plant and grow trees have further promotional opportunities in helping other businesses to reduce their carbon footprint, through offsetting. Remotely, even the local crematorium may agree to promote a natural burial site as the location for cremated remains, and then claim any tree planted as carbon offsetting. A local funeral director, by arranging such a funeral, could make the same claim. If such an approach leads to more trees, the environment and mankind ultimately benefits but offsetting might be considered a form of greenwashing.

There are increasing promotional opportunities through developing car-free funerals. Adjacent public transport would help and might be facilitated by using buses or coaches on funerals. Promoting a cortège free funeral, by collecting the body after a funeral service elsewhere, and interring it without grave-side attendance, is an obvious opportunity. This issue is also considered in section 10.2.

It is also essential to watch trends and identify current media interests. For instance, global warming and ecological threats have continued unabated since the 1990s. Agenda 21 was introduced to counteract this and although still relevant this is now relatively forgotten. In the public mind too much carbon related angst might oversell the issue, so care must be taken to identify the mood and change the message to suit.

9. Potentially reduces cremation disbenefits

Cremation has a high carbon cost, and creates harmful emissions, but it is our scientific ignorance of the overall impact of incineration that is the greatest concern. It is known that the emissions change upon contact with other air pollutants but the dangers to the environment and the food chain are simply not fully understood. People may say that this is the case with much human activity, but the difference here is that there is a safe and proven alternative.

Some would suggest that with abatement, cremation might be more acceptable. This ignores the fact that the sheer cost, both in manufacturing the mass of equipment and the additional fuel costs of abatement, is unsustainable. The sustainability of the raw materials used in manufacture must also be a factor. The process creates virtually no benefit other than expediency, in contrast to the environmental and carbon benefits of natural burial.

Others might take a positive stance against cremation based on its tackiness. Many chapels are shoddily embellished, new crematoria have no architectural merit, and the conveyor belt process is about as spiritual as a car boot sale. With all this potential for adverse criticism

I am surprised that so few natural burial site managers appear to oppose cremation.

Any promotional messages opposing cremation will raise awareness and invite questioning of the process. I would recommend everyone involved with natural burial to arrange to visit a crematorium. This could be by appointment or by attending any Open Day events. This focuses the issues and gives a much better understanding of the process, essential if it is to be adversely criticised.

Part of the problem is the lack of understanding as to why 73% of people choose this form of incineration, whilst 100% of people appear to oppose similar waste incineration. If people choose cremation simply because it is indoors and warm, then their inclination to choose a natural burial site with no facilities will be very low. Promoting a natural burial process which avoids people having to stand at a cold and wet grave side might counteract this response.

Adverse criticism of cremation can be expected to upset people. Where a person has recently chosen cremation for somebody close to them, it is often a decision based on established practice rather than any awareness of the issues, and any criticism can cause them cognitive dissonance. Nonetheless, such an approach is essential in order to move to a more sustainable world. It is fact, not fiction, that we all eat North Sea white fish which contain mercury from the cremation of amalgam from human teeth.

10. Potentially educates about the environment

It might be considered that as the commercialism of a site increases, there is a corresponding reduction in the desire to educate customers on the environmental and carbon footprint impacts related to their service. The reason, in part, is that the private sector tends to be less transparent.

I am aware of at least one natural burial site that includes education in its remit, but this message is generally very rare. To be successful and meaningful, education concerning the environment requires the backing of recognisable and established organisations, who already promote through education. For instance, the marketing potential of the National Trust and RSPB is phenomenal and natural burial on land they own would possess real promotional impact. In the early 1990s, I discussed the possibility of the Woodland Trust offering natural burial but they deferred.

Natural burial associated with food production can be appealing and possesses an educational objective. As sites already exist for orchards and sustainably managed farmland, the use of the concept associated with organic and sustainable production is a message for modern times. As demand for vegetable allotments is rising and local authorities are short of money to buy land, such an association might make an ideal natural burial project. Perhaps only a limited number of people would be comfortable with people working over the graves, so some research would be useful.

A local authority may offer, through their climate change strategy, other green initiatives, or a local green directory, promotional opportunities based on education. It is essential to contact the relevant local authority staff, who are often recent graduates, and both cognisant of the latest climate research as well as the local situation, and devise a promotional strategy. A natural burial site can convey a potent educational message if its raison-d'être is planting trees, which can result in carbon offsetting, or creating other habitats. The guilt implicit in the modern lifestyle of extensive holiday flights might well be assuaged if people choose natural burial as compensation! Climate compensatory purchases might be a new marketing niche!

Climate change is a valid topic for natural burial with habitat as their focus. Site owners and managers can use it as the basis for giving talks to local groups and organisations. Care must be taken in identifying effective local activists. For instance, the Women's Institute can be a very effective lobbying group on green issues. It is also essential to get effective word of mouth support throughout the local green community. This can be very extensive and apart from members of the Green Party, Friends of the Earth and Greenpeace, far more local people will touch on the environment such as beekeepers, organic gardeners, birdwatchers, walkers, cyclists, joggers and possibly dog walkers. It is important not to underestimate the level of interest.

MPs and local councillors should be approached, especially if they are portfolio holders for the local authority climate change or for environmental strategies. At the very least this increases their awareness, and discussion can identify other opportunities. Clearly, commercial operations may well be treated with some circumspection in any contacts, but natural burial Trusts or not-for-profit organisations with social aims can expect a greater level of support. A natural burial site operated by a local authority ought to lobby for support through their council's climate change and environmental policies.

11. Creates a new local business

This is a promotional message from private sites, and possibly sites with charitable or not-for-profit objectives, often called social enterprises. It is principally a message to the local residents, parish council, and other local businesses especially to promote support at the planning stage. If the employment of local people is included in the proposal, then it should carry even more weight.

Once a site is up and running, the message will incorporate community resilience, the issue of both creating and maintaining rural villages and towns, and keeping their identity. It is essential to recognise this role and support other local businesses in developing such resilience. Utilising natural burial for farm diversification fits within this local business perspective.

12. Improves local resilience regarding pandemic

Every district council has a resilience plan to meet the possible excessive deaths if a pandemic occurs. The fact that existing cemeteries and churchyards are short of burial space, and that crematoria are reducing their cremation capacity, was discussed earlier in this book. It is a fact that any proposal to increase designated burial land increases resilience, and has strategic importance. In the event that deaths do increase beyond existing capacity, it would be necessary to resort to trench burial, possibly for a temporary period. The availability of natural burial sites for temporary or permanent burial will avoid the planning complications of using alternative green space.

Consequently, this is a strategic message to the district council in order to promote support at the planning stage. Clearly it would be part of a wider series of promotional messages related to the value of the site, but it might just make a difference. If council support is obtained, it prevents the council being a focal point for opposition, and this might disarm other elements of local dissent.

13. Replaces need to extend local churchyard or cemetery

The provision of a new natural burial site, whether private, charitable or municipal, is much easier to justify if local burial facilities are full, or close to full. As discussed earlier in the book, this is the case in much of the UK. Local research on burial provision would be necessary well before the application to open a new site was prepared.

It would be essential to contact the incumbent and parish council to see whether further burial provision is already secured, and if not, whether support could be given to the natural burial proposal. Often, further provision is impossible as available land simply does not exist, or resources to buy land are not available. Support might be forthcoming if the local town or village name is incorporated in the site name. In addition, the need for burial provision would be supported if any local people could be contacted who sought burial, yet were denied this option by the closure of existing churchyards or cemeteries.

14. Reduces deficits had local cemetery or churchyard been used

Few, if any, local cemeteries or churchyards break even, let alone operate at a profit. Consequently, as grave space runs out the funds to extend the site, assuming that this was locally feasible, rarely exist. Local support might well be promoted if a natural burial site supplemented these facilities by attracting some of the burials, and defers the need to extend their cemetery or churchyard. This message is vital in gaining support from the church or parish council at the pre-planning application stage, as well as in seeking the support of local people in order to grow the business.

Conversely, if it is locally considered that the natural burial site is likely to reduce churchyard or cemetery burial income, the message might need to be given fiscal advantage in order to gain support, or at least reduce opposition. For instance, a supplement could be built into the fee for any natural burial grave sold for donation to the local church. Alternatively, the site could undertake churchyard maintenance, or make improvements on behalf of the parish council, elsewhere in the community. A promotional strategy and messages of this type are all too often ignored and local opposition not taken seriously enough.

15. Potentially supports other local businesses

This is a promotional issue when opening a site, especially where it is private, perhaps less so for charitable or not-for-profit operations. In part the strategy is to support other local businesses (perhaps those involved in grounds maintenance, or gravedigging), in part to create a mutually supporting network that will foster local business, but also to seek local support and advice. The local authority may offer business support or grants, which in itself might counter adverse criticism on the proposals. Longer term, it is essential to operate within all local business networks, e.g. Rotary Club, as such networking is a promotional opportunity.

9.5.2 Promoting niche products

The promotional activity in the above 15 messages can be assumed to relate to the sale of adult natural burial graves, the expected prime purpose of a site. As mentioned earlier in the book, three other niches might need to be promoted.

Cremated remains graves

The commercial funeral process, whether in the form of private or municipal crematoria, or funeral directors, is well geared to selling locations and memorials following a cremation. Financially, they may have nothing to gain in referring clients to a natural burial site for the deposit of cremated remains. It might also be assumed that the cremation applicants, in favouring cremation rather than natural burial, have no interest, let alone awareness, of the concept.

In a competitive sense, it must be assumed that no natural burial site could compete with, say, a crematorium based on memorial choice. Neither does the potential for reduced cost appear to be a promotional opportunity, as many cremated remains are strewn at beauty spots without any costs applying. That said, cremation memorials at private crematoria can be very expensive, so should be researched.

There remain two clear promotional opportunities for attracting cremated remains to a natural burial site. The first option relates to an apparent desire of many cremation applicants to place cremated remains in a meaningful location, perhaps one which has a sense of continuity and purpose. Placing the remains beneath or around a tree on a purchased grave in a natural burial site meets this perspective. Most crematoria exist on matured sites, and little space exists for new tree planting, so tree type memorials are rarely offered. Crematoria memorials are also on very short lease periods. Cremation applicants can only be accessed directly if the natural burial site makes contact with the crematorium, or with any funeral director, who then agree to promote the site as a potential burial location. This may be achieved if the site offers environmental benefits or carbon footprint reductions, based on the trees planted, which can be promotionally used by either or both of the parties. Realistically, it is probably only feasible by offering a financial incentive for every grave sale promoted by them, so this might have to be considered.

The second option for attracting cremated remains relates to the desire of many applicants to return them to their home locality. If the site is part of a large community, especially a community with no local burial facilities for cremated remains, then considerable numbers might be attracted. The competition might be a plaque placed in a remote corner of a poorly maintained churchyard. These competitors need to be researched, and a better product, perhaps a grave under a tree, ought to be devised and promoted. Getting the message out is essential as all too often one hears comments such as, "If only I had known I would have preferred this site". Comments like this are reminders of promotional failure!

Baby and child graves

I have seen no evidence of purpose designed baby or child graves in natural burial sites. Most local authority sites will usually offer a specific plot in one of their cemeteries. Nonetheless, if a need can be recognised, perhaps after contact with the charitable organisations involved, it might be considered. The proximity of a maternity unit must also be an influence on this decision. The provision of graves for fetal remains or stillbirths would be a social benefit to the local community, and their promotion an example of social marketing.

Conventionally, such graves are currently only associated with intensively mown lawns. Natural burial sites that utilise only conservation mowing would have to be innovative in devising a product that could meet the needs of parents, whilst also caring for the environment.

Pet or companion graves

As pet ownership is so high, and pets seen as an important social benefit in the UK, the provision of these graves would appear to have commercial potential. Many of the earlier promotional messages still apply including more choice, a local option, low cost, meaningful funeral, creation of habitats, reduction in cremation disbenefits (the usual process for pet disposal) and creating a local business. Pet burial and pet funerals are an interesting topic for local talks, and an opportunity to stray into human natural burial, which might not be so appealing to the general audience! Pet funerals introduce and educate children about bereavement, and this educational perspective is a social marketing issue.

9.5.3   Getting the message out

Once the product is defined, and the associated messages prepared, the means of getting the message out need to be considered. Promotion is all the communications utilised in the market place, and include:

Advertising

Regular local newspaper and radio advertising is very expensive. It is extremely rare for any local authority to advertise its burial or cremation services and they often leave promotion entirely to local funeral directors. The funeral directors themselves often advertise in every local newspaper copy, and natural burial advertising adjacent to such a section might be feasible. Some newspapers refuse adverts adjacent to funeral directors or obituaries. A short period of advertising when the site opens might at least generate some early awareness.

Local authorities often issue regular newsletters or small newspapers to all homes in the area. All too often these are so politicised that the routine advertising of in-house services, such as a natural burial service, is rare. Local authority bereavement staff need to lobby their council to obtain more promotional coverage.

Public relations

PR is defined as maintaining goodwill and a favourable image with the public. Many new natural burial sites generate their own interest through the planning process, not always favourable, and follow-up reports in the press are usual. This publicity is free, and articles in local newspapers are widely read. The environment, habitats, insects, trees, etc. are all interesting topics so every attempt must be made to submit reports to newspapers, free publications, residents association and other newsletters in the local area. Newspapers often print a green or environmental page, so topics related to this are usually appreciated. Articles should reflect the individual messages previously considered, so that the subject is not exhausted in one combined feature. Natural burial related to the carbon footprint, to habitats, to trees and to local green space, ensure that at least four articles can be submitted, with social issues, air quality, green funerals, etc. adding another three perspectives.

A willingness to talk to local groups, free of charge or for a fee donated to a local charity or cause, must be promoted. Once on the talk circuit, a good speaker, especially one with an interesting slide show, soon obtains an increasing number of requests. Talks on the environment tend to be more favoured than talks on death! That said, many groups, such as the Quakers, Round Table, and WI often periodically consider an important social issue, so death-related topics can then be pertinent. Such talks can be structured around the importance of a will and an advance funeral directive. Talks need to be on offer both

241

during the day, as well as the evening, to accommodate the times when groups meet. As men die younger, a high percentage of funerals are arranged by women, so talking to women's groups ought to be a priority.

Group site visits usually consider the environment, but can be expanded to cover funerals or bereavement generally. Given a broader educational focus, perhaps with a funeral director involved, they might well be arranged for local nursing home staff, and charities involved with the aged, especially if they are free of charge. This could become part of their continuing professional development (CPD) training for their staff.

If the site is large enough, or perhaps on an interesting footpath network, and includes enough points of environmental interest, a walk can be offered to the general public. Site visits and walks are often routine follow-ups to a talk to local groups. They should be free of charge, and ideally with no more than 30 people, as an interactive relationship is more difficult with larger parties. With both talks and walks, a considerable impact can be made by word of mouth throughout an area that will generate interest. Local authorities often include walks as part of annual Cemetery and Crematoria Open Days or similar events, and sometimes use in-house ecologists or environmental staff to lead these. Private natural burial sites might be able to locate similar skilled people, perhaps volunteers, to lead walks.

Direct mail

I am not aware of direct mail usage by any natural burial site, or conventional cemetery or crematorium. The sending of a courteous letter together with a site leaflet could prove effective, but is labour intensive and fairly expensive. A few complaints can be anticipated from people offended by the death topic. A pilot, say of 500 letters, is certainly worthwhile, as the message in the letter can be measured by the number of contacts made. A second or third pilot can be tried with different messages to see whether a specific approach works more effectively.

Personal selling

Personal selling might seem commercial but is perhaps more significant than it first appears. The site manager and staff, when talking to the bereaved and visitors, on the telephone or at the site, are constantly being assessed. A personable character allied to passion for the local environment, and a not-too-obvious commercial intent, can all support and sell the product. A willingness to talk openly to groups is immediately seen as transparent, implies integrity, and is an ideal promotional platform. It is essential that the manager and all staff wear name badges so people can immediately recognise who they are.

Internet promotion

All natural burial operations should have a website. For many products, marketing now ignores the place component of the four Ps, this being replaced by the website. This is not the case with natural burial, where the place, or site, is truly the point of sale. Nonetheless, a website is ideal for photographs of the site and graves, as well as information on prices, coffins, etc. It can be expected that many people will review their natural burial options based on what is presented on the internet, and perhaps create a shortlist on which to visit. Many of the sites I have reviewed are somewhat vague about their environmental policies and rather too little information is given. Details on road directions and access by public transport can also be inadequate.

Word of mouth

Some modern marketers now refer to 'word of mouth marketing'. The importance of word of mouth, defined as 'person to person' cannot be over-emphasised. Without doubt, the funeral services on a natural burial site are the most significant word of mouth promotional opportunity. If the experience is good, word will travel, and it is free of charge. The old adage of first impressions count still holds true. The appearance of the entrance, the site overall, the views, the on-site signage and the availability of leaflets are all part of this shop window experience. The on-site experience can be extended much further if meaningful services can be created. A personable minister or secular officiant, one who can spiritually associate the deceased to the ethos of natural burial, perhaps even to the surrounding views and environment, can create a very emotional funeral experience. The natural burial site is a funeral stage and each service a performance.

Donations and bequests

The promotion of a culture that welcomes, even invites, donations, perhaps as a form of memorial, can be developed. An invitation to create habitat, say a scree garden or butterfly border, build a toilet block, or buy hedgehog hotels, might be considered. Although it could be assumed that such an approach suits the charitable or not-for-profit managed sites, some commercial sites can foster this approach. People are willing to pay for prominent features, especially when it becomes a memorial. Local authorities appear to receive far less this way than in the past. This is perhaps because fewer cemeteries are permanently staffed and management more remote, so personal relationships no longer develop with the bereaved or even with councillors. Bequests were more frequent when facilities were seen as a community resource, and the staff known and appreciated by the bereaved. As such, bequests could be seen as a quality indicator on how the service is perceived in the local community.

Natural burial as a brand

The concept of natural burial suffers from brand confusion. This is due to the broad definition, the wide-ranging types of sites and the absence of defined standards. Unlike McDonalds, people do not know what to expect when they enter a natural burial site. Some might suggest that this reflects choice and avoids excess commercialism; others might suggest that if the concept is to be promoted successfully, a brand is essential.

This lack of identity was recognised by the relatively new pet burial and cremation market. They rapidly created an association and code of practice. A similar approach was taken by the Natural Death Centre (NDC) when they created the Association of Natural Burial Grounds (ANBG) in 1994 and this, to some degree, promoted the concept and supported the site operators. Perhaps because too few joined and were active, the ANBG languished and little has been achieved. The NDC continues to operate but its financial weakness has been an enduring problem. The independence of its consumer advisory service is invaluable in a commerce-dominated market, and putting the NDC on a more secure footing is urgently needed.

It is disconcerting that natural burial sites appear to see each other as competitors rather than partners in a movement for change. There is an urgent need for unity and networking between natural burial sites, manufacturers of biodegradable coffins, compostable wreaths and biodegradable memorials, etc., as well as green funeral directors. Ideally, a levy to support the NDC and ANBG would benefit natural burial in the future.

Few in the movement today realise that in the 1990s the then new natural burial market received constant media attention. Natural burial was promoted as an environmental initiative and it was assumed that biodegradable coffins, no embalming and reduced mowing were fundamental to the concept. In reality, some of the early sites quickly abandoned these high environmental ideals because they depressed sales and income. Since that period many new sites have opened purporting to be natural burial and yet accepting chipboard coffins, embalming and often intensively mowing grass. These sites appear virtuous within the green burial movement yet have been able to set their own operational criteria, often commercially rather than environmentally driven.

As an example of this, in 2008 a newspaper reporter from New York contacted me after attending the opening of such a site, where chipboard coffins and embalming were routinely accepted. Her question to me was, "Surely this site is not natural burial?". I had to agree. Yet it continues to operate under the banner of natural burial simply because it chooses too. Not only have these actions dissipated the concept, it has severely weakened the essential psychological association linking environmental excellence with the concept. The ability for biodegradable coffin suppliers to infiltrate the market has been severely damaged by this commercial element.

The creation of a brand could be promoted by the Institute of Cemetery and Crematorium Management (ICCM) in line with the targets set out in their Charter for the Bereaved. These targets require improved environmental performance for funerals, whether this is through natural burial or demands that cremation meets specific energy and carbon emission reductions. Membership of the ICCM by operators of natural burial sites, especially private owners, is very low. Increased membership would counterbalance the existing domination by cremation and conventional burial operators. The focus, rather than just competitive jealousy between three modes of body disposal, should transfer to the real challenge of identifying the most environmental and sustainable means of disposing of the dead.

For the bereaved as consumers, the natural burial product has become so diverse that a 'buyer beware' situation has arisen. The consumer does not experience this problem with regard to conventional burial and cremation, which are recognisable services with no fudge. The natural burial movement, such as it is, needs to define the brand and market it with far more clarity.

Greenwashing

Green consumerism is increasing and can be expected to continue. The marketing though, is often complicated and obtuse. Products can be environmentally friendly, eco-friendly, recyclable, biodegradable, climate friendly or climate neutral, organic, carbon friendly or neutral, or simply green. Data can now measure a person's carbon footprint and a nation's Environmental Performance Index.

The response is often unsubstantiated and with vague advertising claims, something natural burial must avoid. For instance, it cannot be stated that natural burial is the only sustainable means of disposal, when this is clearly untrue. Graves in cemeteries or churchyards that have the potential to be re-used in the future, with low maintenance regimes, have much to commend them. Where these are adjacent to where people live, the low associated road mileage compared to a rural natural burial site might be a more sustainable option.

Making careless claims for natural burial invites the accusation of greenwashing, a word more familiar in America and Australia than in the UK. The word 'greenwash' is now in the Oxford Dictionary and is defined as:

> *"Disinformation disseminated by an organisation so as to present an environmentally responsible public image."*

I have a particular reason to remember this word because in 2008 a green burial group in the USA described me as a 'greenwasher' on their website. This was because at Carlisle I was offering natural burial in an urban setting. It was also because conventional burial and cremation was still being offered and at the same location. They considered this as a token gesture to the environment whilst continuing to promote the traditional and unsustainable options.

It is essential to avoid trade misrepresentation and false claims, as cases have been brought against firms manufacturing air conditioners, disposable nappies, beer and even toilet rolls. Claims must be substantiated with meaningful data, and if not available, with logic. This highlights the difficulties for natural burial because the necessary data does not exist, for instance the carbon impact differences between green and standard coffins. Nonetheless, a concentration on the use of natural materials, low energy usage and such factors should not create disputable claims.

For the green consumer perhaps the first question to ask is whether the purchase is necessary at all, as many of us are guilty of excessive consumption. But disposing of a body is not an option; it must be carried out and so at least validates the need for a green and sustainable perspective. The savvy consumer will have a series of questions about the purchase, which the site manager must be able to answer. These questions could include:

- How much energy and water does the site use?

- What natural resources are used?

- Is recycled material utilised?

- What toxic substances are used or allowed?

- What toxic substances get into the soil?

- What habitats are created for wildlife?

- Are identified animals, insects or plants protected by the site?

- Are trees planted to lock up carbon?

- Does the site support local businesses and communities?

- Does the site respect human rights and labour laws?

- Does the site focus on one or two environmental issues, but ignore others?

- Is their any evidence to support their green claims?

- Are the lifecycle environmental impacts considered?

- Are any accreditations by external groups or organisations available?

Many of these questions can be difficult to answer. For instance, what toxic substances are used or allowed might require some specialised knowledge. As a gardener, I can recognise when horticultural herbicides are used and I know that embalming fluid is carcinogenic, but few people are so aware. Factual answers to these questions create a potential 'bundle of benefits' which might not initially be recognised by the less savvy consumer when choosing natural burial. In addition, the site manager will be briefed and ready to respond when natural burial is adversely criticised. Being well briefed is essential in order to become an ambassador for the site and the concept of natural burial. The wider the proven bundle of benefits is in meeting sustainability and environmental criteria, the greater the integrity of the product.

An accusation of greenwashing could still be valid if disinformation is evident through highlighting the benefits but ignoring any harmful activities. For instance, the creation of a habitat-rich natural burial site, which otherwise accepts chipboard/MDF coffins and embalmed bodies, is greenwashing. Those supporting this approach argue that it is still greener than the alternatives and that people are unable at present to accept the constraints of natural burial in its purest state. They might also suggest that their approach is more acceptable to commercial funeral directing, and therefore more likely to succeed; and that if successful they then have the opportunity to improve their environmental standards in the future.

It might be considered that no matter how many benefits arise, it cannot justify an evidently harmful activity. There would be no moral dimension were it not for the fact that embalming and chipboard/MDF coffins can be avoided without detriment. In contrast, finding locally sourced flowers and recyclable packaging or wreaths may prove impossible for the bereaved. An accusation of greenwashing in accepting such flowers and plastics would not be fair. Nonetheless, a need to continue educating users on these issues, through advisory leaflets, is essential for the green consumer.

The advice here applies equally to private and local authority sites, although the latter are perhaps more vulnerable to greenwashing accusations where they manage natural burial and other services in tandem. Both cremation and conventional burial avoid the issues and rely on the obfuscation implicit in custom and practice. If these local authorities demand biodegradable coffins and oppose embalming for their natural burial service, but (as is typical) not for cremation, then the accusation might be valid. The desire to avoid conflict with conventional funeral directing, the political dimension, and management and staff taking an ambivalent stance on the environment, are all implicated in this approach.

Sourcing funeral advice

Within the funeral market there is a disinclination to refer to the bereaved as consumers and identify the funeral as a purchased service. Words suited to the purchase of a washing machine appear cold and insensitive in relation to the intensely emotional content of a funeral purchase. The cynical will suggest that mainstream funeral directing prefers the Victorian paternalistic management of the bereaved. This is an assumption that they must be shielded from aspects of death, and this runs the risk of weakening transparency, reduced choice and rights. The caring and friendly 'I know best' stance creates a relationship that confuses and complicates the purchase. Whatever, if funeral advice is within the control of mainstream funeral directing, the danger is that improvements will be stifled. They will ignore the existence of natural burial, especially if it reduces potential income, not least from coffin and memorial sales. This is as good a reason as any to consider how a bereaved person obtains advice on funeral options.

It is difficult to assess overall how well the bereaved are served as consumers, but I suspect it is very poorly. If we assume that on average two people gather advice and arrange a funeral, then around 1.2 million people need advice every year. It is essential for them to obtain early and pertinent funeral advice before being locked into the commercial maelstrom of funeral directing. In my working life the response from the bereaved was too often: "If I had known that, I would have arranged the funeral differently". The process is not the only cause of this failure as the consumer must also have a measure of responsibility. The bereaved, before the death that defined them as such, were the general public and in being indifferent and perhaps frightened of death, contributed greatly to their own ignorance.

When a death occurs, the funeral advice available is often reliant on chance. A death at home might be attended by a GP from a surgery that takes an interest in bereavement, but this is not common. If the deceased died in a hospital where bereavement staff is employed, or a chaplaincy team exists, they might get some advice. Even then it is often limited, as at GP surgeries, to suggesting immediate contact with a funeral director. This advice will usually be given without any reference to ability to pay or the need for a specific kind of funeral. For instance, just a few questions would indicate whether the family wants a green funeral, or that they are secular, or that they might prefer not to use a funeral director. The bereaved are innocents in a sophisticated market!

Consider also the fact that research suggests that a very large proportion of these bereaved people will soon be seeking medical help for depression and ill health provoked by the effects of the bereavement. Because of this, the medical professionals have a vested interest to ensure that the bereaved obtain a meaningful funeral, if for no other reason than to reduce future medical issues and costs.

Up to 20% of the bereaved will be in contact with a coroner's officer. In these cases, the body will have been collected by a funeral director and taken to a mortuary where a post mortem can take place. This funeral director will have been awarded a contract to act for the coroner service. All too often, large funeral directing conglomerates tender for such contracts for free. This is because they are aware that in collecting the body they will obtain the funeral order in the majority of cases, often a significant number in each locality. Do the family order from them because of touting within the process? I have actually seen the funeral directors contact details left at homes when bodies are collected, an action prohibited in most contracts. Is it because the family is embarrassed to ask their preferred funeral director to collect the body from the contract funeral director? I suspect that in most cases it is because the family had no preferred funeral director anyway, and end up with the contract funeral director by default. Whatever, nothing is for free so it must be assumed that the successful contract funeral director is confident of recovering their coroner service costs within the funeral bill to the bereaved family. The practice of tendering for free clearly has an impact which may be against the interest of the consumer and should be prohibited. Under the present situation the coroner's officers cannot be expected to do anything other than direct people towards the contracted funeral director.

The medical services and coroner's officer will ultimately direct the bereaved person to the Registrar of Births, Deaths and Marriages in order to register the death. The registrar is usually aware of all local cemeteries, crematoria and churchyards because they receive confirmation that the body has been interred or cremated from these facilities. Nonetheless, they shy away from the bereaved as a consumer, and recognise them only as informants in a statistical process related to population data. I have met some excellent and well-informed registrars, but their advice is always informal, and varies according to the personal interest and knowledge of the registrar on duty. Also, by the time the bereaved meet the registrar they are usually already contracted to a funeral director.

It is a concern that these three expensive government funded services, i.e. the medical services, coroner and registrar, have so much contact with the bereaved, yet operate independently. The benefits arising from these three units working together as a statutory death management unit would be considerable, but it is a vain hope!

The charities serving the aged give some advice, but they are too often agents for funeral plans, and far from independent. Nursing homes may also have some form of liaison with, or support from, specific funeral directors, so advice can be biased. Citizens Advice Bureau (CAB) is a source of information but the success of the advice can be variable. If the CAB volunteer on duty has personally experienced a funeral then the advice may be pertinent. Overall, charities and nursing homes are only as good as the training their staff receive, and if it is restricted to funeral directors, a degree of bias must be suspected.

The Natural Death Centre offer an advisory service, are independent and the ideal source of advice on natural burial and sustainable options. This, of course, is not unbiased consumer advice. As a charity, their enquiries are often people researching their own demise, and they have little impact on those immediately bereaved.

Cemeteries and crematoria, often under the umbrella of Bereavement Services, are more often than not only involved after the bereaved have contracted with a funeral director, so any advice might be too late to affect the current funeral arrangements but might be helpful for future deaths. It can be anticipated that staff employed just in a cemetery know little about cremation, and vice versa. Similarly, the staff working in conventional burial and cremation rarely know anything about natural burial. Usually, these staff give advice relevant to their facility, but not about caring for the deceased, called last offices, coffins or the actual funeral arrangements.

Some local authorities have adopted the ICCM Charter for the Bereaved, an action that in itself suggests that they recognise the bereaved as consumers. Consequently, they should provide a higher level of service which will be more transparent. This can be identified by such actions as the provision of a funeral advisory service, by allowing the cremation process to be witnessed and by a willingness to assist those wishing to carry out a funeral independent of a funeral director. Less obvious is the fact that they might be very active in providing free training to nurses, nursing homes and charities, in order to help them advise the bereaved at that essential early stage in the process. The best local authorities, like Cardiff, go one step further and provide a genuine fixed price funeral contracted to a local funeral director. That gives the staff direct access and experience of funeral arrangements, and provides the only genuine competition to mainstream funeral directing.

Government agencies are improving but there is a limit to what they can do. Consumer Direct (www.consumerdirect.gov.uk) offers useful advice but it is general and unrelated to local services. It states that a funeral can be done without a funeral director, but if the local authority is not a Charter for the Bereaved member (few private crematoria join), where would an enquirer go? The Department of Work and Pensions through Job Centre Plus issues the useful booklet '*What to do after a Death in England and Wales*', which points enquirers towards the local authority or Natural Death Centre.

The information process is casual and random. There is regrettably, no formal process to identify the bereaved as consumers or provide a universal, independent bereavement advisory service. The government and local authorities do not recognise this as a public need and cede this function to funeral directors. This is understandable except, as outlined in section 10.2, the definition of a funeral director does not include any specific reference to giving advice about the options. In truth, it would be naïve to suggest that they explain options, such as arranging an independent funeral, or a natural burial, which does not use their services, and might lose them a funeral and any associated income.

The Office of Fair Trading (OFT) could formulate a precise definition of funeral directing that made specific reference to giving consistent, relevant advice on all the options. This would replicate the standards set by the Financial Services Agency regarding the giving of financial advice. At the very least, they should be expected to inform the bereaved:

- of their right to do a funeral without a funeral director;
- of the options available at churchyards, conventional burial grounds, natural burial grounds and crematoria in the area;
- that they can source a coffin from any supplier;
- of the process and implications of embalming;
- of the degree of involvement the bereaved can have in the funeral arrangement;
- of the right of the bereaved to a transparent list of charges;
- of the environmental impact of options.

The problem is, such advice requires skilled, time served staff, and is entirely opposed to the current practice of simplifying funeral sales through the non-negotiable funeral package, often set out in an expensive brochure. I experienced in the last two decades of my working life clear evidence that misinformation, disinformation, and entire omission, were commonplace in modern funeral directing.

The OFT could also prohibit funeral directors and companies who sell funeral plans from getting involved with nursing homes and charities dealing with the aged. The current approach of many commercial funeral directors is to levy high charges for individual funerals purely to enable them to give some of this money back to nursing homes and charities as inducements. Because of this furtive activity, the service to the consumer is potentially influenced, and funerals are thereby more expensive.

Without doubt there is a need for a national independent 24/7 advisory service that supersedes any contract with a funeral director. This would be consistent, and prior to the ad hoc advice arising when a death occurs, as outlined above. The potential benefits, in smoothing the process, reducing the dissonance, creating a meaningful funeral, and potentially reducing medication for depression and the other ill effects of a death, such as debt, would be immeasurable.

A local funeral advisory service

This is the provision of information leaflets specific to a site on all aspects of funeral provision. This should enable the consumer to understand how the local process works and how they can obtain a funeral that is meaningful and within their budget. The immediate implication of a funeral advisory service is that it is transparent and shows a concern for the total funeral outcome for the consumer, rather than just commercial interest. The information leaflets need to be specific to a locality and should provide far more detail and contacts than could be obtained in a national guide such as *The Natural Death Handbook*. Such a service also implies that the site manager fully understands how their burial service fits into the existing funeral market.

Information leaflets also save staff work by avoiding the need to repeat the same advice and information to enquirers. I also consider that many bereaved people are distracted by their loss, so find it difficult to absorb all the information given by telephone. Many compliments will arise if they are able to sit down at home and quietly read and consider written information on funerals.

Each handout can deal with a separate part of the process. For instance, a leaflet that outlines a secular service will be helpful for a bereaved person to read before they meet the secular officiant to consider the funeral service. The leaflets are a focus when presenting talks to local clubs and organisations and are useful promotional material to hand out.

The leaflets can be divided into those which are essential, and those which can be added progressively:

Essential

1. Information for the bereaved (this should be the site leaflet outlining terms and conditions).

2. Guide to an independent natural burial without a funeral director.

3. Questions people ask about natural burial.

4. Information on biodegradable coffins, burial shroud, etc.

5. Table of fees.

6. Plan of the site (showing grave plots, water points, etc.).

7. A site environmental travel plan.

Useful backup leaflets

8. Information on using a funeral director.

9. Funeral plans, especially if provided by the site.

10. Environmental issues (embalming, car free funerals, Local Agenda 21, etc.).

11. Information on Charter for the Bereaved and Guiding Principles.

12. Copy of advance funeral directive (perhaps bespoke for the site).

13. Information on the Natural Death Centre.

14. Laying out and caring for the deceased 'last offices'.

15. Outline of a secular service.

16. Information on memorials.

A newsletter and details of walks or other events might be added. Books and other publications that support the site ethos might also be advertised. The leaflets could also be combined if it is preferred to reduce the total number.

Printed leaflets can be expensive so it is important not to include details which will frequently change, such as fees. The table of fees can be maintained as a Word document on a computer, which is readily changed and photocopied. The guide documents, such as number 2 – guide to an independent natural burial without a funeral director, and number 3 – questions people ask about natural burial, are ideally maintained as Word documents. These can then be readily updated when addresses change, or if further information is needed.

To ensure transparency, in-house leaflets should include precise costs. Generic leaflets that constantly refer the reader to the separate table of fees are often confusing, especially to elderly people. All leaflets should be dated and regularly reviewed. For instance, with guide number 2, this would include the current costs of hiring a suitable van or car to transport the coffin, the cost of a coffin, body storage and the individual fees for natural burial on the site.

Leaflets and font size are also a special needs consideration. The minimum font size should be 12, and Arial font, which has evenly spaced letters and figures, is considered the easiest to read. Large print copies can be useful and a video recording of the site could be loaned out. A willingness to visit people at home should be included in promotional material and not just a default option. This is greatly appreciated by the very old and those with mobility problems.

A number of local authority Bereavement Service units work closely with local bereavement support groups such as CRUSE, Compassionate Friends, and SANDS (Stillbirth & Neonatal Death Society). A few units have been merged with the Registrar of Births, Deaths & Marriages. This enables them to establish contact with the bereaved immediately after registering a death, to give them information on the burial and cremation facilities, on bereavement counseling or support groups and even to cancelling rent books and bus passes.

This extended Bereavement Service approach is an example of a new marketing topic called social marketing, typically focused on health and social care. These initiatives highlight the relative strength of local authority bereavement services in supporting the bereaved in comparison to the rather weak social support of private, often isolated, natural burial sites. The private sites need to network with bereavement organisations, consider bereavement support and identify training on this issue.

Competitor analysis

Natural burial sites do not sit in a vacuum, and it is extremely important to both identify and understand local burial and cremation facilities and how they care for the bereaved. Overall, the purpose of the analysis is to identify the weaknesses of the competing services. As all the facilities tend to be used by funeral directors and their staff, they will be a good source of information, certainly at the early stages of analysis.

In all my management posts I periodically checked the number of registered deaths for the area, and then notionally apportioned them to local burial and cremation facilities. This confirmed the percentage using the services I managed and how many, and to where, the other funerals were going, what is termed the market dynamics. Although this sounds a relatively simple exercise, it was often difficult to balance the number of deaths, and a small proportion was always missing. A few bodies were going to anatomical dissection or cryonics, but these were insignificant. In Croydon, the answer was that a considerable number of bodies were repatriated to India and Pakistan, their homeland. Although one might assume this was just a cultural desire, it was a shock to discover that with high burial costs in London, it could prove cheaper to fly the body to India for burial. This is a classic instance of the need to analyse and understand the local funeral market.

A further issue is that people may choose to use other crematoria, and less often burial facilities, outside of the area, perhaps where their family funerals occurred in the past. At Carlisle, a typical rural area, churchyards and parish burial grounds absorbed a varying number of burials, but this was never easy to analyse with confidence. First, there can be a lot of churchyards and parish burial grounds in a large rural district, identifying contacts is time consuming and often the statistics were just not available. Nonetheless, as the standards at such sites often vary from very good to very poor, it is essential to visit and assess them.

A significant future challenge to natural burial sites, as well as to cremation, is the already stated government intention to legalise the introduction of grave re-use, often called 'lift and deepen'. It can be assumed that this will allow graves last used 75–100 years ago, and where no family interest remains, to be exhumed (the lift) and replaced below 6' (183cm) in the same grave (the deepen). The grave can then be re-used for two burials, one above the other, say every 75–100 years, which is sustainable. This will potentially re-open many old cemeteries within heavily populated communities. If these sites utilise urban natural burial, as in section 4.2.14, but with re-used graves rather than reclaimed graves, they could create a very low-carbon funeral.

It appears inappropriate to suggest that trade discount might be used in the funeral market, but private crematoria are reputed to offer this to funeral directors using their services. If so, it could influence the advice given to the bereaved and affect competition.

The dreaded pauper grave

I have a copy of the Memorandum on Planning for Post-War Reform in the Disposition of the Dead issued in 1944 by the National Association of Cemetery & Crematorium Superintendents (now the ICCM). It states that although poor law funerals:

> "have been greatly improved in recent years, in many instances to the point of being indistinguishable from private disposal, past conditions in this respect have brought about a fear of 'pauper burial'. This fear has had the effect of causing much unnecessary expenditure on funerals and burials, even to the extent of lavishness with resultant poverty to the relatives, in order to emphasise the non-pauper nature of the disposal. Social competition in private funeral and burial arrangements has also developed therefrom. It is appreciated that much of the expenditure is occasioned by reverence and the preservation of long established customs, but it is regrettable to have to state that sentimental excesses in private expenditure on the last rites are frequently encouraged as a matter of business."

The Labour Party understood the public shame of the pauper's funeral and it directly led to the introduction of a death grant of £20 in 1949. Because of the abiding fear of a pauper funeral, care needs to be taken in the language used to describe natural burial to avoid any correlation with it. In the early 1990s on guided walks at Carlisle cemetery, a person would occasionally prefer not to enter the woodland burial site. They felt that the long grass and lack of mowing was disrespectful to the dead and reminded them of pauper graves.

The pauper grave is a remarkable hangover from Victorian times. It was a way of punishing those who were unable to buy a grave right and falling on the parish to pay for their burial. The law required the parish to provide unpurchased graves, but this did not extend to the rights expected in a purchased grave. Typically, the bereaved were not allowed to place any form of memorial, neither could they deposit flowers or mementoes on the grave. Private American cemeteries still apply these principles to those who fail to be paying consumers.

In the 1990s I was asked to attend a parish council to defend the case for increasing wildflower conservation areas in a churchyard, one of seven closed churchyards under my management. I had selected an area of graves over 100 years old and after personally checking that none of these graves were visited, bulbs were planted, and mowing restricted to once a year. A resident had contacted the parish council and accused me of insensitivity and no longer caring for the paupers of the parish. I was aware that some, perhaps all the graves were of paupers, but that had not influenced my choice of the area. The parish councillors accepted my plea that the habitat had been greatly improved. The complainant, far from happy, reminded them that I was the man "who had developed a woodland burial option, where all the graves were neglected". The strength of feeling on these issues is very real and should not be ignored.

9.6　THE MARKETING PLAN

The four Ps and other issues in the foregoing pages on marketing are the basis of a marketing plan. It is essential not to see a marketing plan as too complex and shy away from creating one. At its simplest it is a description on how the site is resolving the many problems, environmental, sustainable and perhaps financial, already apparent at conventional burial grounds or crematoria. It can be called 'resolution selling' in that a new kind of grave has been designed, and will be managed and maintained in such a way to resolve these problems.

The products, i.e. the various grave types, must be matched with relevant promotional messages. The more messages that fit the products on offer, the more it suggests an appeal to a wider range of consumers and an increased number of sales. A promotional budget must be set that enables effective communication. The decision then is to ascertain the number of sales needed to break-even, and by when. Without such targets, it is not possible to measure success or failure. There must be a constant monitoring of sales and of operational and promotional costs, as part of the business strategy. It is essential to stay with the marketing plan, and not deviate from it.

A marketing plan at the very least defines targets over a set period. If promotion is failing in some way, a plan might suggest why. At review stages, the plan should then be changed to reflect the new strategy, and then monitored over the set period.

I have not mentioned staff, or team performance, which are a vital part of marketing. There is a need to lead, but also to know when to listen and when to delegate. People visiting a natural burial site quickly appreciate a good team and they must not encounter disenchanted and disengaged staff. The team also includes the site designer, environmental advisor, the financial advisor, the staff who clean the toilets and those who attend funerals. For the bereaved, they may not separate the on-site team from the funeral director, minister or secular officiant, as they are all part of the delivery process. If one fails, it reflects upon everyone.

9.7   HOW GREEN IS YOUR FUNERAL?

The culmination of the marketing topic, and the focus of this book, is to highlight the myriad issues that lie behind the phrase 'natural burial'. The most effective natural burial is one that embraces a biodegradable coffin, and avoids embalming, hothouse flowers, extensive road mileage and mowing. In this sense it is highlighting many of the weaknesses typically evident in conventional burial and cremation. The fact is, a natural burial is just one funeral component, and the other components could create a hefty carbon footprint. In order to be more objective, I have created a chart to measure carbon impacts such that both burial and cremation based funerals can be objectively compared.

The majority of natural burial sites are rural and a funeral could involve more road miles, especially if many subsequent visits to the grave occur. Consequently, on balance, such a natural burial could have a higher carbon footprint than a cremation organised in the immediate vicinity of the deceased. This is complicated further because many choosing natural burial do not use the grave as a shrine, and rarely visit subsequently. As they often reject embalming, choose a biodegradable coffin and oppose the use of air-freighted flowers then accrued benefits after accounting for road miles to the site might still create a low footprint. This virtuous choice will be challenged where grave re-use, and reclaimed graves (the latter currently legal only in London) are locally available in a conventional cemetery.

To be objective it is essential to account for all carbon and waste costs as well as harmful emissions without prejudice to any particular form of disposal. Consequently, I have compiled a simple score sheet with all funeral components listed vertically starting at the top with embalming. By scoring each topic, negative score to the left and positive score to the right, a total is obtained. In choosing either burial or cremation, a further nine other components of a funeral are listed. This enables a total score of -100 for the worst case scenario and +100 for the best. Needless to say, -100 is only possible by arranging a conventional cremation, and +100 by arranging an ecologically sound natural burial. These high or low scores are less important than the real purpose of the exercise. This is to enable people to move away from a minus score towards a plus score by recognising the impact of each component of a funeral, and if any one of these is greened the environmental impact is reduced.

For example, even though a conventional cremation scores very poorly its environmental impact can be significantly reduced. A cremation score of +30 can be attained if embalming is rejected and a biodegradable coffin used. This score also requires a collection for charity in lieu of floral tributes, choosing a Book of Remembrance memorial and limiting road miles. With similar components, a reclaimed grave in a London cemetery could attain approximately +65. It would be wrong to assume that where the bereaved choose natural burial they will automatically exceed these scores. For instance, if embalming is used together with a chipboard coffin, air-freighted flowers, at a site over 20 miles from the home, with a stone memorial and high road miles, the natural burial score can dip to -50. In such cases a local green cremation may have less impact on the environment. This suggests that the score sheet is not biased towards natural burial and provides a balanced assessment.

It needs to be recognised that the reclaiming and re-use of graves in conventional burial grounds is disadvantaged. This is because the older plots where grave reclaim or re-use will occur are generally poor due to derelict memorials and roads, and often lack trees. If this results in the bereaved rejecting that option, then the opportunity to create a local funeral, with low road miles, is no longer realistic. This suggests that authorities intending to pursue urban grave re-use, with its high environmental and social potential, should be putting together a strategy to raise standards immediately, as it cannot be achieved overnight.

Finally, I am conscious that any assessment that suggests disapproval of wreaths at funerals, or that measuring the number of visits by the bereaved to a grave, is sensitive. It could upset the bereaved and no doubt, attract adverse attention from the media. Nonetheless, the waste resulting from death is just as serious as that resulting from life. It is financially expensive to dispose of, and as it contains considerable organic material such as peat and soil from pot plants, turf and other waste which rots, it is a major source of methane in landfill. This scoring process is merely a disinterested assessment of what might be considered custom and practice, which all too often is not subject to scrutiny. The assessment also highlights the need for all site managers to survey visitors and identify, amongst others, the type of flowers left on graves, number of grave visits and distance travelled.

9.7.1 Assessing the environmental impact of a funeral

Less environmentally friendly more intensive and less sustainable		*More environmentally friendly less intensive and more sustainable*	
EMBALMING (often called hygienic treatment)			
-10	Using formaldehyde base		
-5	Using a less harmful chemical (still requires the unacceptable disposal of 5 litres of blood down the drains)		
		No embalming, body refrigeration over 5 days prior to disposal	+5
		No embalming, body refrigeration up to 5 days prior to disposal	+10
CHOICE OF COFFIN			
-10	American casket/coffin made of rainforest timber or metal		
-5	Conventional coffin made of particle board/chipboard/MDF with plastic handles, fittings, lining, etc.		
		Cardboard, bamboo, etc. non-locally produced sustainable material	+5
		Locally produced wicker, papier-mâché, FSC approved, etc.	+10
FLORAL TRIBUTES			
-10	Air-freighted flowers in plastic frames		
-5	Air-freighted flowers with recyclable frames and all green material composted		
		Locally produced flowers in recyclable frames and with all green material composted	+5
		No wreaths and/or money donated to charity or use of garden flowers with no frames and with all green material composted	+10

DISPOSAL BY BURIAL			
-10	Burial in wet grave creating anaerobic conditions and potential for water pollution		
-5	Burial above the water table		
		Burial in reclaimed grave or natural burial site where grass is intensively mown	+5
		Burial in natural burial site where ecological standards apply	+10
OR: DISPOSAL BY CREMATION			
-10	Same day cremation in conventional chipboard/MDF coffin resulting in maximum gas use and emissions		
-5	Cremation in biodegradable coffin reducing emissions by 50% and with metal residue recycled		
		No plus score as cremation not sustainable and emits proven harmful emissions	nil
FINITE ENERGY USE ON DISPOSAL OF BODY			
-10	Conventional cremation using cremator managed inefficiently		
-5	Cremation with efficient process utilising shifts/holding coffins, etc. so that gas usage is minimised		
		Burial with grave excavated mechanically using fossil fuel	+5
		Burial in grave manually excavated	+10
ROAD MILES ON FUNERAL			
-10	Funeral over 20 miles from home		
-5	Funeral 10–20 miles from home		
		Funeral within 10 miles of home	+5
		Funeral within 5 miles of home/or using no fossil fuel private vehicles on funeral	+10

	MEMORIAL		
-10	Memorial in stone quarried and shipped from India or some other foreign source		
-5	Memorial in stone quarried from UK source		
		Memorial as small plaque/in recycled stone or wood from sustainable source	+5
		No memorial, or Remembrance book type made of sustainable paper/ electronic	+10
	GRIEVING WASTE		
-10	Visits to grave over 150 times p.a. leaving air-freighted flowers, plastic pots, peat, etc.		
-5	Visits under 150 times p.a. leaving air-freighted flowers, plastic pots, peat, etc.		
		Regular visits to site but leaving UK grown flowers and/or other green products and/or recycles all waste	+5
		Low visits to site, maximum two per year (e.g. visit at Christmas and anniversary)	+10
	GRIEVING ROAD MILES		
-10	Visits to grave over 150 times p.a.		
-5	Visits to grave under 150 times p.a.		
		Infrequent visits to site, say under12 per year	+5
		No visits to site or using public transport/walks or cycles	+10
	SITE MANAGEMENT		
-10	Intensive weekly mowing and high level of horticultural operations, bedding, etc.		
-5	Less intensive fortnightly mowing and/or 25% of site under ecological standard		
		Over 50% of site under ecological standard	+5
		Entire site under ecological standard/ no chipboard coffins or embalming allowed	+10

Chapter 10

FUNERAL DIRECTING

10.1   INTRODUCTION

The issue of conventional funeral directing is not a topic for this book. Nonetheless, the fact that some natural burial sites have integrated funeral directing into their service suggests that funeral procurement should be considered. There is also an element of resistance by many funeral directors to burial generally, perhaps due to the increased time involved compared to cremation. In addition, if the bereaved wish to arrange a natural burial funeral without a funeral director, the process must be understood.

The funeral market is dominated by mainstream funeral directing, as they continue to be the first point of contact and advice for the bereaved. This role makes them gatekeepers, because they stand between the bereaved and the place of burial. Whether a natural burial or not, any new option that promotes the separate procurement of coffins, reduced motor vehicle use, memorial free funerals and opposition to embalming is going to attract continuing antipathy. Why would they support any change to the detriment of their income, even if it does reduce overall funeral costs?

Funeral directing organisations maintain their influence through the All Party Parliamentary Group for Funerals and Bereavement at Westminster. Their principal focus is to remove the cap on government funeral payments from the Social Fund and fend off pricing competition and transparency. They show virtually no interest over innovation in funerals or on issues related to the carbon footprint or sustainability. Apart from a few new green funeral directors and the NDC widening the availability of biodegradable coffins, neither the OFT or books on improving funerals, or the small number of activists, has made any significant inroads into changing the process. Also, the ICCM is not mandated to lobby against a commercial funeral process, and no other means to challenge mainstream funeral directing is evident.

As local authorities are experiencing an increasing number of residents refusing to arrange a funeral, a funeral procurement strategy is necessary to address this increasing risk. Low-cost funerals will continue to be demeaned by the private sector, costs will rise, and those unwilling or unable to pay will fall on the local authority.

Before considering the issues, the definition of a funeral director and their role needs to be reviewed.

10.1.1 Definition and role of a funeral director

The precise definition of a funeral director is difficult. An internet search will suggest that he/she is 'one whose business is the management of funerals'. This is vague in that it could equally apply to a cemetery sexton or to any natural burial site manager. A second definition, 'the person who actually does the carrying of the deceased, whether vehicularly or by hand', is slightly nearer the truth. This is because the motor or horse drawn hearse is designed purely to carry bodies, and is only used by funeral directors on a day to day basis. Nonetheless, this suggests that any person carrying out a funeral without a funeral director, perhaps hiring just a hearse, qualifies, and yet they do not do this contractually or as a means of business.

I first researched this definition when considering whether a local authority could provide its own funeral directing service. Council legal officers came to the decision that the transport of the body was the determining factor in being defined as a funeral director, and this specific element of a funeral was *ultra vires*, that is, outside the powers of a local authority. This prevented the authority from transporting bodies and thereby qualifying as a funeral director.

The funeral director might be considered an agent, rather similar to a travel agent. The travel agent pulls together the various components of a holiday, and creates a holiday package. The funeral director similarly procures the various components to create a funeral package. The funeral director often does not employ the people involved including the embalmer, coffin maker, florist and even the carriage master to supply the hearse and cars, including the drivers and bearers. The fact that they often do employ them is purely related to commercial considerations, as well as the fact that this makes integration of all the components easier and probably more efficient for them. This suggests it is more accurate to define a funeral director as 'an agent who is contracted to bring together various components to create a funeral service for remuneration'.

This definition does not include an explicit requirement to give the bereaved timely and pertinent advice on the various components.

Yet, this is ever more necessary with increasing options and choices, related to the environmental, sustainability and financial implications of their decision. Consequently, the potential for incorrect advice (misinformation) gets ever greater. As natural burial sites could be owned by the funeral directing company involved, and they might have other commercial interests in the funeral process, the potential for advice that deceives or misleads (disinformation) is similarly high.

10.2   CAN AN INTEGRATED FUNERAL SERVICE BE PROVIDED?

In the 1990s a number of new private natural burial sites came close to failure when implicit promises of support by local funeral directors failed to materialise. In desperation, these site owners realised that the only way to survive was to offer the full funeral package, and they integrated funeral directing into their service. A private natural burial site working in partnership with a (green) funeral director, or with explicit support, would not have such concerns.

Most people are unwilling to face death, and the skilled funeral director is undoubtedly valuable in removing the burden of the arrangements. Many funeral directors and their staff are professional, sympathetic and personally dedicated to their work. Nonetheless, it might be considered that current mainstream funeral directing is anachronistic in perpetuating Victorian funeral practices in the face of serious social and environmental challenges. For example, the body is moved between the deceased's home, the mortuary, the funeral director premises and the burial site. The process promotes the status of using high horsepower, polluting vehicles e.g. the Rolls Royce hearse, and the creation of cortèges on congested roads. There is no commercial incentive to reduce the use of vehicles, in replacing current coffins with biodegradable types, or providing only locally sourced biodegradable floral tributes. This might change if there is more competition and a more responsible attitude is taken by consumers.

Private sites often open in areas where established local authority crematoria or cemeteries already exist. As supplementary facilities, the funeral director can utilise their gatekeeper role and either ignore their presence or advise against them, perhaps based on spurious information. The integrated service removes this gatekeeper role, facilitates innovative funeral procurement options and opens up many social and environmental promotional opportunities, in themselves a unique selling proposition (USP).

Local authorities possess similar opportunities in offering an integrated funeral directing option. This can allow total control of both funeral costs and disbursements and would also be a USP. The legal constraints on a local authority, which do not apply to private sites, require a different approach. The reality is that all the components of a funeral can be brought together in other ways and the role of the funeral director reduced or replaced by a more efficient process based on, for want of a better term, a 'one stop shop'.

10.2.1 A local authority integrated funeral service

The word 'integrated' is misleading related to the local authority situation because, as already stated, they do not possess the trading powers to act as funeral directors. They can, though, contract a funeral director to provide a transparently priced funeral service to complement their burial or cremation service. This ensures the bereaved can obtain a full funeral at a competitive price that meets the environmental objectives of the local authority. To achieve this, the local authority has to prepare a specification and a green funeral option can be written into this. The specification would prohibit embalming, suggest a selection of biodegradable coffins and perhaps encourage the use of locally sourced, biodegradable floral tributes. A shortcoming of a contracted funeral service is that it is inevitably off-site and therefore does not limit vehicle use.

A further disadvantage with a contracted funeral service is that the specification often allows some flexibility for the funeral director who wins the contract. In a previously arranged contract I managed, the successful funeral director demeaned the cheapest coffins they offered and persuaded the bereaved to upgrade. This resulted in the advertised low-cost funeral increasing by an average of £200.00 (2001).

10.2.2 A private site integrated funeral service

A private natural burial site could also contract out, or provide an in-house funeral directing option to provide a transparently priced funeral package. If located on-site, it meets the principles of a one stop shop, which is outlined below. A site with an integrated funeral service can still accept burial bookings from other funeral directors, but resistance can be anticipated from the mainstream, perhaps working through their trade associations. Funeral directors, especially rural businesses, often cover a very limited area and for a natural burial site to succeed it may need to draw burials from perhaps 50 or more funeral directors in the area. The integrated service would need to be promoted over a similar area if local funeral directors do not use the site, and an equivalent number of burials were required.

A model integrated funeral service has two principal requirements: it must be transparent regarding pricing and operation, and it must be unified with natural burial to provide a full green funeral. Ideally, with all the components provided on site, including body storage and celebrant's hall or chapel, it would represent a one stop shop intergrated service. These two requirements are now considered in more detail.

Transparency

The Office of Fair Trading (OFT) conducted a number of inquiries into the funerals market in 1989, 1995 and 1998. The reports were carried out due to ongoing concerns about the lack of transparency and market distortion in the funeral industry. As the OFT found it difficult to find actual evidence, the reports were often inconclusive and did not bring about solutions. In part this is because of the secrecy endemic in the business. The OFT wrote to me on the 27th August 1998 stating that they were conducting a funeral industry inquiry, and that this would focus on:

- The structure of the market.

- Vertical links between funeral directors and crematoria.

- The extent to which leading companies are able to exercise market power.

- An assessment of detriments to the economic interests of consumers.

The letter stated:

> "one of the principal conclusions of the Office's 1989 report was that consumers needed more information about the cost of funerals and the services provided. It was recognised that this was particularly important at a time when consumers are under emotional stress, and therefore at their most vulnerable and least likely to shop around in the same way that they might for other services. The report noted that the manner in which interviews were conducted by some funeral directors, and the way in which information was given, might not

encourage consumers to consider whether the funeral on offer was what they really wanted."

Accusations of a lack of transparency usually relate to the all-inclusive funeral package, the so-called 'take it or leave it' option. The package components are not individually priced so it is impossible to identify how the total price is costed. Even worse is the fact that even if a component can be deleted, the price is not reduced pro rata. There is also the danger of those hidden extras, the ones not included in the package, which so often increase the final price.

To achieve transparency it is essential to offer a simple menu of priced components, each capable of being justified by a logical costing process. This list of components and fees should be printed and available to all users and enquirers. The components could be advertised as a funeral package in order to assist the consumer, providing they can readily remove components, and their associated cost. For instance, the consumer might prefer to procure their own coffin from the internet, make their own coffin or perhaps to lay-out and wash the body.

Transparency is not just essential for commercial operations. Charities, Trusts and co-operatives, as well as local authorities, although they do not seek profit, ought to offer a menu of prices and exhibit transparency.

The one stop shop integrated service

A one stop shop service replicates what funeral directors sometimes advertise as a basic funeral, a description intended to denigrate the offer in the eyes of consumers. It comprises of six components, each of which could be transparently priced:

1. Funeral arrangement fee – the bereaved will be interviewed at home or on site, the order taken and the funeral arranged, including the minister or secular officiant, music, etc. in the celebrants hall.

2. Collection of body fee – a telephone call can initiate the collection of a body in a suitable but not ostentatious vehicle such as a people mover, perhaps with a promotional livery, with two staff using a stretcher.

3. Storage of body fee (per night) – the body will be stored in a cool room or body fridge at the natural burial site. It will be washed and dressed and placed in a coffin.

4. Provision of coffin fee – for a basic biodegradable coffin, perhaps with more expensive alternatives.

5. Viewing of deceased fee (per occasion) – the bereaved to visit the site to view the body at an agreed time in working hours.

6. Provision of bearers fee (per bearer) – if required for the funeral on site.

These basic six components can readily form a package which will be added to the grave costs to create the funeral price. The bereaved could complete any element themselves and delete the associated cost, including dispensing with viewing. Arrangements to visit the Registrar of Births, Deaths and Marriages, floral tributes and obituaries would need to be arranged by the family. If preferred, fees to assist with any of these elements could be charged and included in the fees table.

On the day of the funeral the bereaved will travel to the site in their vehicles, public transport, etc., to attend the service and burial. Staff who normally receive funerals on-site can meet the bereaved as pre-arranged and act in lieu of the funeral director. With minimal staff, no need for hearse, limousines or cortège, reduced road travel and the dual use of site staff and their offices, overheads are kept to a minimum.

This innovative process is a USP, which can be further differentiated, perhaps by providing women only funerals, an in-house horse-drawn carriage, funeral teas, etc.

With the facilities in place, a low-cost 'body disposal service' might be offered, an option highlighted when the Dead Citizens Charter was being considered. This would entail collecting a body, placing it in a basic coffin and interment without attendance of mourners, body viewing or even a funeral service. Rather than the mainstream funeral directing intent of making the funeral arrangements appear complex to validate higher charges, this approach simplifies the entire process and makes low-cost funerals a reality.

Providing an integrated funeral service ensures that the total funeral income is retained by the natural burial site, and not shared with a conventional funeral director, an issue highlighted in section 9.4.

Although the facilities and equipment needed are fairly modest, the real cost and commitment is in maintaining a 24-hour service seven days a week, especially in the early days when funeral numbers at new sites are low. Staff can be placed on a call-out rota in order to reduce costs, which is how funeral directors manage.

10.2.3 Pricing an integrated funeral service

The reason why mainstream funeral directors prefer package funerals is that it equates to a known level of staff and administration input, and ensures a pricing structure applies that guarantees a profit. If the package is broken into components, each of which can be deleted at will, it makes the charging process difficult.

To overcome this, the profit can be included in (item 1) the funeral arrangement fee, which also includes all overheads, administration, attendance at funeral, etc. The remaining five fees (items 2–6) can be charged at cost. The benefit of this approach is that any of components 2–6 can be deleted at will without the danger of not recouping the profit. This also removes the need for salesmanship in that there is no commercial need to sell components 2–6 in order to increase profits. This is consistent and transparent, but because the funeral arrangement fee covers considerable behind the scenes work, and all profit, it can seem an expensive component to the consumer.

Site owners could alternatively treat funeral directing as a means to an end, a commodity service supporting what they might consider as a more lucrative sale, that of grave rights. The funeral components 1–6 could be offered at cost, perhaps even below cost, with overheads and profits absorbed within grave right fees. This is less complex but also less transparent, and it suggests that a high profit exists within grave sales. Nonetheless, in the early stages of a new site the low-cost funeral may be a way to attract burials and develop a business. Over time a proportion of the overheads for the natural burial site can progressively be apportioned back into the funeral service.

HM Revenue & Customs (VAT) treat the funeral package provided by conventional funeral directors as exempt. Any site providing funeral services ought to obtain accountancy advice to ensure that the site qualifies as a funeral director and that the exempt status is applicable.

Funeral plans

Those sites providing an integrated funeral service may consider offering pre-need Funeral Plans, a specified activity mentioned earlier under section 11.4. It would be essential to ensure all monies are protected and specialist advice would be necessary.

10.3   WHAT ARE INDEPENDENT FUNERALS?

A natural burial site can expect, at some stage, a request from a family to complete a funeral without a funeral director. They need to decide whether they will accept this, and if so, how they will manage it. In the UK, these funerals are referred to by various names including independent, DIY or family-centred funerals. In the US they are simply called home funerals.

The local authority reaction to such requests can vary considerably. It can be outright refusal or acceptance without offering any help (unfacilitated), or acceptance along with advice and physical support (facilitated). As recent as 2009 I am aware of private crematoria refusing to accept a funeral booking unless made by a bona fide funeral director. Both private and local authority managers may feel that assisting the bereaved in this way, especially if it is overt and known, will create conflict with mainstream funeral directors.

10.3.1 Unfacilitated funerals

This occurs when the site will accept a family member or friend of the deceased acting as a token funeral director, but leaves them to manage the funeral without overt assistance. The site manager will still need to give more advice and help than if a conventional funeral director was in charge. The person arranging the funeral will make the provisional booking, then complete the interment notice, and perhaps pay the burial fees in advance. This person will have to ensure the death is registered and deliver the Coroner's Order or Registrar's Certificate to the site prior to the burial.

This person then needs to make or procure a coffin, collect the body and place it inside, and store the coffin at home. In practicable terms, it is easiest to procure the coffin, then collect the body from the mortuary on the morning of the burial. Later that same day, the body can be transported to the natural burial site, where the service and burial can occur.

This unfacilitated approach suggests that such funerals will not be promoted or mentioned in any site leaflets and that they will be accepted only when specifically requested. These are likely to be few because the practicalities can present many difficulties, not least the fact that the mortuary might not be willing to retain the body for the period, and that a vehicle to accept a 7' (214cm) coffin and able-bodied bearers are needed.

10.3.2 Facilitated funerals

A small number of burial services in the UK, especially ICCM Charter for the Bereaved members, offer a local funeral advisory service as highlighted under section 9.5, which might include:

- Providing a leaflet called *'How to arrange a funeral without a funeral director'*. This must be specifically tailored for the local area regarding details for registration, mortuaries, and other useful addresses and contact details.

- Stocking one or more biodegradable coffins. This would also overcome possible damage in transit if ordered via the internet.

- Providing a body storage facility for the period leading to the funeral, preferably where the family can view and/or attend to the body. This might be overnight in a chapel, or longer in a refrigerated unit.

I am not aware of any site that routinely provides the following services, but they would facilitate such funerals:

- Coffin transport – providing a vehicle sufficiently large to carry the coffin, or the details of a local hire firm with suitable vehicles.

- Provision of bearers on-site and/or to help with bearing off-site.

A charge for these services can be included on the fees list. As these may not constitute a funeral package, standard rate VAT may apply. The provision of a minister or secular officiant is outside the scope of VAT. It is also remotely possible a local funeral director will agree, for a fee, to provide some or all of these services on behalf of the site.

Where an integrated funeral service is provided it should be transparent enough to allow people to pick and mix the various components of a funeral. This might remove the need for an independent funeral because the overall cost is controlled and any preference for a more hands-on experience by the bereaved will be met.

Appendix

CONTACT DETAILS

Institute of Cemetery & Crematorium Management (ICCM)
Contact: Tim Morris, FICCM (Dip), Chief Executive ICCM
Address: ICCM National Office and Jill Rodican Training Centre
City of London Cemetery
Aldersbrook Road
Manor Park
London E12 5DQ
Telephone: 07811 169600
Email: timiccm@btinternet.com

Burial & Cremation Education Trust (BCET)
Contact: Nicky Birt
Telephone: 01400 251332/07977 273479
Email: flrt@laughtonsfarm.co.uk

Living Churchyards Project
Address: The Arthur Rank Centre
Stoneleigh Park
Stoneleigh Road (B4113)
Warwickshire CV8 2LZ
Telephone: 020 7685 3060
Email: admin@arthurrankcentre.org.uk

Cemetery of the Year Award
Address: MAB (The Memorial Awareness Board)
c/o ONE
19 Heddon Street
London W1B 4BG
Telephone: 020 7993 3833
Email: mab@oneismore.com

The Shaw Trust
Address: Shaw Trust Ltd. Registered Office
Shaw House
Epsom Square
White Horse Business Park
Trowbridge
Wiltshire BA14 0XJ
Telephone: 07852 266127
Public Relations Email: rawle.beckles@eopps.org

Natural Death Centre

Address: Natural Death Centre
The Hill House
Watley Lane
Twyford
Winchester SO21 1QX
Telephone: 08712 882098
Email: contact@naturaldeath.org.uk

Association of Natural Burial Grounds (ANBG)

Contact via Natural Death Centre

Ministry of Justice

Address: Coroners and Burial Division
Ministry of Justice
102 Petty France
London SW1H 9AJ
Telephone: 020 3334 6388
Email: Paul.Ansell@justice.qsi.gov.uk

Federation of Burial & Cremation Authorities (FBCA)

Contact: Duncan McCallum (FICCM Dip)
Address: The Federation of Burial and Cremation Authorities
41 Salisbury Road
Carshalton
Surrey SM5 3HA
Telephone: 020 8669 4521
Email: fbcasec@tiscali.co.uk

Environment Agency (EA)

National Customer Contact Centre
Address: PO Box 544
Rotherham S60 1BY
Telephone: 0870 850 6506
enquiries@environment-agency.gov.uk

Association of Burial Authorities (ABA)

Address: Waterloo House
155 Upper Street
London N1 1RA
Telephone: 020 7288 2522/2533
Email: aba@burials.org.uk